MODEMS MADE EASY

David Hakala

Osborne **McGraw-Hill**

Berkeley New York St. Louis San Francisco
Auckland Bogotá Hamburg London Madrid
Mexico City Milan Montreal New Delhi Panama City
Paris São Paulo Singapore Sydney
Tokyo Toronto

Osborne **McGraw-Hill**
2600 Tenth Street
Berkeley, California 94710
U.S.A.

For information on translations or book distributors outside of the U.S.A., please write to Osborne **McGraw-Hill** at the above address.

Modems Made Easy

67890 DOC 9987654

ISBN 0-07-881962-8

Acquisitions Editor
Bill Pollock

Associate Editor
Emily Rader

Technical Editor
Nick Anis

Copy Editors
Ann Krueger Spivack
Paul Medoff

Proofreaders
Vanessa Miller
Kayla Sussell

Indexer
Valerie Robbins

Computer Designer
Michelle Galicia

Illustrator
Marla Shelasky

Cover Designer
Compass Marketing

Quality Control Specialist
Joe Scuderi

To the memory of the man who introduced the author to the magic of modems, starting in 1985. He was a kilt-wearing kook, a cherished friend, and a patient mentor to every lost rookie online from Denver to Singapore. May this book carry on his good works among the modem-deprived.

```
Caller ID:  Terry Travis

Logged on:   February 13, 1956
Logged off:  March 23, 1993

<click>

NO CARRIER...

OK
```

CONTENTS

INTRODUCTION

This book is for people who want to learn how to use and *enjoy* using modems. It is written for people who want to get online and have fun, without worrying about what their modem is doing. Technophiles who delight in learning the microscopic details of *how* things work will be better served by other books, such as *Dvorak's Guide to PC Telecommunications* by John Dvorak (Osborne/McGraw-Hill, 1992).

The Ultimate Purpose of This Book

Throughout this book, the emphasis is on fun, discovery, and personal empowerment. I hope you will approach *Modems Made Easy* as an adventure, a chance to enjoy a larger and richer life.

I believe life is an exciting and rewarding adventure, a process of repeatedly putting oneself in unfamiliar, challenging situations, and growing by making the unknown a familiar part of your life. Adventures are more exciting and less frightening when shared with faithful guides. *Modems Made Easy* is meant to be your trusty companion as you adventure in the limitless online universe.

Contacting the Author

Please! Contact me at one of the following online addresses. I look forward to learning from you how to improve the next edition of *Modems Made Easy*.

David Hakala
Denver, Colorado
CompuServe ID: 74720,3377
Internet Address: david.hakala@boardwatch.com
July 7, 1993

Special Mail-In Offer from the Author

The very last page in this book is my own special offer to my readers: the *Modems Made Easy* Bonus Disk set. Mail in this coupon along with a check or money order for $12.95, and you will receive two high-density disks full of current software and information addressing the needs of novices and experienced modem users. See the coupon for the specific contents of the disks and ordering information.

CHAPTER

1

WHY MILLIONS OF OTHERWISE NORMAL PEOPLE ARE BUYING MODEMS

Are you discouraged when you overhear incomprehensible discussions about modems, online services, and bulletin board systems? Do you wonder what all the technobabble about baud rates, parity, protocols, and IRQs is about?

Maybe you do know the jargon, but you do not understand why people are so excited about modems. When you say "I never found any use for a modem," friends look at you like you said "refrigerator" instead of "modem." The $250 modem you bought in 1985 never worked right twice in a row. The first month in use, it ran up a phone bill the size of your mortgage payment. You unloaded the devil's tool at a garage sale, and swore you'd never be suckered into that aggravating money-pit again.

Yet, everywhere you go, someone is singing the praises of modems.

"You just gotta get this thing!," insist a legion of baby boomers in TV commercials. The "thing" is Prodigy(sm), an online service developed jointly by Sears and IBM. All it takes is a personal computer, a modem, and approximately $39.95 to get started, and a mere $15.95 per month thereafter.

"Why on earth should I spend all that money?" you ask. The chorus urges a dozen reasons on you, with the evangelical logic of a ten-year-old explaining why shoes aren't worth tying unless Michael Jordan signed them and they cost $120.

"It's got an encyclopedia!" they gush. Well, so does the library, and Junior doesn't use that, either. They persist: "You can play games on it! Pay your bills on it! Shop without leaving the house! Buy and sell stocks at night! Send letters without going to the post office!"

Mentally, you edge away from these people. They must have a virus genetically tailored by Madison Avenue to induce such fevered, quivering consumerism. Someday, when there is a practical, cheap use for a modem, you'll try one.

That day is now. One in every seven U.S. households now harbors a modem. One estimate maintains that 9,500 people per day buy their first modem. Vendors are finally taking the modem market seriously. Modems and communication software are now cheaper, more reliable, easier to use, and more powerful than ever before.

There are now more places to call with your modem. Today's electronic pilgrim can choose from over 50,000 bulletin board systems, commercial networks, and community online services. No matter where you live, an online community is just a local call away.

Competition, especially from home-based, lean-and-mean "info-preneurs," has driven the prices of online services down to a very reasonable range. Many online services are free; most cost no more than a magazine subscription, while delivering far more value.

Consumers are no longer limited to what a few vendors want to sell. You can find exactly what you want among the thousands of info-boutiques out there. In case you don't yet know what you might want, let's take a look at how people are using their modems these days.

What People Really Do with Modems

Forget what those folks on TV told you about the wonders of 'round-the-clock shopping. IBM and Sears thought they were going into the retail sales business. So did CompuServe, GEnie, and other heavily marketed online "mega-malls." The idea was to create a market of millions of affluent, free-spending yuppies by offering "low" access fees, then charge other vendors for space on the mall and a percentage of all revenues.

It didn't work. Even after five years of trying, online catalog sales are so embarrassing that none of the major mall owners will quote hard figures, although they will gladly note that sales are "up 150 percent over last year." It's not hard to post such improvements when you start near the bottom.

People voted with their dollars, and the mall owners had to redefine themselves and their businesses to provide what consumers really wanted.

People Who Need People Need Modems

The real value that 10 million people find online every day lies in each other's company. Think of a nightclub versus a library, or a party versus an automated teller machine. Where would you rather spend your time and money?

The astounding growth in modem use is fueled by people who want to talk to each other. They talk about work and hobbies, their dreams and their problems, their pasts and their futures. They cry on and comfort each other—by the millions!

The Big Three in online services (Prodigy, CompuServe, and GEnie) have reluctantly realized that they are in the hospitality business, not the retail game. All three have posted their biggest gains in users and revenues via electronic mail traffic, and all have introduced low-cost "basic" messaging services to meet the demands of their customers.

Turning to a computer for contact with other people may seem paradoxical, but there are a number of good reasons to do it.

Beating the Time Crunch

After an eight- or ten-hour workday, few of us have the energy to dress up and go out. Childcare further complicates any plans to escape that Mom and Dad may want to make, even on weekends.

A significant part of the precious free time spent "getting out" is actually spent "getting ready," traveling to the destination, and finding a parking space once there. Getting back home takes an equal effort.

All too often, the world doesn't keep to our hectic schedules. Show times are too early or too late. Reservations for dinner can't be had during prime time. Friends can't come over on Tuesday night. The last plane for Aspen leaves while you're still at work.

Modems let users beat this time crunch in two ways. First, you can forget about preparation and travel time. Just fire up your modem, dial a phone number, and you are there! Don't spend an hour hunting up a baby-sitter; just keep an ear open for the sound of too much mayhem (or too much silence). You needn't worry about how you look or what to wear, either.

Second, modems don't let you miss any of the fun. If you don't check in at your favorite online hangout for a couple of days, weeks, or even months, you won't miss anything. All the conversation, news, and entertainment are available long after they actually happened. This suspension of "the action" until you are ready for it is one of the most satisfying aspects of belonging to the online community; finally, time *does* wait for man, woman, and child!

Having an Adventure a Day

Radio, magazines, and TV bring faraway places and interesting people into our living rooms—along with a lot of mental popcorn. Why do we put up with so much junk in our homes and our minds? Because each and every one of us is starved for adventure: something new, exciting, and perhaps a bit alarming in our humdrum lives.

Modems provide infinite opportunities for adventure. Who could pass up a place with a name like "The Hot Muddy Duck," a bulletin board system in south Florida? While Chinese students were under siege at the University of Beijing, many of us in Colorado were there with them via modem. Long before CNN cameras arrived in Florida, Hurricane Andrew victims told us directly about their travails via radio-linked modems. The poignancy of such first-person accounts cannot be matched by professional postmortems.

Thousands of adults-only systems cater to every imaginable fantasy, fetish, and frivolity. "Computer sex," though mostly rather boring and juvenile flirtation, accounts for over 60 percent of all the traffic on MiniTel, France's nationalized modem network.

Changing Your Identity to Suit Your Mood

You can be whoever you want to be in the online universe, just as you can on a tropical cruise. "Dagney Taggart," a formidable female character created by Ayn Rand, is incarnated as a red-haired minor government employee here in Denver. One of the most salacious and hotly admired of all X-rated electronic couples turns out to be a grandmother and her paraplegic son.

Conversely, you can truly be yourself online; in fact, you must be whoever you really are at any given moment. All of the visual and audible cues that trigger prejudice or just unwarranted assumptions (good or bad) about who you are and how valuable you are as a person simply don't exist in the online world. Accents and skin colors don't come across. No one can see your bad complexion, balding pate, or Gucci loafers. The inner person—the real person—comes through without help or hindrance.

Being accepted exactly as you are is *normal* when you join the online community. That may well be the most exhilarating, alarming, and desirable adventure of all, one we enjoy far too seldom.

The Last and Widest Frontier of Freedom

Many of us chafe under the constraints society, government, and corporations place on our lives. At every turn, some convention, law, policy, or "market reality" limits our freedom to express our thoughts, earn our living, or fight back against oppression.

Take this book, for example. A lot of people have the power to interfere in my choice to write it and your right to read it. Someone at the publisher can change or delete anything, even decide whether these pages are ever printed. If this book is published, every wholesaler, retailer, and librarian between you and me will decide whether or not you get a chance to read it.

Most letters to editors are never published. Talk show hosts control who is heard on the air. The cost of reaching a significant portion of any audience with your message, product, or service is beyond the means of most individuals and small businesses. Control of traditional mass marketing and communication channels therefore defaults to governments and large corporations.

Modems obliterate nearly all barriers between an individual and the masses. No matter what you want to say, no one can stop you from being heard by millions of people around the world. The printing press gave individuals a taste of such power, until the size and cost of mass-market publishing exploded. Modems deliver a lifelong feast for the price of one candy bar.

Solitary programmers have become millionaires without spending the $500,000 or more dollars to penetrate traditional marketing channels. Shareware programs are simply copied and passed from person to person on a voluntary and highly informal basis. If you like a program, you send the author the fee he or she requests, which is much less than you would pay if the product were shrink-wrapped and heavily advertised.

I could publish this book myself for the cost of a local phone call. Indeed, electronic publishing and informal distribution of entire books via modem is a small but firmly established and growing industry. Books on unpopular or esoteric subjects that would *never* make it to the retail level are being distributed through phone lines. No matter what we think of a book's "significance" or viewpoint, the fact that every author can reach his audience is a precious freedom for us all.

Governments are powerless in the face of modem power, as the example of the Chinese students in Beijing demonstrates. The U.S. government was thwarted in its attempt to keep an electronic encryption technique out of the public's hands; someone simply released a program implementing the method as no-cost shareware. The Federal Communications Commission was swamped with 10,000 faxed protests in one week after word got out that the FCC was considering a tax on modem use. The notion was dropped.

Corporations no longer have an "information edge" over consumers, or even their own employees. A bad experience with a company's product can be shared with hundreds of thousands of readers in the "Product Warnings" echomail conference, a kind of consumer-authored Consumer Reports. The U.S. General Accounting Office has established a "whistle-blowers" bulletin board system, where employees of government contractors can anonymously report illegal behavior by their employers.

Big business can no longer monopolize mass markets. Anyone with $1,000 worth of computer, modem, and software can challenge IBM and Sears, as Bob Mahoney did with his basement-brewed EXEC-PC bulletin board system. While the corporations spent over $800 million to bring Prodigy online, Mahoney quietly went from one line to over 350, serving more than 10,000 subscribers at an average of $60 each per year. Then Mahoney ran an ad in *Boardwatch* magazine that read, "Sorry, Prodigy!" Perhaps he's referring to the fact that Prodigy doesn't expect to turn a profit until sometime in 1995.

If You Need "Practical" Reasons to Buy a Modem

Adventure and romance, even personal convenience, aren't enough for some people. Here are some hardheaded, practical reasons to buy a modem and use it:

✦ You'll save a fortune on software. For $20 to $60 a year, you can have your pick of over 80,000 shareware programs from a local bulletin board system. Many are better than the shrink-wrapped stuff for which you paid $300 or more.

1

✦ You'll find more and better advice on any purchase or investment through the online community than you'll get from the folks who want to sell you something.

✦ You'll save paper, ink, and gasoline. I once let my printer stay broken for over six months, yet collected reams of magazine articles, statistical tables, and correspondence via modem. Though I live 20 miles from the main library, I didn't spend a nickel on gas or parking to "get" there.

✦ You'll do business faster and better. Access to online databases and government-sponsored services like the Small Business Administration's BBS will make your business more competitive and productive.

Chapter 2 will provide an overview of the many benefits of modems and telecomputing.

CHAPTER

2

AN OVERVIEW OF MODEMS AND TELECOMPUTING

In this chapter you will learn what modems do and the general uses you can get from a modem. Six essential technical buzzword are explained here: protocols, data bits, baud rate, stop bits, parity, and communication parameters. Read this chapter if any of these terms are new to you or if you are unfamiliar with asynchronous data communication.

This chapter also introduces you to the four basic things you can do with a modem:

9

information retrieval, electronic mail, file exchange, and real-time interaction with a remote computer. These are the basic building blocks from which all of the thousands of different online wonders are built.

Telecomputing is a term coined to describe interacton with any computer from a distance (tele: Greek, "far off."). Automatic teller machines are telecomputing devices. When you select options from a computerized voice-messaging system's "menu" by pressing keys on your touch-tone phone, you are telecomputing. See? You already telecompute! Modems are just another way to skin this cat.

The word *modem* comes from the term "MODulator/dEModulator," which would aptly describe what modems do if everyone understood the term "modulation." In English, a modem is a *translator*. It "listens" to your computer, then translates computer-talk into telephone-talk so that what your computer says can travel over an ordinary telephone line. At the other end of the line, another modem translates the telephone-talk back to computer-talk, so the computer to which yours is talking can understand what your computer "said."

Your telephone does the same thing for your voice and ear. The mouthpiece translates airborne vibrations (sound) into the type of electrical signals the telephone system can carry. The speaker in the earpiece translates these signals back into sound so you can hear what was said.

Novice modem users often complain about the complexity of using a modem, "Why can't it be as simple as using a telephone?" Actually, modems *are* as simple to use as telephones, but we have forgotten how complicated telephones are because we use them so often. Hand a phone to a two-year-old and really pay attention to what happens: the poor kid gets as frustrated as any first-time modem user. The technical steps and buzzwords necessary to use a modem are no more overwhelming than those associated with an ordinary telephone. To make a regular phone call, you must remember to follow these steps:

1. Hold the handset right side up, so your voice goes into the microphone and the returning sound goes into your ear.
2. Wait for a dial tone (and know what "dial tone" is) before trying to dial out.
3. Press the right combination of buttons, which can vary considerably depending on where you're calling from and where you are calling. Anyone who has used an unfamiliar office phone system or tried to dial an international call knows how complicated it can be.

4. Speak loud enough and slow enough so that the person on the other end can hear you.

5. Follow the subconscious rules of conversation that let people talk to each other in words and sentences. These rules include such taken-for-granted things as, "Does that two-second period of silence mean that it's my turn to say something, or that Joe has hung up on me?"

6. Listen to what comes back over the line, and try to filter out line static, background noise, and other distractions.

7. Hang up the phone properly to end the connection. Most of us also follow unspoken rules about saying goodbye, so the other party is not left hanging there.

And this doesn't even consider what it takes to assemble and install a telephone!

So you see, using a telephone is a pretty complex skill. Yet we learn all the rules and have no difficulty talking over telephones. You *can* learn to use a modem just as naturally as you use a telephone.

Asynchronous Communications: You Already Do It!

Most of the time, you will communicate via modem in much the same way you talk to someone in person or over a telephone. The technical term for this style of communication is *asynchronous communication,* which basically means that the flow of conversation can start and stop, and include varying intervals of silence or "inactivity," without confusing the speaker or listener.

You have asynchronous conversations all the time, in which each party pauses between sentences or individual words to think before speaking, or to wait for a noise to subside, or to do something else before continuing the conversation. The listener might ask you to pause for a moment while he attends to some other matter on his end. No problem, right?

There are some essential technical concepts you need to know in order to use a modem, but they are no more difficult than what you need to know about telephones. We will stick with the bare essentials here. The nitty-gritty technical details, should you need them, are in Chapter 1 of my last book, *Hot Links: The Guide to Linking Computers* (Osborne/McGraw-Hill, 1993).

Asynchronous Versus Synchronous Communication

Asynchronous communication is most commonly used in the modem world, for the same reason it is most common in person-to-person communication: People more often engage in two-way, give-and-take conversations than in one-way monologues.

Synchronous communication, by contrast, is not so relaxed and informal. One party starts talking and doesn't stop for anything. If the listener is distracted, part of the message may be lost. Listening to a lecturer or watching a TV broadcast is an example of synchronous communication. It is a more efficient way to move data from Point A to Point B than asynchronous communication, but the listener must pay very close and constant attention. Synchronous communication via modem is typically employed for one-way, high-volume exchange of data, such as transmitting a large program file.

Protocols: Rules of Conversation

The buzzwords associated with modem async communication (a common abbreviation for "asynchronous") have their counterparts in oral communication. Take this conversation as an example:

Sally: "Good morning, XYZ Inc! This is Sally."

Joe: "Hello! This is Joe Blow and I want John Smith."

Sally: "I'm sorry, I didn't catch that; could you repeat what you said more slowly?"

Joe: "Hello...this is Joe Blow...I want John Smith."

Joe and Sally just established a *communication protocol*, the set of rules by which each party interprets what the other is saying. The following sections relate Joe and Sally's familiar protocol to the minimal technical rules modems must follow.

Data Bits: How Many Letters Will Be in a Word?

Computers and their various peripheral devices, including modems, all use the same alphabet. This alphabet consists of only two digits, zero and one; hence it is called a binary digit system. Each zero or one is called a *bit*, a term derived from BInary digiT. A complete character consists of a set of 0 and 1 bits arranged in a specific pattern. The capital letter "A," for example, is defined by the bit pattern 1000001. The term data bits refers to this set of bits which carries the intended message from one modem to another.

Two modems must agree upon *how many data bits* comprise a character. Async communication uses eight data bits to represent each character.

Baud Rate, Bits Per Second: How Fast Are We Talking?

Joe's first attempt to convey a message was too fast for Sally to understand, so the two of them negotiated a slower speed at which to speak. Presumably, they will both talk at this negotiated speed throughout the conversation.

Modems go through a similar negotiation whenever they connect. One modem begins by sending information as fast as it can. If the receiver can't keep up, it interrupts the sending modem, and the two must negotiate a lower speed before starting over again.

The speed at which modems communicate is commonly called the *baud rate*, though it is more technically accurate to say *bits per second* or *bps*. A "2400" modem can communicate at a maximum speed of 2400 bps; you will often hear and read "2400 baud."

The fastest modems can race along at 9600 bps or better. Speeds in the thousands of bits-per-second range are often expressed in kilo-bits-per-second or *Kbps*; "kilo" is Greek for thousand. When you read about a 9.6, 14.4, 19.2, or 38.4 Kbps modem, multiply the figure by 1,000.

Stop Bits: Are You Finished Speaking?

This book, and all others, inserts a blank space between words and different forms of punctuation. Without the blank spaces, it would be difficult (though probably possible) to read a book the way an author intended it to be read. Modems also need a way to tell where one meaningful group of data bits stops and another begins.

Async communication uses *stop bits* and *start bits* to mark the end and beginning of each transmitted character. Like the period at the end of a sentence and the two spaces at the next sentence's beginning, start and stop bits are not part of the message; they are merely markers that indicate where one character ends and the next one begins.

Two bits, one to start and one to stop, plus eight data bits per character, add up to ten bits required for every single character transmitted. That is a lot of "blank space" to include in a data transmission, but the benefits outweigh the extra time required to send start and stop bits. Just look at this paragraph; could you read it without all the punctuation marks and blank spaces between words?

Parity: Does What I Heard Add Up to What You Said?

Let's rejoin Sally and Joe's conversation:

Sally: "John's not in, may I take a message for him?"

Joe: "Tell him...(blah, blah, blah)...and have him call me at 303-555-1234."

Sally: "I only wrote down nine digits: 303-555-123. Would you repeat that phone number?"

Sally just employed *parity checking* to verify that she did *not* hear Joe's phone number correctly. She knows that there should be a total of ten digits in a telephone number; since she heard only nine, she knows there was an error and asks Joe to repeat his phone number.

Synchronous Communication: More Efficient and Demanding

Synchronous communication relies on timing rather than start and stop bits to keep track of when one character ends and another begins. If two modems agree to communicate at 2400 bps, and to use eight data bits per character, they don't really need start and stop bits. They can just synchronize their clocks and interpret every 8/2400th of a second's worth of received data as one character.

Synchronous communication doesn't allow any hesitation; you have to keep pitching and catching data bits at a constant rate all the time. Like two jugglers tossing Indian clubs, the slightest loss of synchronization can bring the whole act to a crashing halt.

Synchronous communication saves two bits per character, so it is inherently more efficient than async communication. But most modem sessions include many starts and stops, and many switches between sending and receiving data (like an oral conversation between two people). Async communication is better suited to such two-way interaction, because it provides frequent opportunities for each party to let the other interrupt or reply.

Modems used to rely on parity checking to detect errors, but more recent error-correction protocols make parity checking largely unnecessary. Still, instructions for calling an online service frequently include "No parity," Even parity," or "Odd parity." Just assume "No parity" in the absence of specific instructions.

Communication Parameters: Putting It All Together

All of the foregoing technical details come together very compactly in the *communication parameters* that tell you how to set up your modem before calling another modem's phone number. For example, you might see an entry like this in a list of bulletin board systems:

Boardwatch magazine: 303-973-4222, 8-N-1

The last item, 8-N-1, tells you everything you need to know before you call this modem. You should set your modem to use

+ 8 data bits
+ No parity checking
+ 1 stop bit

Don't worry about baud rate. Unless both modems are "locked" to specific, different speeds, the modems will negotiate a mutually satisfactory speed once they connect to each other.

Now that we have covered the tedious details, let's look at the useful things you can do once you master them.

Things You Can Do with a Modem

Think of all the useful things you can accomplish in an ordinary telephone call. You can give someone information and get information in return. You can ask the listener to take a message and carry it to someone else, or save it

8-N-1: All People Need to Remember

The communication parameters 8-N-1 (8 data bits, No parity checking, 1 stop bit) are the most widely used protocol in PC-to-PC modem calls. When connecting to mainframe computers, 7-E-1 (7 data bits, Even parity checking, 1 stop bit) may be required.

for someone else to pick up later. You can give another person instructions to do something for you, either now or at a later time. A modem lets you do the same things with a computer, but much faster and often with a higher probability that what you request will be done correctly.

There are four broad categories of modem-based activities: information retrieval, electronic mail, file exchange, and real-time interaction.

Information Retrieval

You, the caller, receive information that is stored on the computer you are calling. Sometimes you have to look it up through database search and retrieval, and sometimes it is automatically presented for your passive consumption, but essentially, you are receiving some information that was already prepared and waiting for you.

Electronic Mail

The object is person-to-person communication, with the computers and modems acting as letter carriers and post office boxes. Electronic mail, or *e-mail,* can be addressed to specific persons or to a group of nearly any size, such as "everybody who sees this."

File Exchange

You can retrieve files (packages) of text, software, pictures, and even audio recordings from the hard drive of the computer you are calling, or send such files to another computer for storage. When you send a file to another computer, later callers may retrieve your file to their computers.

Real-time Interaction

Games, catalog shopping, and electronic banking are examples of person-to-computer interaction that is done in *real time,* meaning you type something, wait for the computer to perform a task and send you the result, then respond to what is sent. Teleconferencing, commonly called electronic "chat," involves person-to-person, real-time interaction. A number of people can conduct conversations as if they were gathered around a table in one room instead of being scattered all over the world.

These basic functions often can be combined to provide more useful and convenient services. For example, you might write an e-mail message to me, then attach a file to the message so I will get both the file and its "cover letter."

You can send and receive fax messages if you have a modem with fax capabilities. Others don't even need a modem to receive your fax or send one to you; they can use ordinary fax machines.

Real-time interaction includes remote control of another computer—the ability to use its resources as if you were sitting right in front of it instead of at a keyboard one room or one thousand miles away.

2

Places You Can Call with a Modem

Literally hundreds of thousands of computers are waiting for you to call. Their owners may be corporations, government and nonprofit agencies, small businesspeople, or your neighbor's teenager. While the trend is towards full-service facilities that offer all four major types of activity, there are some specialized types of online services: database providers, e-mail and fax services, online malls, and bulletin board systems.

Database Providers

Database providers retrieve information—all other activity is secondary. Your local library may let you look up books, magazine articles, and access other information. You probably will not be able to send e-mail or transfer files. Real-time interaction is limited to telling the computer what to look up, then waiting for the information to be found and displayed.

E-mail and Fax Services

The new breed of postal workers, e-mail and fax services specialize in moving written messages from sender to addressee. Often they go beyond modems to deliver the mail, transmitting your message to a service center nearest the addressee, and then printing it for normal postal delivery. Many services that began just offering e-mail now provide fax delivery, local printing, postal delivery, and even file exchange.

Online Malls

The "big three" nationally know services—CompuServe, GEnie, and Prodigy— started with the idea that they would be the landlords and take in a percentage of retail sales earned by electronic shopkeepers, who would rent space on expensive mainframe computers connected by private modem-only networks. Today the "big three" still focus on real-time interaction, specifically catalog shopping and credit-card transactions, but all three have found that it takes electronic mail, file exchange, and other non-purchasing options to attract callers.

Bulletin Board Systems (BBSs)

Bulletin board systems are the entrepreneurial renegades of the modem community, and the source of most of the innovative ideas online today. All it takes to start a BBS is a spare PC, a modem, some cheap (under $50) shareware, and a phone line. Most BBSs are full-service "corner stores" offering file exchange, e-mail, chat, games, information, and the opportunity to buy something—even if it's only an annual membership for full access to all the BBS' goodies.

Separate chapters later in this book cover each major type of online service. For now, you should realize that you have a very large range of options in online services.

But to exercise those options, you need a modem. Chapter 3 helps you choose a modem that will meet your needs and fit your budget.

CHAPTER

3 BUYING A MODEM

You have a lot of choices when buying a modem. That can be good or bad depending on whether you like making lots of choices. This chapter first recommends some "standard" modem packages for various intended uses such as electronic mail, file transfers, sending and receiving faxes. If you prefer to skip the details, you can choose from this list.

A more detailed discussion of speed standards, error-correction options, data-compression features, fax standards, and "convenience" features such as status lights and voice/data switching occupies the bulk of this chapter. Buyers who like to develop a detailed wish-list before shopping will find this section useful.

Modems are often bundled with valuable software and/or trial subscriptions to online services such as CompuServe, Prodigy, and others. The savings on such bundled extras may exceed the price of the modem itself, so it is a good idea to shop for them. This chapter describes some of the most common and enduring bundles.

Finally, you will learn a great deal about *where* to shop for a modem. The same package is often available at widely varying prices through retailers, mail-order houses, manufacturers, and such untraditional channels as your local computer user group.

Choosing the Right Modem for Your Needs

From the typical consumer's standpoint, there are three major uses for modems:

✦ Two-way personal interaction with a remote computer—that is, reading and writing electronic mail or searching a database.

✦ One-way "machine-level" interaction in which a person starts a process and the two computers take it from there, sending or retrieving large files.

✦ Fax sending and receiving; a modem can replace a bulky fax machine and eliminate a lot of paper.

The concerns of someone providing online services to consumers are similar but include other factors; these are discussed in Chapter 12.

Budget-Minded Modems for E-Mail and Database Searching

Speed, expressed in bits per second (bps or baud rate) is the primary factor affecting the cost of a modem. Every time a new, higher-speed modem becomes widely available, the prices of all lower-speed modems go into free-fall. It makes sense to start your online career with the lowest (cheapest) speed that will satisfy your needs.

"Live" interaction rarely requires the fastest speed available. When reading and writing e-mail online, the limitation is your speed, not the modem's. A 2400-bps modem can display what you're reading or send what you're typing at about 240 characters per second. That's a typing speed of 2,880 words per minute—probably faster than the person at the keyboard!

NOTE: "bis" indicates an enhanced version of an earlier standard.

3

Quick-Buy Recommendation

If you want a modem primarily for e-mail and database searching, buy a model with these features:

◆ 2400 bps maximum connect speed

◆ v.42bis data compression/error correction

Price range: $50 to $100

Budget-Minded Modems for File Transfers (Up/Downloading)

"Machine-level" interaction can benefit from high-speed modems. When you send a file via modem, the computer does the "typing," feeding characters to the modem as fast as the modem can handle them—which is not fast at all by the computer's standards. The faster your modem can pass data, the less time the entire process will take.

Modem speed is critical if you plan to frequently transfer files to and from other computers, especially over long-distance telephone connections where every minute costs money. A 300K file (a typical shareware program or an 800 x 600 graphics image) will take at least 21 minutes to transfer at 2400 bps, but only 5 minutes and 30 seconds at 9600 bps. If your long-distance telephone service costs 12 cents per minute, the difference between 2400 bps and 9600 bps is $1.86 every time you call another computer long-distance and transfer a 300K file.

High-speed modems—9600 or faster—currently cost $200 or more. The lowest price will probably fall to $150 by the time this book is printed, as even faster modems are being announced as "available soon."

A 9600-bps modem is four times faster than a 2400-bps model, and only costs two to three times as much. If you can afford it now, a 9600-bps modem is clearly a better choice for long-distance file transfers.

Currently, the fastest modems operate at 14,400 bps, 150 percent faster than a 9600-bps modem. But at this time, there are not that many 14,400 bps modems in service, so you will have few opportunities to take advantage of the speed gain. This situation is rapidly changing as the price of 14,400 bps swiftly approaches that of 9600 bps.

Quick-Buy Recommendation

If you believe you'll spend more than 10 percent of your online time transferring files, paying long-distance charges to do it, buy a modem with these features:

✦ 9600 or 14,400 bps connect speed

✦ v.42bis error correction/data compression

Price range: $200 to $1,200

Budget-Minded Modems for FAX-aholics

A *fax/data modem* can send and/or receive the specially encoded data that fax machines use, as well as the types of files we normally think of as "data." A document you just wrote with a word processor can be faxed directly from your hard drive. Incoming faxes can be routed to a printer, saved to disk, or both.

Fax modems come in send-only, receive-only, and send/receive models, as well as in several different speeds. When you add in all the possible combinations of speed, data compression, and error-correction features on the data side of the modem, buying a fax/data modem can get very confusing.

3

Quick-Buy Recommendation

When buying a fax/data modem, get one with these features:

◆ Send *and* receive capabilities

◆ Group III (9600 bps) or Group II (14,400 bps) fax speed

◆ 2400, 9600, or 14,400 bps data speed

◆ v.4bis data compression/error correction

Price range: $70 to $200 for Group III fax/2400 bps data; $200 to $1,000 for Group III fax/9600 bps data; $250 to $1,200 for Group II fax/14,400 bps data

Translating Modem Techno-Talk

If you have no previous experience with modems, earlier discussions about data compression, v.42bis, error correction, and so on, probably did not mean much to you. You can now buy a modem just by looking for the appropriate set of features listed in the boxes in the preceding "Choosing the Right Modem" section, but you may well wonder "What am I buying?"

This section of the chapter takes an in-depth look at the options available in modems. It explains the arcane terms in plain English. It also describes some "hidden" features found in better modems that cost little or nothing extra, yet make using a modem more convenient.

Should You Buy an Internal or External Modem?

Internal modems are bare circuit boards that plug into an expansion slot inside your PC. Only the modular phone jacks needed to connect your phone line and telephone handset are visible once the modem is installed, and these are flush against the case of your PC. You will not need any cables or connectors. Internal modems draw electricity from the PC's power supply, so you will not need to worry about an electrical outlet for the modem.

Internal modems have serial ports built right into them, so you won't have to buy another serial port card if all of your existing serial ports are in use. See Figure 3-1.

Right now, all you need to know about serial ports is whether the modem you buy already has one; internal modems do, external modems don't. For the details on why you need a serial port, see Chapter 5.

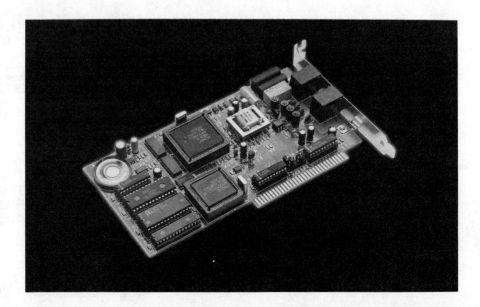

Internal
modem card
photo
Figure 3-1.

External modems occupy their own separate cases, and are linked to your PC by serial cables and connectors. Your PC must have an available serial port into which the modem can be plugged. External modems draw their own power through an AC/DC transformer, so you will need a separate electrical outlet for the modem's power supply. The modular phone jacks are in the modem's housing.

The external case and power supply add about $10 to $30 to the price of a modem. All else being equal, this is money well spent. *Buy an external modem whenever possible.* The only circumstances under which an internal modem makes better sense than an external model are when:

+ You have no available serial ports and cannot afford both a modem and a $15 add-on serial port card.

+ There is no way to reach an electrical outlet for an external modem's power supply.

+ Your PC is kept in a public, unattended area where theft is a real possibility.

+ You move your entire PC setup at least once a month.

External modems are easier to install than internal models; you do not have to remove the cover from your PC and squeeze another circuit card into a tight-fitting slot. But more importantly, you will not have to reverse the process if the modem is set up wrong the first time you install it! If an external modem needs service, you just unplug it. Removing an internal modem requires "major surgery."

Another advantage of an external modem is that you can watch what it's doing via the status indicators on the front of the modem's case. See Figure 3-2. These blinking lights (and in some modems, printed messages) are invaluable troubleshooting aids. Internal modems are no help at all when something isn't working right.

Speed Standards: v.22, v.22bis, v.32, v.32bis

No matter what vendors may tell you about their modems' "effective throughput," there are only four *real* speeds you should consider when buying a modem: 1200, 2400, 9600, and 14,400 bps. Check the modem's maximum *connect speed* (the highest number of bits-per-second it can send over a phone line) by looking for the highest *CCITT standard* it supports, as shown in the following table:

Maximum Connect Speed	CCITT Standard
1200 bps	v.22
2400 bps	v.22bis
9600 bps	v.32
14,400 bps	v.32bis

It is better to look for these CCITT standards designations (v.##, v.##bis) than to rely on a vendor's claims of "effective throughput up to...." CCITT standards are clear and internationally recognized, while other speed claims may be based on proprietary methods that assume two modems of the same brand are connected, or that both modems are using the same type of data compression. (See the next section on data compression.)

Some vendors offer modems that can achieve connect speeds of 16,800 or even 19,200 bps; U.S. Robotics Corp., Telebit Corp., and ZyXel Corp. are examples. But they do it using proprietary methods that require the same vendor's modems on both ends of the connection. Unless you know in advance that you will be calling only modems made by these vendors (an unlikely assumption), you should stick with the universal CCITT standards. The vendors just mentioned also support CCITT connect speeds in their modems, so it is perfectly safe to buy their modems for connecting to other vendors' wares.

External modems showing panel lights
Figure 3-2.

3

Cables and Connectors for External Modems

You need an RS-232C serial cable to install an external modem. Many modem vendors do not include a serial cable with their products. The reason for this omission has more to do with the variety of serial port connectors found on PCs and the variable length of cable each buyer needs, than with a vendor's cost-consciousness.

A serial cable will cost about $10 to $12 for 8 feet. Any Radio Shack or other electronics/computer store will have what you need.

It is vital to get the right types of connectors on both ends of the cable. External modems generally have *female* (holes to accept pins) DB-25 serial port connectors, so your cable must have a *male* (pins sticking out) DB-25 connector on the modem's end; that takes care of one end of the cable.

Your PC may have a 9-pin or 25-pin serial port connector, but it will almost certainly be a male connector (pins sticking out). Your serial cable will need a connector with 9 or 25 holes to accept these pins: a female DB-9 or DB-25 connector, as shown here:

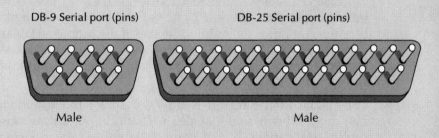

DB-9 Serial port (pins)   DB-25 Serial port (pins)

Male   Male

Data Compression: MNP-5, v.42bis

Your modem's connect speed can be augmented by using fewer bits to carry the same amount of information. If you could make 2400 bits carry 9600 bits worth of information, then a 2400-bps modem would be "as good as" a 9600-bps modem, right? *Data compression* is a combination of techniques that make it possible to transmit more information in a given number of bits.

One way to pack more "good stuff" into a given volume is to eliminate unnecessary space during shipment, then return it when the receiver needs it. Anyone who buys frozen concentrated orange juice understands how this technique works. Six small cans of concentrated juice are a lot easier to carry home than six half-gallon jugs of the original juice.

Part of data compression rests on the ability to eliminate "redundant" characters in a block of data before sending it through a phone line. The one blank space and the period that precede this sentence, for instance, could be replaced by a single character that represents "one blank space and a period." When the receiving modem gets that special character, it replaces the special character with one blank space and a period. Voila! One transmitted character just did the work of two.

Another way to compress data is to use a form of shorthand. Suppose you and I agree that the characters "!@" will represent the phrase "data compression" from now on. We could save 14 characters' worth of ink and paper every time we needed that phrase. The Gregg shorthand system allows secretaries to compress virtually every common word and phrase into single-character codes; thus, they can take dictation much faster than they could write in longhand. Similarly, data compression allows modems to transmit information much faster.

Many modems now have data compression capabilities built into them. Microcom Corp. developed the first method to achieve widespread use; it is called MNP Level 5, or just MNP-5 for short. CCITT later developed an international standard called v.42bis, which improved on MNP-5's compression ratio (the ratio of the size of uncompressed data to its compressed form's size). The v.42bis standard incorporates MNP-5 too, so a modem equipped only with MNP-5 can still achieve data compression when connected to a v.42bis modem.

This v.42bis/MNP-5 feature is fairly widespread today, and virtually every new modem being sold includes it. That is important, because *your* modem can't take advantage of data compression unless the modem to which it connects is also equipped with the same data compression method. A secretary can't take dictation in shorthand unless the person who will later type the letter can *read* shorthand, right?

Some types of data compress better than others. Ordinary text, such as a word processor document sent via electronic mail, can be squeezed down to roughly 25 percent of its original size. That means 1,000 bits can carry 4,000 bits' worth of information. So you *can* achieve "effective throughput" of 4 x 2400 = 9600 bps using a 2400 bps (connect speed) modem equipped with v.42bis/MNP-5—if the receiving modem also has v.42bis/MNP-5 capability. Database files, such as the *.DBF files dBase creates, are also highly compressible.

Executable files (those ending with the extension .COM or .EXE) have less "white space" in them and fewer "standard words" that can be compressed. An executable program file might compress to only 50 percent or 75 percent of its original size. Effective throughput for such files will be considerably less than the maximum claimed by the modem vendors.

Once you get online, you will find a lot of files that are *already* compressed before you retrieve them, using archiving utilities such as PKZip. A v.42bis/MNP-5 modem won't transmit these files any faster than the modem's true connect speed.

Data compression adds little, if anything, to the cost of a modem. Make sure your modem has data compression even if you only plan to use it for electronic mail and database searching. It will save a substantial amount of long-distance time over the long run. Just don't be disappointed if your 2400-bps v.42bis modem doesn't always achieve 9600 bps "effective throughput."

Error-Correction Protocols: MNP 1 Through 4 and CCITT v.42

Ordinary telephone lines are designed to carry voice signals, which are much more forgiving of transmission errors than data. A slightly annoying hiss in the background won't ruin your conversation with Mom, but such line static can cause serious problems in a data transmission: unreadable garbage characters, corrupted data files, even software that won't run after you receive it. Bad static can cause both modems to lose their connection and hang up on each other.

Error-correcting protocols were developed to counteract the errors inserted into data transmissions by the less-than-ideal conditions found in telephone lines. The error-correcting process essentially works like this:

1. Modem A takes a block of data and performs a calculation based on the number of 0 and 1 bits in the block, according to a CCITT standard method such as v.32, v.32bis, etc.

2. Modem A sends the block of data to Modem B and tacks on the result of its calculation.

3. Modem B performs the same calculation on the block of data it receives.

4. Modem B checks its result against the result sent by Modem A. The two results should match if the block of data reached Modem B without errors.

5. If the two results don't match, Modem B signals Modem A to stop sending new data and re-send the block that contained an error.

Two error-correction schemes have achieved widespread use: MNP Levels 1 through 4 (MNP 1-4) and CCITT's v.42. The v.42 protocol incorporates MNP 1-4, so modems equipped only with MNP 1-4 can achieve error-free connections with v.42 modems. (v.42bis is a newer, more efficient version of v.42, quickly replacing v.42 in new modems.)

Error correction achieves data integrity at the cost of transmission speed. The need to send an extra few characters (the result of the error-correction calculation) along with each block of data lowers the amount of "keepable" data transmitted per second. But the overwhelming benefits of an error-free transmission make this small sacrifice well worthwhile.

Other Features to Look for in a Modem

External modems include a row of status lights that provide some visual indication of what the modem is doing; these are standard on virtually every external modem. It takes some practice to decipher the meaning of the various blinking colored lights. Some modem manufacturers, such as Supra Corp., also include LED displays that show in plain English what connect speed has been established, whether the connection includes data compression and/or error correction, and other information that can help you estimate the quality of your connection or diagnose problems.

Both internal and external modems usually include a small speaker that can transmit the dial tone, connection signals, and even the sound of an entire online session to your ears. The quality of such speakers is usually awful, and modem noises are not the stuff of symphonies anyway. Many people disable their modems' speakers. Sometimes, it is worthwhile to leave the speaker turned on to monitor the progress of a call, particularly when using an internal modem that provides no visual feedback through panel lights.

Make sure the modem's speaker volume can be adjusted via software commands. Internal modems always include software commands that can adjust the volume of the speaker up or down, and turn it off entirely or after a firm connection is made. External modems should include such software commands, but a few models rely on a manual knob or switch to adjust speaker volume. This switch is almost always in the most inconvenient place possible, and rarely allows fine adjustments.

Many modems include a voice/data switch, which allows the user to manually change from data-transmission mode to voice-conversation mode and back again. Few people use this feature; it is not worth a higher price than a comparable modem without a voice/data switch.

A line quality test function is included in some modems, such as Practical Peripherals Inc. (PPI), ZyXel, and some Supra models. Entering the correct command or simply pressing a button gives you a signal-to-noise ratio displayed on your monitor or on the modem's LED if it has one. This information is invaluable when you are having trouble making a good connection; it can pinpoint or eliminate your telephone company's service as the source of the problem.

Modems are starting to suffer from "featuritis," the tendency of vendors to add on features that 90 percent of consumers don't need or use in order to maintain their products' price and profit margins. Don't buy a modem just because it includes Caller-ID (the ability to tell you the phone number of the party calling you), a 20-number internal dialing directory (you'll generally store your phone numbers in your own software), callback capability, or other esoteric bells and whistles.

The Best Places to Buy a Modem

Buying a modem directly from a manufacturer generally means you will pay full list price for no good reason. Computer dealers and mail-order houses used to be the only other places to buy modems, but today you can find excellent modems at deeply discounted prices in office supply stores (such as BizMart, Office Club, and others), computer warehouse stores (Comp USA), and even general-merchandise discounters like Kmart, Target, and WalMart. Mainstream department stores such as Sears and J. C. Penney generally do not have the best prices on modems.

Computer Shopper is the direct-mail computer buyer's best friend. Hundreds of manufacturers and distributors advertise their best prices in this thick monthly publication. Regional shoppers' guides also carry good values. You can find these publications at supermarkets, bookstores, newsstands, and computer dealers.

Discount catalogs such as DAK and Damark routinely carry manufacturers' overstock and discontinued inventory, or buy very large quantities of an item to secure an exceptionally low price. You'll find modems of every kind in these catalogs.

Software Etc., a chain of over 200 nationwide stores, recently set a new price floor for 14,400-bps v.42bis modems: an incredibly low $199 for an internal modem (about $20 more for an external version).

Prodigy(sm), the IBM/Sears online mall, sold over 150,000 2400-bps modems bundled with its service startup kit (list price $39.95) for just $50 during the summer of 1992. Prodigy is planning to upgrade its network to allow 9600 bps access, and at this writing is rumored to be preparing a $100 package for a v.32 modem and Prodigy starter kit—a deal you can't beat, even if you never use Prodigy!

CHAPTER

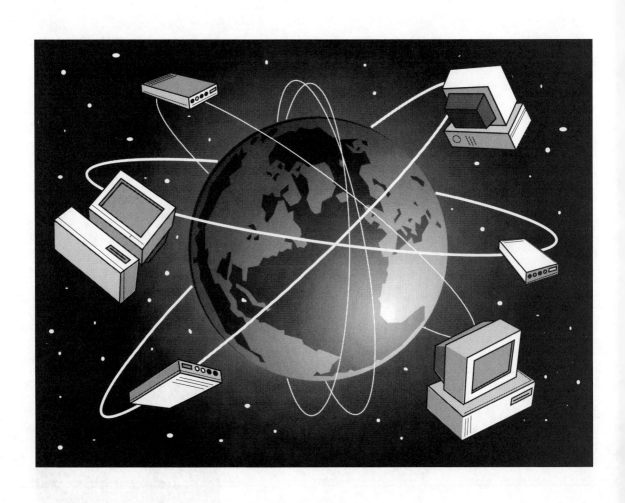

4

SOFTWARE FOR YOUR FIRST MODEM

You are the captain of your computer-ship. Telecommunications programs act as your second-in-command, automatically taking care of routine matters, conveying your specific orders to the modem, and reporting to you what the modem has accomplished.

There are different types of telecommunications programs for different missions. Most specialty telecommunications programs can do general duty as well, but their strengths lie in one particular type of telecommunications mission. Your specific needs beyond general use determine which type of program you'll select. Choosing a telecommunications program is like hiring a first mate for a voyage; an experienced mate can handle most aspects of any journey, but if your ship is headed into combat you probably won't hire a mate from a cargo ship.

 ## Two Primary Types of Programs

This chapter discusses the two most popular types of telecommunications programs: terminal emulation software and fax software. The first, *terminal emulation* software, is so essential to life online that virtually every modem sold comes packaged with one of these programs. Terminal emulation software (also known as just terminal software) lets you set up your modem, control its operation, connect to other modem-equipped computers and interact with them, and transfer files through modems. This chapter describes terminal emulation software for MS-DOS, Windows, and Macintosh users.

 NOTE: Terminal software sometimes suffers from "featuritis," a proliferation of options that can confuse first-time buyers. The most important thing to learn from this chapter is what functions are essential in general-purpose terminal emulation software, and what luxury features are worth buying.

Fax software is the second type of telecommunications program examined in this chapter; it turns your computer and modem into a send/receive fax machine. The most advanced fax programs offer Optical Character Recognition (OCR), the ability to convert the graphics dots of a fax into data other programs can readily use. Fax/OCR is such a useful capability it has joined word processing, database management, and other major computing processes as an essential industry function. But OCR technology is still in its infancy; few OCR programs reliably do all their manufacturers claim they will. This chapter shows what you can realistically expect fax/OCR software to do.

Other specialty telecommunications programs are designed for sending and receiving electronic mail, PC-to-mainframe communication, remote control of other computers, hosting incoming modem calls, and running bulletin board systems. These more specialized programs are discussed in later chapters.

Terminal Software

4

A terminal program's basic job is to send what you type over a modem to a remote computer and tell you what comes back—an easily accomplished task if you're not too finicky. Charles Petzold wrote a tiny (just 49 bytes!) program appropriately named TINYCOMM.COM that does these two things, and virtually nothing else.

But Petzold's program lacks amenities. It requires you to memorize and accurately type arcane commands to control the modem. It may lose characters if you go faster than 300 bps. If you press the (Enter) key, the cursor will move to the beginning of the line (basically performing a "carriage return") but it will not move down to the next line until you type in a "line feed" character. It won't allow you to transfer files from one machine to another.

At the other end of the size spectrum are commercial programs such as Crosstalk, Procomm Plus, and Qmodem Pro, which consume megabytes of disk space and cost from $150 to $300. Learning to use all the features packed into these programs may require months of daily study and experimentation.

Taking that much time to learn an elaborate terminal program may not be worthwhile for you; most people never use more than 10 percent of the features that high-end terminal software offers. This chapter covers that critical 10 percent that you will need most.

Between these extremes are dozens of shareware terminal programs such as Telix, Telemate, Unicom for Windows, and ZTerm for Macintoshes. Because they are usually written by people who use terminal software quite often, these programs are generally as good as (and often much better than) their shrink-wrapped retail counterparts. More than 75 percent of true modem maniacs use shareware terminal programs, according to a survey of over 11,000 self-professed online addicts conducted by *Boardwatch* magazine, the leading chronicle of the online scene.

Shareware: Pay for It Only If You Like It

Shareware is software that may be freely copied and shared, unlike shrink-wrapped commercial software. Shareware authors get free distribution of their products, and users get a chance to test-drive the software before sending any money (a registration fee) to the author. Shareware Marketing is all done on the honor system. (Yes, many shareware authors actually make their living this way—some have become millionaires!)

Registration fees are typically 20 to 50 percent of equivalent commercial software prices. The author saves advertising, packaging, store markup, and other costs associated with putting a product on the retail market.

Voluntary payments by satisfied users keep shareware authors in business. *If you keep and use shareware, be sure to pay for it!* Registration fees can bring you free lifetime upgrades, spiral-bound illustrated manuals, and personal support from the author.

Features You Really *Need*

The array of features available in terminal software can be bewildering, especially for first-time buyers. Until you actually use a modem, it is hard to decide what you really need in a terminal program.

The following sections describe the critical features to examine when choosing terminal software. This material includes specific recommendations based on my own experience gauging the needs of both novices and moderately proficient modem users. Your own needs may differ; for instance, if you already use COM1 through COM4, you will need a terminal program that supports COM5 or above. (See the following section on COM port support.)

A section later in this chapter, "'Luxury' Features You'll Really Appreciate," tells you about nonessential but time-saving, fun-enhancing possibilities.

COM Port Support: COM1 Through COM4

Modems communicate with your computer through serial ports. Other add-on devices use serial ports, too, so most computers provide more than one serial port. Serial ports are named COM1, COM2, COM3, and so on, so your computer knows where to find each serial port device.

NOTE: Terminal software must be able to use the same COM port your modem does.

Early terminal software supported only COM1 and COM2 (surprisingly the original relaease of Windows 3.0 supported only these two ports). Make sure the terminal software you buy supports the highest-numbered COM port address to which you are likely to assign a modem. Most people find COM1 through COM4 sufficient.

4

Terminal Emulation Types: TTY, ANSI/BBS, VT100

Just as you have to tune your television to the right channel in order to see anything worth watching, you will have to set your terminal software to the right "channel" in order to successfully communicate with a remote computer. These "channels" are known as *terminal emulation types.* A little history explains why they are necessary.

Before desktop computers, *dumb terminals* (a keyboard and monitor, with no built-in "brains") were the only way to communicate with mainframes, minicomputers, and other "intelligent" machines. The computers were programmed to communicate only with specific manufacturers' makes and models of terminals. If you hooked a Wyse Model 50 terminal to a computer that was programmed for DEC model VT100 terminals, things wouldn't work very well at all. The F1 function key on your Wyse terminal might mean "Next page, please" to you, but to the computer that thinks it is talking to a DEC terminal, F1 could mean "Hang up the phone."

Dumb terminals are still widely used, so most telecommunicating computers still require a desktop computer user to *emulate* (imitate) one of the dumb terminals they support. Most general-purpose terminal software can emulate at least TTY, ANSI-BBS, and DEC VT100/101/102 terminals. These terminal types are supported by virtually every public-access online service. If you know you will be calling a computer that requires a specific terminal type, be sure the software you buy includes it. Modern terminal software includes many common terminal types; see Figure 4-1.

Plain Old TTY Versus Color/Graphics Terminal Types   The TTY terminal type emulates an old-fashioned Teletype keyboard and printer. It doesn't produce fancy output or give you many features—just plain, unadorned black-and-white text. This lowest common denominator is supported by every online computer, and is handy when you can't find a match between your terminal types and the more sophisticated ones supported by the remote computer.

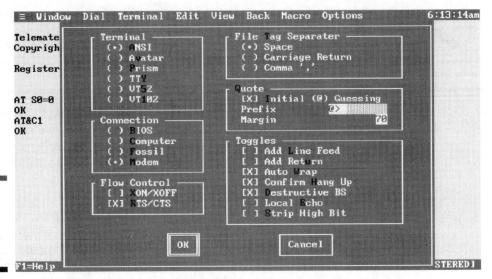

Telemate
offers a rich
selection of
terminal types
Figure 4-1.

ANSI/BBS is the next step up the terminal-type features ladder, and is almost
as widely supported as TTY. ANSI/BBS supports ANSI (American National
Standards Institute) color and cursor control codes. Online menus and text
displays take on vivid life compared to drab TTY displays. Cursor control
makes full-screen editing possible, so you can "jump" to the next word, top
of screen, end of file, and so on, much like using the word processor on your
local computer. Many online systems use cursor control to format displays,
and even to show you animated pictures!

Figure 4-2 shows a typical menu screen in ANSI/BBS terminal mode. Figure
4-3 shows the same screen in TTY mode; you can see the difference IBM
graphics make, although the color (not shown in this book) is even more
impressive!

Other terminal types, such as DEC VT100, include color and cursor control
and add their own special functions. Unless you regularly call a computer
that takes advantage of the special functions of a particular terminal type,
ANSI/BBS should provide all the color and cursor control you need. Enough
online computers *do* take advantage of DEC terminal types to make it a good
idea to choose terminal software that supports the VT family of terminals.

File Transfer Protocols: ASCII, Xmodem, Ymodem, Kermit, Zmodem
File transfer, the ability to sit back and let your computer and the remote
computer swap blocks of data (files) at the highest possible speed, saves you
time, money, and labor. You wouldn't want to send a 100,000-byte file by

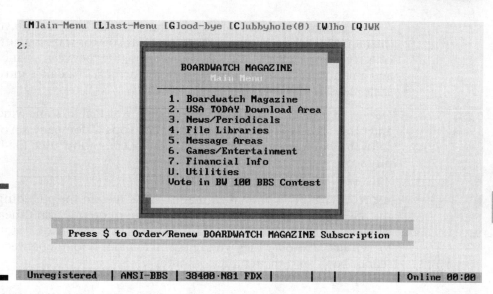

[M]ain-Menu [L]ast-Menu [G]ood-bye [C]ubbyhole(0) [W]ho [Q]WK
2;

4

A typical
ANSI/BBS
terminal
emulation
Figure 4-2.

typing in every character while connected to a remote computer at
long-distance prices, especially if the file already exists!

File transfer is an intricate, demanding dance that both computers must
perform in perfect synchronization. Your terminal software and the remote
computer's software must agree on which file transfer "dance" they will
perform.

```
j
[M]ain-Menu [L]ast-Menu [G]ood-bye [C]ubbyhole(0) [W]ho [Q]WK

   BOARDWATCH MAGAZINE
       Main Menu

1. Boardwatch Magazine
2. USA TODAY Download Area
3. News/Periodicals
4. File Libraries
5. Message Areas
6. Games/Entertainment
7. Financial Info

U. Utilities
Vote in BW 100 BBS Contest

Press $ to Order/Renew

Command:
```

Same menu as
Figure 4-2, but
TTY terminal
type.
Boooorring!
Figure 4-3.

A *protocol* of any kind is a set of rules that two parties agree will govern their interactions with each other. There are protocols for waltzing, jitterbugging, country swing dancing—and for transferring files between your computer and a remote computer. Obviously, both partners in a dance must know the same steps!

Dozens of different file transfer protocols are available, some widely used and others barely known outside their developers' companies. Your terminal software should include the following most commonly used file-transfer protocols.

ASCII   Like TTY terminal emulation (described in the preceding section), the ASCII protocol is a lowest common denominator. It isn't the most efficient or the most error-resistant protocol by a long shot, but it is useful for sending text-only files when no other match is found between your "dance book" and the remote computer's.

NOTE: Do not use ASCII to send anything except plain-text files! The ASCII protocol will not transmit programs (COM or EXE files), spreadsheets, database files, graphics, word processor documents, archived files (ZIP, ARC, LHA, ARJ, and so on), or any other file that contains control or high-bit characters.

Xmodem   Xmodem provides error correction, making it suitable for file transfers in which the data must get there in exactly the same form in which it was sent. Xmodem was the first error-correcting protocol developed for personal computers (see Chapter 7 for Xmodem's origin). It is the most widely available error-correcting protocol, but it is rather slow.

Ymodem   Ymodem is an improved version of Xmodem that yields higher file-transfer speeds. Several variations of Ymodem include other nice features. *Ymodem-Batch* lets you send several files in a row, without repeating the file-transfer setup process for every single file. *Ymodem-G* is designed to take full advantage of modems that provide all the error correction in their hardware. (See Chapter 3 for a discussion of error-correcting modems.)

Kermit   Kermit was developed at Columbia University to be a Swiss-Army knife sort of file-transfer protocol—ready to handle any situation. Kermit's strength lies in its ability to transfer data over any kind of serial connection between virtually any type of computer. This extreme flexibility comes with a price: Kermit is very slow even compared to Xmodem, though Kermit does offer automatic filename reading, which Xmodem lacks.

Zmodem   Zmodem is the most recent of the file-transfer protocols discussed here, and it is fast becoming as "standard" a feature of terminal software as power steering is in automobiles. Zmodem is extremely fast, rock-solid in error correction, and provides many user-friendly features. These include batch-transfers (like Ymodem), automatic downloading when an incoming file is detected (so you don't have to manually set up to receive); automatic reading of filenames (like Kermit) so you only have to tell the remote computer what to send, and Zmodem tells *your* computer what it is receiving; and *download-resumption*: the ability to save the portion of an aborted file transfer that came through, and pick up where it left off in the next transfer attempt. You'll really appreciate download-resumption when you receive almost all of a 500K file before someone in the house picks up an extension phone and kills your modem connection!

There are dozens of other file-transfer protocols (see Figure 4-4), but Xmodem, Ymodem, Kermit, and Zmodem are widely considered the essential protocols. Many terminal programs offer "hooks" to which you can attach *external protocols* that are not built into the terminal software itself.

The Dialing Directory

Most people need an address book to keep track of all of their contacts. Any terminal software worth using lets you create a *dialing directory*, a database that serves as an address book for your frequent online stops. But good terminal software includes more than just names and phone numbers; it can act as a personal secretary, and even help your modem perform routine functions in your absence.

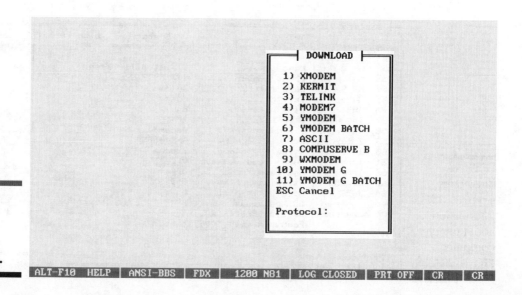

Procomm's suite of file transfer protocols
Figure 4-4.

Figure 4-5 shows a Dialing Directory setup screen that facilitates basic and "luxury" functions. The basics include

✦ *Remote Computer's Name* You can search for part of a name to quickly find the right entry to dial.

✦ *Phone Number* An obvious essential.

✦ *Communications Settings* The terminal type and file-transfer protocol normally used with this particular remote computer, the port speed (computer-to-serial-port speed) to use, and the essential data bit, parity, and stop bit settings.

✦ *Password* You can store a password associated with each entry in your dialing directory. If you use a different password on every remote computer you call, this feature keeps track of them for you.

✦ *Linked Script* This file contains instructions that you want executed every time this remote computer is called. See the "Script Recording" section later in this chapter for details.

✦ *Dialing Prefix* Here you enter predefined characters that you want sent to the modem just before it dials the phone number for this entry. Prefixes can save quite a few repetitive keystrokes when you are building your dialing directory. Multiple prefixes can be defined elsewhere in the terminal software. Examples include "9~~" (which tells the system to dial 9 for an outside line and wait two half-seconds to get it before dialing the phone number) and simply "1" (which tells it to dial 1 before trying to dial this long-distance number). If you travel, a third prefix might

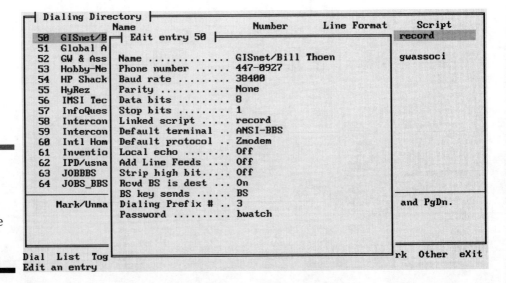

Dialing directories store information about remote computers

Figure 4-5.

send your calling-card number along with appropriate pauses and codes, saving a *lot* of repetitive keypunching!

The other items in this dialing directory entry are routine "set once and forget" configuration items. Rarely will you need to change these defaults when creating a new dialing directory entry.

"Luxury" Features You'll Really Appreciate

The following features are not essential, but they do make life online a whole lot easier, less time-consuming, and generally more fun! Most shareware and commercial terminal software include these features to some degree—their ease of use and efficiency will vary between systems. Learning to use them is easy and well worth the trouble.

Session Logging: Saving a Transcript of What You See

An online session often gives you much more information than you can remember, or would care to stop and read while paying by the minute. Sometimes you will have problems interacting with a remote computer. The first thing you need to know is "What keys did I really press, and exactly what were the results?"

Wouldn't it be nice to have a personal transcriptionist record everything that crosses your screen? That is exactly what *session logging* does! When you turn on session logging, it opens a file on your disk that captures a copy of everything you type to the remote computer and everything that comes back to your screen; hence the alternative name *disk capture*.

Session logs of data tables (items arranged in rows and columns) generally can be imported into spreadsheet and database programs, eliminating the need to print hard copies and rekey all that data. Direct importation eliminates typing errors as well.

Macros: Saving Little Bits of Time, Lots of Times

Each time you connect to a remote computer, you have to enter some little scrap of information: your name, password, address, telephone number, birthdate, and so on. *Macros* let you store such trivia and transmit them with a single keystroke.

For example, I call my local library's online catalog several times a day. It always asks for my library card number and last name. The [F2] key, which is the one I've set up for this particular macro, sends these 22 characters for me without error, every time.

Script Recording/Programming: "Smart" Macros

A macro does the same thing every time you press its function key. Macros cannot "decide" whether to send your last name or your first name first, based on what the remote computer requests. *Scripts* are special programs that add nearly-intelligent capabilities to your terminal software.

A script can do basic repetitive chores, such as signing on, entering your name and password, and stopping at the Main menu. Complex scripts employing IF...THEN...ELSE logic and looping can deal with busy signals, bad connections, waiting mail, and other uncertain events without you even being at the keyboard. Scripts can even call other scripts, so your modem can "make the rounds" of numerous online services with no help from you at all!

If you take the time to learn your terminal software's *script programming language,* you can write "intelligent" scripts that can appropriately respond to varying conditions, like the possibility of a busy signal, the absence/presence of new mail, or unexpected disconnections.

Non-programmers in particular should look for *script recording* when choosing terminal software. When you turn on the script recording feature, your keystrokes and the remote computer's responses are recorded and compiled into a script program. Thereafter, a single keystroke can dial a number, wait for the "Enter your name" prompt, enter your name and password, get you to the Main menu, check for new files, and do other complex tasks that are beyond the abilities of simple macros.

Recorded scripts follow the same routine every time they are run. If your script dials a number and gets a busy signal instead of a log-on prompt, it won't know what to do. If there are no new files since your last call, you don't want your script to try to download anything. Recorded scripts cannot detect such common variations between reality and what they expect.

Macintosh Terminal Programs

Most of the personal computers in use today (over 100 million) are IBM-compatible computers running Microsoft's MS/DOS operating system. Therefore, it should be no surprise that online services and software are heavily IBM oriented. This state of affairs is not a slight to Macintosh owners, merely a result of the relative sizes of the IBM-PC and Mac markets.

Mac owners can fully enjoy IBM-oriented online services if they choose terminal software that supports ANSI color/cursor control codes and IBM graphics characters. Without these features, Mac owners will be limited to TTY (plain text) terminal emulation when calling IBM-oriented online services.

ANSI color/cursor control was discussed in the "Features You Really Need" section earlier in this chapter. IBM graphics are not as important to online enjoyment as ANSI, but they do make screen displays more readable and fun.

IBM graphics are often called *high-bit characters*. The standard ASCII character set consists of 127 characters, which can all be represented by just seven of the eight data bits found in an asynchronous character. The eighth bit, also called the "high bit," can give the 127 characters entirely new looks. Adding the eighth bit to a seven-bit ASCII character is the same as adding 127 to the decimal number that represents the seven-bit character. Try the following exercise to see how high-bit characters look and correspond to seven-bit characters:

4

1. Hold down the ⟨Alt⟩ key and press the number ⟨6⟩, followed by the number ⟨5⟩ (⟨Alt⟩-⟨6⟩⟨5⟩). The letter "A" should appear when you release the ⟨Alt⟩ key.

2. Now do the same thing using the number 192 (65+127). You should see a Û graphics character. This is the high-bit version of ASCII character 65 (the letter "A," in upper case).

IBM designed these high-bit characters into its original PC, which is how they became known as IBM graphics characters. These characters include line-drawing elements such as the little "box corner" you just saw, patterned boxes that can provide shadow effects, "smiley faces," and other special characters for decorative purposes. IBM graphics are widely used in the design of online services. They make menus more readable, and games more entertaining.

Most commercial terminal software for Macintoshes support ANSI color/cursor control and IBM high-bit graphics; often this is indicated by the phrase "ANSI/IBM" in the features list on the box. Three shareware Mac terminal programs are very popular. You can find them online, in shareware catalogs or stores, or by contacting these authors directly:

✦ *White Knight* Freesoft Co., 105 McKinley Road, Beaver Falls, PA 15010. 412-846-2700 (voice)

✦ *Teamworks* c/o James Rhodes, 401 Eastwood Place, Lufkin, TX 75901

✦ *ZTerm* c/o David P. Alverson, 5635 Cross Creek Court, Mason, OH 45040

Windows 3.0 & 3.1 Terminal Software

The Windows *graphical user interface* (GUI, pronounced "gooey") is taking the computer world by storm; over 1 million copies are sold every month! Windows is called an *operating environment*, a new "way of doing things" under the venerable MS/DOS operating system. Windows alone won't cold-start your computer; MS/DOS must be loaded first. In this respect, Windows is different from the Macintosh, which includes a stand-alone operating system.

But *operating* your computer under Windows is as different from operating under plain old DOS as driving an automatic transmission car is from driving a standard stick-shift. The driver has to make far fewer motions to accomplish the same thing, and has far fewer things to worry about. (The same praise can be heaped on Macintoshes.)

Instead of pressing keys to search for a dialing directory entry, Windows lets you use a mouse to scroll through lists and select the entry you want with a single click. Downloads can be started with a similar point-and-click technique. About the only time you must type text is to create a dialing directory entry or change the modem's initialization string.

Multitasking, the ability to do several things at once, is another key benefit of Windows-based telecommunications. You can start a lengthy file transfer, switch to your favorite word processor or Windows game program, and get some work or play done while the bytes fly in the background. (Lately, I have been keeping one eye on cable television in one Windows window while reading my e-mail or editing this book in another, thanks to the Watchit!TV card from New Media Graphics—a sinfully delightful example of multitasking!)

Alas, telecommunications has never been a high priority with Microsoft Corp., the developer of Windows. Terminal, the built-in Windows communications program, is a stripped-down version of DynaComm, sold by Future Soft Engineering, Inc. The medical definition of "terminal" best describes the convenience and performance of what is left in Terminal for Windows. The program lacks ANSI color/cursor control and IBM graphics; graphic box characters, often used in menu borders of online services, look like Greek letters (see Figure 4-6). File transfer protocols include only the two slowest options: Xmodem and Kermit.

Fortunately, third-party software developers have come to Windows' rescue. Here are some good alternatives to Terminal suffering:

✦ *Crosstalk for Windows* Digital Communications Associates Inc., 1000 Alderman Dr., Alpharetta, GA 30202; 800-348-3221, 404-442-4000 (voice). Crosstalk, in whatever flavor, is one of the most popular and powerful communications programs ever sold; more powerful, in fact, than most people need.

✦ *MicroPhone II v2.0 for Windows* Software Ventures Corp., 2907 Claremont Avenue, #220, Berkeley, CA 94705. 800-336-6477,

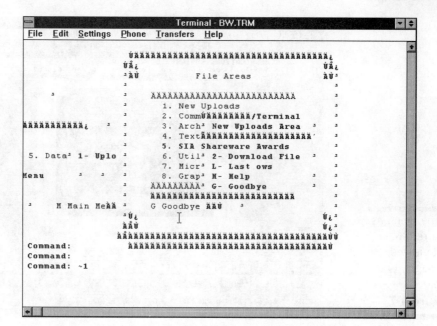

Online menu
viewed
through
Windows'
Terminal

Figure 4-6.

510-644-3232 (voice). Originally a Macintosh program, MicroPhone adapted very well to the Windows GUI environment.

✦ *Procomm Plus for Windows* DataStorm Technologies Inc., P. O. Box 1471, Columbia, MO 65205. 314-443-3282 (voice). Procomm started as shareware and went commercial. There is no Windows shareware version. The program was designed by modem maniacs *for* modem maniacs; a good bet! (See Chapter 15 for a review of Procomm Plus for Windows.)

✦ *Terminal Plus* Future Soft Engineering Inc., 1001 S. Dairy Ashford, #101, Houston, TX 77077. 713-496-9400 (voice). From the folks who brought you Windows' Terminal, but don't let that scare you. Terminal Plus includes Xmodem, Kermit, Ymodem-Batch, Zmodem, and CompuServe-B file-transfer protocols, a decent script language, script recording ability, and other standard features.

✦ *Unicom v3.0* Data Graphics, P.O. Box 58517, Renton, WA 98058. 206-932-8871 (voice). A shareware upstart that is giving the shrink-wrapped packages a run for their money. The current version *requires* Windows 3.1. See Figure 4-7.

Fax/Data Modem Software

Adding fax capabilities to a modem opens up a whole new world of options for business and personal telecommunications. More people have fax

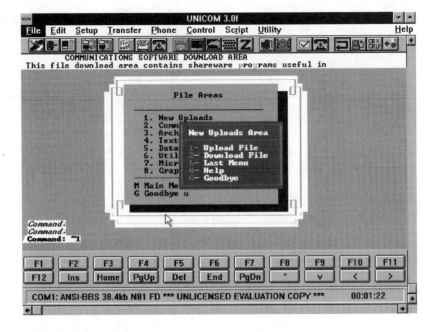

Same menu as
Figure 4-6,
but viewed
through
Unicom
Figure 4-7.

machines than have modems. More information is available on faxable
paper than on hard drives.

A modem that can send and receive both asynchronous data and facsimile
data is called a *fax/data modem,* or simply "fax/modem." Ordinary terminal
software serves just fine on the data side of a fax/modem, but special
software is required to drive the fax capabilities. Fax/modem software
generally includes both fax and terminal emulation functions.

A fax machine ideally is always ready to receive incoming faxes. When using
a fax/modem, that means the fax software must always be running, even if
you need the computer for something else. MS-DOS fax software solves this
dilemma with *Terminate and Stay Resident (TSR)* software, which stays active
"in the background" while you load and run other programs. A TSR fax
program constantly "listens" for incoming faxes, and handles them without
your intervention. You can go on processing words or spreading sheets of
numbers.

But things can get pretty crowded in your MS/DOS computer's limited
(640K) conventional memory. Facsimile software is complex, and takes up
a lot of RAM (Random Access Memory). You may find that some larger
programs that you need to run while the fax software is loaded simply won't
fit into memory.

TSR fax software can conflict with your foreground application for access to the disk drive when the fax software is spooling an incoming fax to disk. The fax software can't wait; data is pouring in. So your foreground application may suddenly "freeze up" until the fax is done; in the worst case, trying to load a spreadsheet may abort both the fax and the spreadsheet program.

Windows 3.*x* solves these problems much better than DOS can. Windows running in 386 Enhanced mode provides each active application with its very own "virtual machine," effectively dividing the megabytes of RAM that an 80386 processor can address into several partitions that act like separate computers with up to 640K of RAM each. Fax software needn't squeeze out your spreadsheet. Windows was designed from scratch to arbitrate conflicting demands for disk access, and it does so quite well.

One of the most exciting developments in fax software is Optical Character Recognition (OCR), the ability to translate the dots that comprise a fax into ASCII characters that standard database, spreadsheet, and word processing programs can recognize. Many incoming faxes must be retyped into computers; OCR promises to eliminate all that labor.

Promises, promises... the truth is, OCR is still an infant technology, with an infant's tendency to make messes and become cranky. Even the manufacturers promise only "99 percent accurate" translation of faxes into ASCII text. That means in a typical 2,000-character page, you can expect 20 errors under ideal conditions (10-point nonproportional type, in a single column). Most OCR software is far less accurate when translating two-column pages, proportionally spaced type, or text mixed with pictures on a page. Don't expect too much from the current generation of OCR software.

While the whole world seems to be moving into Windows, not everyone is there yet. Most fax software shipped today comes with both DOS and Windows versions. Some titles include:

✦ *Faxit* From Future Soft, makers of Terminal Plus described above. Faxit can be had bundled with Terminal Plus for $195.

✦ *WinFax Pro* Delrina Technology, Inc., 895 Don Mills Road, 500-Z Park Centre, Toronto, ON M3C 1W3, Canada. 416-441-3676 (voice). $129.00.

✦ *UltraFAX* ZSoft Corp., 450 Franklin Road, Ste. 100, Marietta, GA 30067. 404-428-0008 (voice). $119.

4

Choosing Terminal Software Is Like Choosing a Car

Many people (myself included) don't drive their cars much, so they feel fine with just basic transportation. But traveling sales reps and other "road warriors" want automotive comfort and convenience proportionate to the amount of time they spend behind the wheel.

Similarly, if you won't use a modem except for basic, occasional use, the terminal software that came with your modem may be all the software you'll ever want. People who spend a lot of time online wisely spend a lot of time choosing their terminal software.

You choose a car by trying it out. The seats, mirrors, air-flow vents, lighting, even the steering wheel tilt and interior colors can all be purchased or adjusted to suit your personal comfort. Few people are overwhelmed by the choices and possibilities of all these options. Indeed, most car buyers would be very unhappy if they *couldn't* get everything exactly the way they want it!

Most modem users interact with their terminal software as intimately and constantly as they do with their cars when driving them. The more customizable your software is, the more you will enjoy your trips along the online highways.

CHAPTER

5

SETTING UP YOUR MODEM

This chapter helps you install an internal or external modem quickly and correctly. The information that this chapter gives about how modems connect to your computer will help you avoid 99 percent of hardware installation problems. (Appendix B goes into great detail about that last 1 percent of installation situations.)

Here you will find tips on avoiding interpersonal conflicts as well as hardware problems. People who share your modem's phone line (for incoming or outgoing calls) must be considered when setting up your modem.

Modems often must cooperate with other devices attached to your phone line. This chapter gives simple, inexpensive ways to avoid problems.

General Considerations for Internal and External Modems

Some installation issues are the same for internal or external modems. This section explains serial ports, COM ports, IRQs, and how to set up your modem so it works with your existing computer system. Later sections focus on the differences between installing internal and external modems.

Serial Ports: Traffic Cop and Waystation Between the Computer and the Modem

All data passing between your computer and modem goes through a *serial port,* a hardware device that acts as a traffic cop and temporary storage area for incoming and outgoing data.

You will occasionally hear this device called an *RS232C port* or a serial *I/O (Input/Output) port.* Don't let it throw you; a serial port is a serial port.

Serial Connectors: the Visible Aspects of Serial Ports

When serial ports are installed, the only visible evidence of them are *serial connectors* sticking out of the back of your computer, in the same general area where you plug in printers, monitors, and other external devices.

Two types of serial connectors may be found; the only practical difference is the number of pins sticking out of them. (See Figure 5-1.) If you have an older IBM PC or PC XT computer, your serial port probably includes a 25-pin connector. More recent PC AT class machines use smaller, 9-pin serial connectors. Some computers have both 9-pin and 25-pin serial connectors.

COM and IRQ Memory Addresses: the Invisible Aspects of Serial Ports

In order to allow your modem to talk to your computer, you need to give the modem a "direct line" to your computer's memory. Imagine that this direct line is a telephone line and think of your serial port as an ordinary telephone. The serial port must do two things for your computer that a

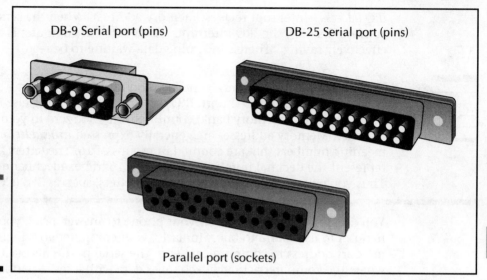

9-pin and 25-pin serial port connectors
Figure 5-1.

DB-9 Serial port (pins)　　　DB-25 Serial port (pins)

Parallel port (sockets)

phone does for you: 1) get your computer's attention, and then 2) exchange data with your computer. Telephones get your attention by ringing, and exchange sounds with you through the handset. Computers and serial ports do much the same thing through separate memory locations in your computer. See Figure 5-2.

The ringer in your phone signals anyone listening that someone is trying to call you. The ringer interrupts whatever you are doing to focus your attention on the phone. The ringer's equivalent in a serial port is called an

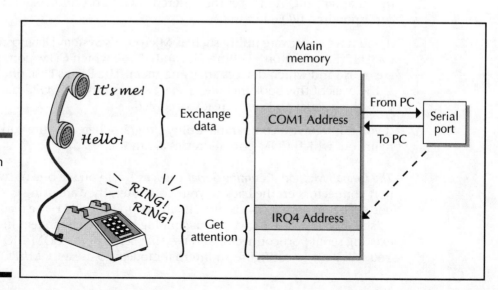

Serial ports "ring" through the IRQ; computer "answers" through the COM port
Figure 5-2.

It's me!

Hello!

Exchange data

RING! RING!

Get attention

Main memory

COM1 Address

IRQ4 Address

From PC

To PC

Serial port

IRQ address, (InteRrupt reQuest memory address). When the serial port activates its IRQ, the IRQ interrupts whatever your computer is doing, effectively saying, "There's incoming data waiting to be read."

 NOTE: A *memory address* is the location of the first byte in a block of bytes used by a COM port, IRQ, program, or anything else residing in your computer's memory bank, counting from byte zero in your computer's memory. Memory addresses are generally expressed in *hexadecimal* numbers, meaning numbers that are counted in groups of 16. The letters *A* through *G* represent the decimal numbers 11 through 16 in hexadecimal notation. Thus you will see "numbers" that include letters, such as 2F8 (COM1).

You don't pick up the *ringer* on your phone to answer a call; you lift the handset to listen and to talk. Similarly, your computer goes to another memory address to communicate with the serial port. This place in memory where the computer actually exchanges data with a serial port is called a *COM port address.*

IBM-compatible computers are designed to accommodate multiple serial ports. Their memory addresses are labeled COM1, COM2, IRQ3, IRQ4, and so on. Every serial port you use must be assigned a COM port address and an IRQ address.

Finding a COM Port Address for Your Modem

The first step toward an ideal installation is to determine which COM port addresses are already used by the devices on your system. (A section later in this chapter, "IRQ Addresses for Different COM Port Addresses," discusses corresponding IRQ addresses.)

If you have a software utility such as Microsoft's System Diagnostics (MSD.EXE) or Norton's Utilities, it can tell you which COM port addresses are in use and which devices are using them. The Bonus Disk offered by mail at the back of this book includes a shareware utility, SNOOP, that will tell you which serial ports are already occupied.

If you don't have a comparable utility program, here are three other ways to figure out which COM port addresses are in use.

The Eyeball Method: Counting Serial Devices If you see one or two serial port connectors on the back of your computer, they are using two COM ports. The first serial port is most likely set up for COM1; the second (if it exists) probably uses COM2. You can plug an external modem into an existing serial port connector and use that serial port's COM/IRQ settings. You will have to configure an internal modem to use a COM/IRQ combination that is not used by any existing serial ports. (The section "Installing an Internal Modem," later in this chapter, gives information on configuring internal modems.)

NOTE: If you plug your external modem into an existing serial port, but do not know whether it is set for COM1 or COM2, you can quickly find out by trying to "talk" to your modem. Just use the DOS COPY command to send any small (under 1,000 bytes) file to the COM port you think the modem is using. COPY SMALL.TXT COM1, for instance, will send the file SMALL.TXT to COM1. If the external modem is connected to COM1, you will see a flurry of blinking lights on the LED panel. If the modem is using COM2, it won't receive SMALL.TXT and nothing will light up.

If you have a *serial* mouse (as opposed to a *bus* mouse), it takes up a COM port whenever your mouse driver software is loaded. Local area network adapters also monopolize COM ports. If your system includes such serial devices, you will have to determine from their software settings or user manuals which COM ports they are using. Eliminate these COM ports from your list of potential modem settings.

It is possible, though unlikely, that your system has no existing serial ports, and no other serial devices. If this is the case, you can use COM1 for your internal modem. Count any serial port connectors too. Each uses a COM port, even if nothing is plugged into them.

The DEBUG Method   You can use one of MS/DOS' standard utilities to determine which COM port addresses are currently in use. The subdirectory containing all your other DOS command files, such as COMMAND.COM, COPY.COM, and so on, usually contains DEBUG.EXE. If your DOS files are in a subdirectory named C:\DOS, switch to that directory and start DEBUG.EXE by typing the following at the DOS command prompt (press the (Enter) key at the end of each line):

```
CD C:\DOS
DEBUG
```

A simple hyphen will replace the DOS command-line prompt on your screen, indicating that DEBUG is loaded and ready. Now type the following and press the (Enter) key:

```
D40:00
```

DEBUG should display several lines of numbers. The very first line tells which COM port addresses are in use.

In Figure 5-3, the first four pairs of numbers to the right of 0040:0000 represent COM1 through COM4. A non-zero pair of numbers, such as "F8 03," indicates that a COM port is being used by a serial device; in this example, COM1, COM2, and COM3 are all in use. The fourth pair of numbers in Figure 5-3 is 00 00, indicating that COM4 is available for your modem.

The DEBUG method should be used with the eyeball method; neither is totally reliable by itself. If your visual inspection tells you three serial devices are in use, but DEBUG shows only two (or vice versa), see Appendix B.

The MODE Command Method   The MODE.COM command, like DEBUG.EXE, is a standard MS/DOS utility. You can use it to see if a specific COM port is active. Just type the following and press the (Enter) key:

```
MODE COM# (where # is 1, 2, 3, 4, etc.)
```

If COM# is occupied, MODE COM# will yield this display:

```
Status for device COM#:
-----------------------
Retry=NONE
```

If COM# is empty (available for a modem), MODE COM# will display this:

```
Illegal device name - COM#
```

One of these methods—a utility program, the eyeball method, DEBUG, or MODE—should tell you which COM port address(es) are available for your modem.

IRQ Addresses for Different COM Port Addresses
Because every COM port address needs a corresponding IRQ address, manufacturers have developed default standards for the first four COM ports:

DEBUG
display of
COM port
addresses
Figure 5-3.

```
0040:0000   F8 03    F8 02    E8 02    00 00
            ‿‿‿      ‿‿‿      ‿‿‿      ‿‿‿
            COM1     COM2     COM3     COM4
                                       unused
```

✦ COM1 and COM3 use IRQ4

✦ COM2 and COM4 use IRQ3

These default assignments are much like having two phone lines in your house, one for the adults and one for the kids. The important thing is to avoid fighting over who will use the phone at any given moment!

If your modem will share an IRQ with other devices, remember that *only one device at a time can use an IRQ address.* This makes sense: only one person can answer a ringing phone, and while that person is using the phone no one else can hear the phone ring.

If you will use your modem on COM2/IRQ3, you can set up your mouse (or other serial device) on COM4/IRQ3. But you must *unload the mouse's software from memory before using the modem!* Otherwise, the mouse software will be using IRQ3 when you try to use the modem, and an *IRQ conflict* will keep your modem offline.

5

NOTE: Windows 3.x stores a list of serial ports that it uses in the Windows WIN.INI file. Load this text file into a word processor and search for COM1, COM2, and so on, to learn which ports Windows uses.

CAUTION: Be careful not to change the WIN.INI file in any way.

If you run into an IRQ conflict that you cannot solve with the information in this chapter, see Appendix B.

Plugging in Phone Lines

Every modem, internal or external, includes two modular telephone jacks. (Some modem manuals call them RJ-11 jacks, the technical term.) Usually, one jack is labeled Line; the phone cord running from the wall socket plugs into the Line jack. The other jack is generally labeled Phone. You can plug a telephone's cord into this jack if you wish, and use the line for regular telephone calls when the modem is not in use. Figure 5-4 shows how a phone and internal modem share a line.

It is important to plug the right cord into the right jack. Even experienced modem maniacs catch themselves trying to dial out through a jack that is connected to the phone on their desk, not to the telephone network. Nothing serious, or even humorous, will happen if you make this mistake; you just won't get a dial tone.

Some modems label the LINE jack WALL. A few modems have no labels on the jacks (like my Galaxy UFO modem); it doesn't matter which cord goes where on such modems. The modem figures out what is on the other end of each cord; the one plugged into the wall carries the telephone network's electrical current.

Whereas COM ports, IRQs, and phone lines are common to both internal and external modems, there are specific installation procedures for internal and external modems; the rest of the chapter shows how to install each type.

Installing an Internal Modem

Internal modems plug into one of the expansion slots inside your computer. Because internal modems have their own serial port circuitry built in, they do not take up any existing serial port connectors. If all of your serial port connectors are in use, consider purchasing an internal modem.

The first step when installing an internal modem is to remove your computer's cover.

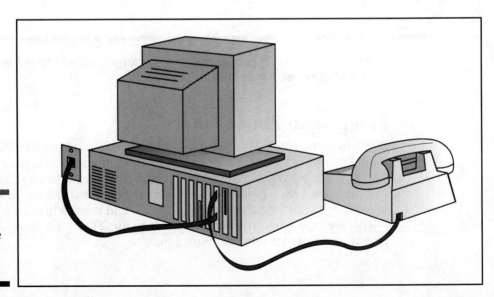

A telephone and a modem can share one phone line
Figure 5-4.

Next locate a vacant expansion slot. Figure 5-5 illustrates an expansion slot with an internal modem card poised to slide down into it.

In Figure 5-5 you see an 8-bit card about to slide into a 16-bit slot; notice that the slot extends in a second row of gripper teeth beyond the end of the card's connector. If you have a short, 8-bit slot in your computer, save the longer 16-bit and 32-bit slots for cards that really need them.

NOTE: If at all possible, choose a slot relatively removed from other cards. Modems generate a moderate amount of heat, and any extra ventilation will extend your modem's life span.

Once you select a vacant slot, unscrew and remove the vertical protective plate that covers the hole in your computer's rear panel, right in front of the slot. Then turn your attention to the modem card itself.

5

Configuring an Internal Modem's COM and IRQ Addresses

Before installing your internal modem, make sure its COM port and IRQ address settings do not conflict with those of other devices already in your computer.

An expansion slot with internal modem poised above it
Figure 5-5.

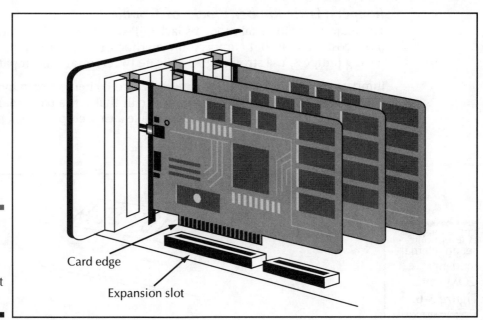

Card edge

Expansion slot

CAUTION: Read your modem's manual to determine its factory-default COM port and IRQ settings! Your modem could have been shipped set up to use anything from COM1 to COM4.

If you expect a conflict with the modem's default COM/IRQ setting and another device in your computer, use one of the methods described next to change your modem's settings.

DIP Switches: Little Light Switches All in a Row

High-quality internal modems use a row of very tiny toggle switches to set up COM port addresses. These *DIP switches* look like regular light switches that have been shrunk to about 1/16th of an inch. Figure 5-6 shows DIP switches. Using a ballpoint pen, a narrow screwdriver, or other blunt-pointed tool, you can flip the switches on or off to match one of the patterns shown in your modem's manual; each such pattern corresponds to a COM port address and its default IRQ setting.

WARNING: Never use a pencil to change DIP switches. The lead in pencils is an electrical conductor, and any shavings that get into the switch's circuitry might short it out.

Jumpers: Little Rubber Blocks of Trouble

The majority of internal modems lack DIP switches, relying instead on a more cost-effective but cumbersome method of setting COM ports. When setting jumpers, use strong light, delicate tweezers, and great patience.

Jumpers are pairs of pins on the modem card. When covered by a *jumper block*, the pins complete an electrical circuit that sets a particular COM port/IRQ setting. A jumper block looks like a tiny chip of black plastic with

DIP switches set an internal modem's COM port
Figure 5-6.

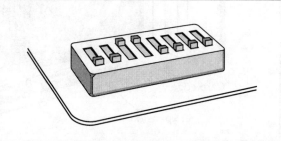

two metal-lined sockets for the jumper pins. Figure 5-7 illustrates these troublesome devices. Diagrams in your modem's manual will show which pins should be connected by jumper blocks in order to configure each COM port/IRQ setting.

"Switchless" Software-Configured Modems

Some modems don't have physical DIP switches or jumpers. Instead, they are configured entirely through software commands that you issue to the modem from your keyboard, using your terminal software. The settings you choose can be stored in the modem's own memory, so you need not enter these commands more than once.

Physical switches do have one advantage over software switches: a physical switch is relatively indifferent to electrical interference. If a power surge scrambles your modem's memory, the physical switches will still "remember" the basic default settings you need to get back online. In the event of a power surge, switchless modems may lose their settings and need to be configured again from scratch.

Inserting a Modem Card into Your Computer

Ease the modem card into its slot, making sure that the gold "tooth" connector along its bottom edge is perfectly aligned with the slot below. Press slowly but firmly to seat the card in the slot. See Figure 5-5.

 NOTE: If you encounter any solid resistance, stop and see what is causing it. Usually, the gold edge and the slot are not perfectly aligned, or the metal "tongue" at the bottom of the silver backplate is not aligned with its slot on the bottom back edge of your computer's case.

Your modem card includes a tab that will be screwed down to secure the card to the back edge of your computer. (See the top of the card in Figure 5-5.) This tab should fit flush with its matching hole. The top edge of the modem card should be perfectly level, indicating that the gold edge along

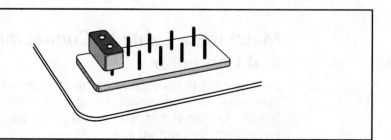

A jumper block and jumper pins
Figure 5-7.

the bottom of the card is inserted to the same depth all along the length of its slot.

Before securing the tab, check the modular telephone-style jacks that now peek out from the back of your computer. Make sure you can insert and remove phone cords in each jack with ease. If the jacks are out of alignment—partially hidden by the backplane's edge—gently move the card from side to side just a tiny bit until you can insert and remove phone cords easily. Hold the card in that position while you screw down the retaining tab.

NOTE: Theoretically, you are now finished. But don't replace the computer's cover until you have read Chapter 6, installed your terminal software, and made sure that the card's COM port is properly configured. Otherwise, you may have to start all over.

Installing an External Modem

External modems can be a plug-and-play breeze compared to their internal cousins. If you have an empty serial port connector, all you need do is plug the right cable into the serial port connector and your modem, insert the phone lines, and connect the modem's power supply.

Adding an Internal Serial Port Card for an External Modem

If your existing serial port connectors are all occupied, you will need to buy a serial port add-on card and install it inside your computer, or remove one of the devices taking up an existing serial port. A simple two-port card should cost about $15; you can buy them at any computer or electronics store.

Most add-on port cards come configured for COM1 and COM2. You may have to fiddle with jumpers to set the new ports for COM3 and COM4. Install the serial port card as described in the "Installing an Internal Modem" section earlier in this chapter.

Matching a Cable to Connectors on the Modem and Computer

Because modem manufacturers don't know what kind of connectors you will need, most external modems do not come with a cable that connects the modem to a serial port. You probably will have to buy a cable at an electronics or computer store.

When buying a cable for your modem, ask for an *RS232C serial cable, wired "straight through,"* meaning pin 1 on one end of the cable is wired to pin 1 on the other end, pin 2 is wired to pin 2, and so on. Do not accept a *null-modem* cable. This type of cable is wired a bit differently, for directly connecting two serial ports without modems between them.

The connectors on each end of the cable must match the connectors on your modem and computer. Most modems have 25-pin female connectors (holes in the connector), so the modem end of the cable must have a 25-pin male connector (pins sticking out).

Your computer's serial port connector will most likely be male, so that end of the cable must be female. But the computer's serial port connector may have 9 or 25 pins; make sure the computer's end of the cable has the same number of holes!

5

NOTE: Gender-changing adapters let you fit a cable you may already own to just about any type of modem or serial port connector. They cost about $5 to $8 (instead of $12 to $20 for a new cable).

Eliminating Problems with Shared Phone Lines

If you use the same phone line for regular telephone and modem calls, two common problems may arise. Both are easily avoided.

Call Waiting

The click heard when call waiting tells you someone else is trying to interrupt your current call will usually end a modem connection. At the very least, this line noise will scramble the data your modems are exchanging. Eliminate call waiting if you can (it's an abominably rude thing to do to your current caller, in our humble opinion). But if you absolutely cannot give up call waiting, configure your modem to temporarily turn it off each time the modem places a call. See Chapter 6 to learn what initialization strings are and how to set them.

Extension Phones

If someone in another room picks up an extension phone while you're sending or receiving a modem transmission, it will have the same effect on your connection as call waiting; the modem will quickly disconnect. The other person will get an unpleasant earful of modem "squeals." Neither event is good for domestic tranquility, which is probably why one-third of modem users eventually add another phone line exclusively for their modem's use.

You can solve your modem's problem (though not that of the other person who wishes to use the line) with an inexpensive device sold at phone stores, electronics shops, and even department stores. An *extension blocker* will prevent a modem's transmission from being interrupted when another phone is picked up elsewhere in your home.

Protecting Your Modem from Power and Heat Damage

All modems generate a fair amount of heat. External modems are designed to dissipate heat through a system of slots cut in their cases. Don't block these slots with stacks of paper, floppy disks, or other things. Place your modem so that air will readily circulate around it. Do not put it on top of a monitor or other device that puts out even more heat!

Power surges can also damage a modem's delicate circuits. The normal power coming in through your phone line is harmlessly weak. But modems, designed as they are to operate with weak power signals, are vulnerable to relatively strong surges in phone line power. Your modem's circuitry can be permanently damaged by a lightning bolt striking the phone line. A less disastrous but more common occurrence is loss of default settings stored in your modem's memory, a serious though rarely terminal nuisance. If this happens, you have to type all those default settings into your modem and save them again. Loss of stored settings can be triggered by power surges much weaker than lightning strikes.

A *phone line surge protector* installed between the wall plate and your modem's modular jack can head off such calamities. Surge protectors are often built into master power control switches and protectors that protect all of your sensitive computer equipment, but they can also be purchased as standalone devices that serve only modems.

Don't forget to provide surge protection for an external modem's power supply! Often this bulky box won't fit in any receptacles on a master control power switch, and people just plug it directly into the wall. Power conditioning and surge protection devices that plug directly into the wall socket and provide outlets for your modem's power supply, are often the best solution. Some models also provide modular jacks to guard your phone line as well as the electrical line.

Electrical and radio interference can be particularly troublesome with inexpensive, poorly shielded modems. Avoid putting your modem on top of a radio, near a fluorescent light, or within a foot of any electrical motor.

High-intensity, low-energy halogen lights generate a phenomenal amount of radio frequency interference. Try tuning in an AM station on a radio that is in the same room with one of these modern lights. The static will be especially impressive if the light is dimmed to a relatively low intensity. Turn off the halogen lamps in the room where you use your modem, or better yet, move them into another room.

When Everything Is Plugged in and Screwed Down

Modems are finicky about how they are initially installed, but once snuggled in, they seldom give any trouble. The only thing to remember is that your computer now has a new serial device installed in it. It's an excellent idea to keep a written record of which devices are installed on each COM port and IRQs, to make installing future add-ons easier.

5

Now that the hardware setup is out of the way, turn to Chapter 6 to learn how to set up the software that will let you control your modem.

CHAPTER

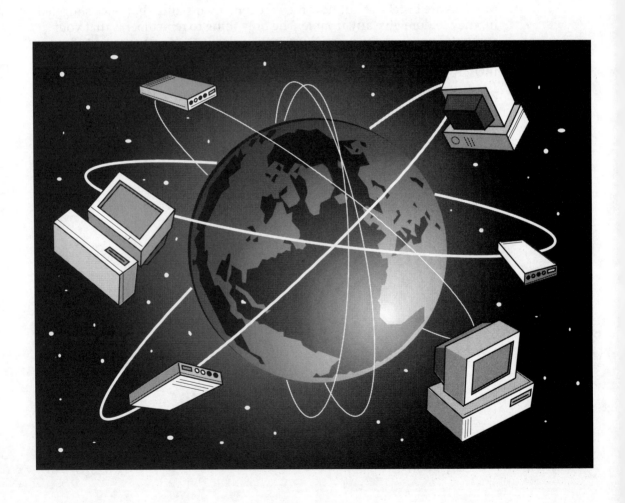

6

SOFTWARE INSTALLATION: INTRODUCING YOUR TERMINAL SOFTWARE TO YOUR MODEM

This chapter explains how to set up (configure) your terminal software to work in harmony with your modem. The first section, "General Software Setup for All Modem Types," deals with software settings that all types of modems require. You must get these settings right in order to make a successful modem call.

The second section, "Special Considerations for High-Speed or Data-Compression Modems," explains special configurations required by high-speed (9600 bps or faster) modems and modems of any speed that provide *data compression*: the ability to squeeze more useful information per second through a modem link of any given speed. Read this section if your modem has a top speed of 9600 bps or more *or* if your modem includes MNP, v.42, or v.42bis data compression regardless of its speed.

The third section, "Fine-Tuning Your Terminal Software Configuration," discusses the finer points of configuring your modem, including how to program it using the *Hayes AT command set* and the *initialization string* (commands your modem executes every time it is powered up or reset). These two issues baffle many novices, so this section explains them thoroughly. The third section also shows how to change the amount of time your modem waits for an answer before giving up; how to get your terminal software to dial 9 and wait for an outside line, enter calling-card codes for you, and handle other special dialing conditions; how to overcome sudden disconnections caused by call-waiting signals on your phone line; and other ways to deal with your unique circumstances.

General Software Setup for All Modem Types

Before tinkering with your terminal software, read its instruction manual to see if there is an easier way to configure your software and modem. Many manufacturers now include setup utilities that can make it very easy to set up many types of modems. Figure 6-1 shows a setup utility menu.

If your terminal software has a setup utility, be sure and run it since it may include your make and model in its list of modems. If your modem appears in the setup utility's list, all you need do is answer a couple of questions about COM ports and you'll be off and running!

If your terminal software did not include a setup utility or your modem is not listed in the setup utility's list of modems, follow the guidelines in this section to manually configure your terminal software.

COM Port Selection

You must tell your terminal software where to find your modem—that is, which COM port address the modem is using. Figure 6-2 shows Telix's Terminal Options screen, where you can select the right COM port. (Chapter 5 discusses COM ports in detail.) Your terminal software will not be able to exchange data with the modem unless both use the same COM port.

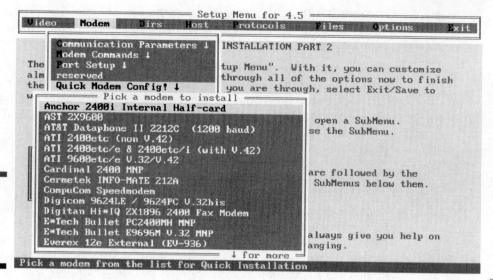

Qmodem
modem
definition
screen
Figure 6-1.

Most terminal software comes preset to assume the modem is using COM1. If your modem is using another COM port, change the software so it uses the same COM port.

Communication Parameters: Data Bits, Parity, Stop Bit

Most of the time, you will use eight data bits, no parity, and one stop bit (8-N-1). The only other common choice is 7-E-1, generally used only when

```
┤ Terminal options ├

A - Port COM1    Baud 38400    Parity None    Data bits 8    Stop bits 1

B - Emulate before translate table... Off
C - Default terminal type .......... ANSI
D - Status line .................... Bottom
E - Local echo ..................... Off
F - Add Line Feeds after CRs ....... Off
G - Strip high bit (incoming data) .. Off
H - Received Backspace destructive .. On
I - Backspace key sends ............ BS
J - XON/XOFF software flow control .. Off
K - CTS/RTS hardware flow control ... On
L - DSR/DTR hardware flow control ... Off
M - Compuserve Quick B transfers .... Off
N - Zmodem auto-downloads .......... On
O - Answerback string (ENQ) ........

Change which setting?        (Return or Esc to exit)
```

Telix Terminal
Options setup
screen
Figure 6-2.

Alt-Z for Help | ANSI | 38400-N81 FDX | | | Offline

communicating with mainframe computers. The 8-N-1 combination is so widely used that most terminal software comes configured for it. See Chapter 2 for a complete discussion of communication parameters.

If you need to change these communication parameters, read your software's manual to find the right menu. Each communication parameter—data bits, parity, and stop bit—can be changed individually. Many terminal programs also offer a one-key toggle that switches from 8-N-1 to 7-E-1 and back. Figure 6-3 shows Procomm's very convenient way of setting all communication parameters in one step.

Terminal Type Selection

The Qmodem terminal type selection screen, shown in Figure 6-4, has all the terminal type options most people need. ANSI/BBS is the most commonly used terminal type, and most software that supports ANSI/BBS uses it as the factory default. ANSI/BBS is ideal for general BBSing; it features ANSI color/cursor control and IBM graphics character support.

VT-100 terminal emulation is the second most widely used terminal type. It also offers color, cursor control, and graphics. If you are not familiar with the VT-100 keyboard, you may find that some keys don't behave as you expect them to. Read the manual or online instructions of any online service that requires VT-100 terminal emulation; it should tell you which keys have been assigned unusual functions.

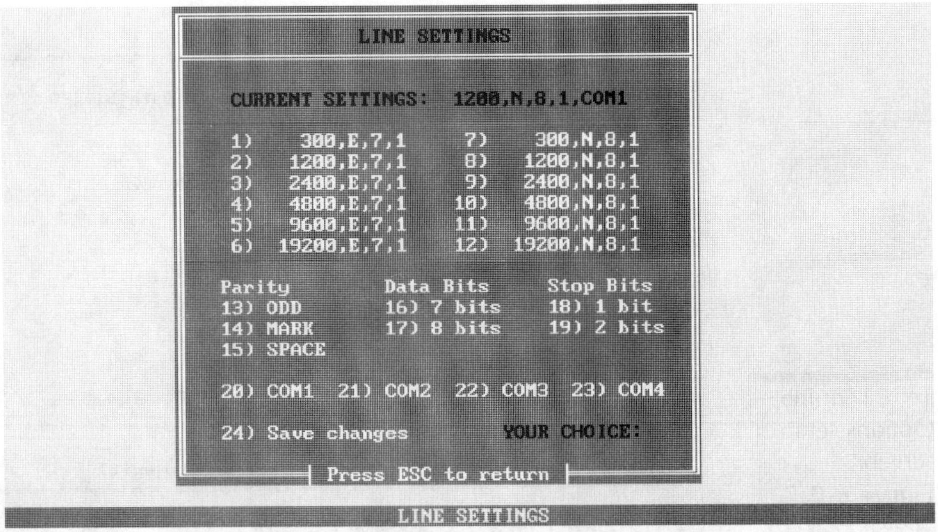

Procomm
communication
parameters
screen
Figure 6-3.

```
                      LINE SETTINGS

      CURRENT SETTINGS:   1200,N,8,1,COM1

       1)     300,E,7,1      7)      300,N,8,1
       2)    1200,E,7,1      8)     1200,N,8,1
       3)    2400,E,7,1      9)     2400,N,8,1
       4)    4800,E,7,1     10)     4800,N,8,1
       5)    9600,E,7,1     11)     9600,N,8,1
       6)   19200,E,7,1     12)    19200,N,8,1

      Parity           Data Bits         Stop Bits
      13) ODD          16) 7 bits        18) 1 bit
      14) MARK         17) 8 bits        19) 2 bits
      15) SPACE

      20) COM1   21) COM2   22) COM3   23) COM4

      24) Save changes          YOUR CHOICE:
                 | Press ESC to return |
                      LINE SETTINGS
```

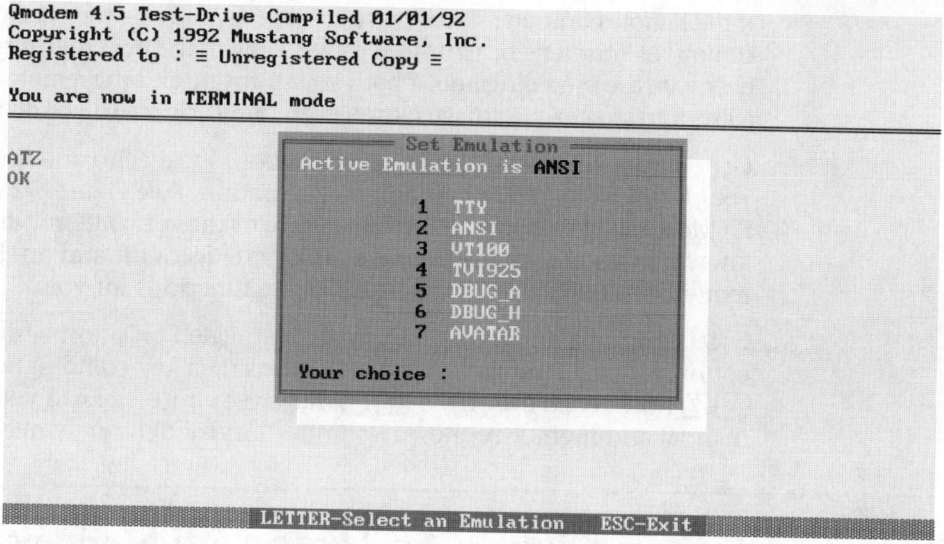

```
Qmodem 4.5 Test-Drive Compiled 01/01/92
Copyright (C) 1992 Mustang Software, Inc.
Registered to : ≡ Unregistered Copy ≡

You are now in TERMINAL mode

                        ══════ Set Emulation ══════
ATZ                     Active Emulation is ANSI
OK
                               1  TTY
                               2  ANSI
                               3  VT100
                               4  TVI925
                               5  DBUG_A
                               6  DBUG_H
                               7  AVATAR

                        Your choice :


                   LETTER-Select an Emulation    ESC-Exit
```

Qmodem
terminal type
selection
screen
Figure 6-4.

Local Echo and Line Feeds

You should understand what local echo and line feeds do, so you can
quickly recognize during an online session whether you need to turn them
on or off. These two options make or break the readability of your online
session.

Local echo means that everything typed to the remote computer also appears
on the screen at which you're working. When using a terminal program,
what you type goes directly to the serial port, not to your display screen.
Turning local echo on means your software duplicates on your screen what
it sent to the serial port. Knowing only that, it seems sensible to turn local
echo on. *Don't!*

Most remote computers send the keystrokes they receive from your keyboard
right back to you (called *remote echo*), so they are displayed on your screen
anyway. If local echo is turned on, you will get an echo of each character
you type from *two* sources, aanndd iitt wwiill llooookk lliikkee tthhiiss!!

A *line feed* moves everything on your screen up one line, presenting a fresh
blank line under your cursor. When you press the Return key on a
typewriter, two things always happen together: the carriage moves to the
left and the paper roller feeds a new line of paper up to the printhead. In
telecomputing, a carriage return and a line feed are two distinct things;
either can be done without doing the other. As with echoing what you send
to the remote computer onto your local screen, some coordination is
necessary to determine whether your software or the remote computer will
provide line feeds.

If the remote computer "returns the carriage" by moving the cursor to the leftmost column of your screen, a line feed must follow or the next line of type will overwrite the preceding line. If both your software and the remote computer add a line feed after each carriage return, everything you see will be double-spaced.

Generally speaking, it's best to turn off both local echo and line feeds in your terminal software's default configuration. (See Figure 6-2, items E and F.) Most remote computers will take care of these two items. But you need to know how to quickly turn local echo or line feeds off and on, just in case the remote computer does not perform these functions for you.

Local echo and line feeds can usually be toggled on or off while you are connected to a remote computer, by pressing a key combination such as Alt-E (local echo on/off) or Alt-F (line feeds on/off). Read your software's manual and memorize these two important though rarely needed keystrokes.

Software Setup Checklist for All Modems

◆ Is software set to use the same COM port that the modem uses?

◆ Do communications parameters match those of the remote computer? (8-N-1 for general use, 7-E-1 for mainframes)

◆ Has the appropriate terminal type been selected? (ANSI/BBS for general use)

◆ Is local echo turned off?

◆ Is line feeds turned off?

◆ Do you know which keystrokes will turn local echo or line feeds on if you need them in a hurry?

Port Speed: How Fast Software Talks to a Serial Port

The *port speed* option in terminal software determines how fast your terminal software communicates with your serial port. Figure 6-3 shows a baud rate of 38,400; this is the port speed, not the speed at which your modem will attempt to connect over a phone line.

Your serial port passes data back and forth between modem and software. The serial port can "talk" to the modem and the software at different speeds, just as you can speak slowly to one person and rapidly to another in the same conversation. The serial port will communicate with your modem at the highest speed your modem can handle.

Before the arrival of data-compression techniques (which you'll learn about in the following section), the port speed you selected for the terminal software had to be no higher than the modem's highest speed. It could be lower, in which case communication would proceed at the lower of the two speeds.

If you own a 2400-bps modem without any advanced hardware features, your software's port speed should be set to match the modem's highest speed—2400 bps.

Special Considerations for High-Speed or Data-Compression Modems

Two features found in late-model modems—high speed and data compression—vastly increase the speed and efficiency of telecomputing. But terminal software must be properly configured to take advantage of these innovations.

6

Software Setup for Data-Compressing Modems (MNP, v.42, v.42bis)

As you learned in Chapter 3, data compression lets the modem squeeze data into smaller packages before sending it over the phone line, or decompresses already compressed data that it receives before passing the data through the serial port to your terminal software. If your terminal software is properly configured, data will appear to fly through your modem as much as four times faster than the modem's rated connect speed (which is the highest bits-per-second speed at which the modem can pass data to another modem).

If your modem is equipped with data compression, set your terminal software's port speed four times higher than the modem's connect speed. Specifically, set the port speed to 9600 bps for a 2400-bps modem, to 38,400 bps for a 9600-bps modem, and to 57,600 bps for a 14,400-bps modem.

Most terminal software has an *auto-baud* option, which when active automatically changes the software's port speed to match the modem's connect speed. Turn auto-baud off so the port speed stays where you set it. Otherwise, you will lose all the benefits of data compression.

NOTE: Turning auto-baud off is the same thing as *"locking" the port speed,* a term found in some terminal programs. Another common phrase is "locking the *DTE (Data Terminal Equipment)* speed."

Software Setup for High-Speed Modems (9600/v.32, 14,400/v.32bis)

High-speed modems need direct control over the flow of data through the phone line. Your terminal software must be configured to let the modem handle flow control.

Flow Control: What Is It and Who Does It?

Flow control is how modems tell each other to temporarily stop sending data or to restart a stream of data previously put on hold. Flow control is necessary because modems hold incoming data in a *buffer* (block of memory) and sometimes cannot empty the buffer as fast as it is being filled. (The modem may be waiting for a file to be written to disk, for example.) If more data pours into an already-full buffer, the data will be lost forever. Flow control lets the receiving modem tell the sending modem to pause while the receiver empties the buffer.

There are two ways your modem can send these start/stop flow control signals to the remote modem: the modem itself can send them or your terminal software can send them. But if *both* modem and software are sending flow control signals, your setup is inefficient at the least. Often, such duplicate signals will abort an online session or "lock up" your computer.

Modem and software must each be told which one will handle flow control. The following sections describe how to give your modem and software their instructions about flow control.

Software Flow Control: XON/XOFF

Software flow control relies on your terminal software to send the start/stop signals. Your modem signals your software that the modem's buffer is almost full, and your software sends a special character called *XOFF* ("transmit off") to the sending modem, halting the flow of data. When your modem catches up, it again signals your software that the modem is ready to receive more data. The software sends the character *XON* ("transmit on") to the sending modem, telling it to restart the flow of data.

This roundabout method of flow control is inherently inefficient. It takes more work on the part of both modem and software, and the XON/XOFF characters lower your modem's overall rate of transmission of usable data. But software flow control does offer one advantage under specific circumstances. When multiple modems are active, as is often the case on computer networks, the computer that controls all the modems must be aware of each modem's buffer status, and handle all flow control.

Read your terminal software's manual carefully to identify where and how software flow control is turned on and off in your software's configuration menus. Different terminal programs (Telix, Procomm, Qmodem, and so on) refer to software flow control by different names. See Figure 6-2, item J.

Hardware Flow Control: RTS/CTS   Hardware flow control uses two of the wires that connect your modem to your computer to regulate the stopping and starting of data transmission. (These wires and others are in an external modem's cable; internal modems use circuit-board paths as wires.) Hardware flow control is faster and more efficient than software flow control, because there are no XON/XOFF characters to handle, and the electrical signals used are very simple and straightforward.

In hardware flow control, one wire sends the *RTS* (Ready To Send) signal from your computer to your modem at the command of your terminal software. As long as your computer keeps the RTS signal turned on, your modem will keep receiving data and passing it to the computer. If your computer turns off the RTS signal, your modem stops sending data to the computer and tells the sending modem to temporarily stop sending data.

6

The other wire used in hardware flow control sets the *CTS* (Clear To Send) signal on or off. Your modem uses CTS to tell your computer and terminal software to start/stop sending data to the modem, exactly the reverse of what happens in RTS. The combination of RTS/CTS wires ensures that both modem and computer can halt or restart data transmission at any time.

If hardware flow control is used, your terminal software must check the CTS signal before sending data to the modem, to make sure CTS is turned on. Likewise, your modem must constantly check the RTS signal before sending data to your computer.

If you use a 9600-bps (v.32) or 14,400-bps (v.32bis) modem, turn software flow control off in your terminal software and turn on hardware flow control. Most terminal software configuration menus refer to software flow control as XON/XOFF, and refer to hardware flow control as RTS/CTS. See Figure 6-2, item K.

NOTE: The DSR/DTR (Data Set Ready/Data Terminal Ready) option frequently is confused with RTS/CTS, possibly because most terminal software lumps the two side by side on configuration menus. DSR/DTR is not used for modem-to-modem communications; it only comes into play when directly connecting two computers with a serial cable. If DSR/DTR is not turned off by default, turn it off manually.

Whenever possible, use the more efficient hardware flow control method instead of software flow control. Most modern 2400-bps and faster modems can use hardware flow control. A 2400-bps modem may be preset at the factory to use software flow control; the modem's manual should tell you how to set the modem to use hardware flow control. Faster 9600- and 14,400-bps modems invariably come from the factory preset to use hardware flow control. A few ancient 300 to 2400 bps modems can use only software flow control. Read your modem's manual before selecting a flow control method.

Configuring Terminal Software Checklist

Use this checklist when configuring your high-speed or data-compressing modem.

◆ Is software port speed set higher than modem connect speed?

◆ Is software flow control turned off? (XON/XOFF = OFF)

◆ Is hardware flow control turned on? (RTS/CTS = ON)

◆ Is auto-baud speed adjustment turned off?

Fine-Tuning Your Terminal Software Configuration

This section touches on the most useful fine-tuning options found in most terminal programs and introduces the (almost) universal language that is used to program modems.

Easy Options

Some fine-tuning can be done without learning the language of modems. A couple of these easy options are discussed here. Figure 6-5 shows some examples.

Redial Time and Redial Pause

Redial time is the amount of time the software waits for the modem to make a connection before issuing the hang-up command. Thirty seconds is typical. More time may be needed if you frequently call a computer that takes a long time to answer.

Redial pause is the number of seconds after disconnecting that your software will wait before dialing the same number again. One second is usually

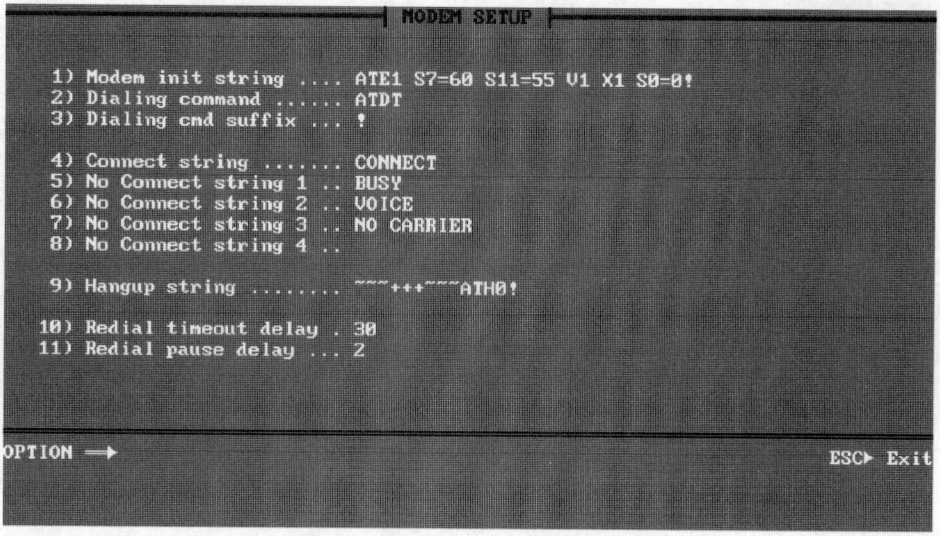

```
                       ┤ MODEM SETUP ├

   1) Modem init string .... ATE1 S7=60 S11=55 V1 X1 S0=0!
   2) Dialing command ...... ATDT
   3) Dialing cmd suffix ... !

   4) Connect string ....... CONNECT
   5) No Connect string 1 .. BUSY
   6) No Connect string 2 .. VOICE
   7) No Connect string 3 .. NO CARRIER
   8) No Connect string 4 ..

   9) Hangup string ........ ~~~+++~~~ATH0!

  10) Redial timeout delay . 30
  11) Redial pause delay ... 2


OPTION ➔                                        ESC▶ Exit
```

Procomm
modem setup
screen
Figure 6-5.

6

sufficient for the modem to reset between attempts. A longer interval is optional.

Dialing Prefixes

The environment in which you use your modem and terminal software—at home, at the office, at a pay phone—can have an impact on ease of use and performance. For example, an office phone system often requires you to dial a 9, then wait a half-second or so for an outside line before dialing the number you want to reach.

A *dialing prefix* is the string of commands sent to the modem right before the phone number you want to call is sent. Multiple dialing prefixes can be set up to accommodate the fact that you may be using your modem from different types of phones and under different conditions. You can assign a specific dialing prefix to each entry in your dialing directory.

We already mentioned the "dial 9, then wait for a line" use for dialing prefixes. Other common uses for dialing prefixes include

✦ Entering an account code before dialing CompuServe, so your phone system can track where you spent last month's budget.

✦ Entering that lengthy calling-card number when you are calling from a client's office or a pay phone.

✦ Entering the "1" before long-distance calls, so you do not have to add a "1" to every long-distance dialing directory entry.

✦ Disabling call waiting by entering *70 before dialing. The click call waiting makes always breaks a modem connection. The *70 prefix disables call waiting only for the current call; when you disconnect, call waiting is reactivated.

Read your terminal program's manual to see how dialing prefixes should be set up and used in conjunction with the numbers stored in your dialing directory.

AT Commands: The Language of Modems

The deeper you delve into the options offered by your terminal software, the more you will need a basic understanding of the language used to control modems. This section gently introduces this command language and some of its simplest uses.

Hayes Microcomputer Products Inc., one of the earliest and now the dominant maker of modems, developed a set of commands that has become the standard for modem command languages.

Today, virtually all modems sold are "Hayes-compatible" in that they all use the basic set of commands developed by Hayes. Many advanced modems have added "extended Hayes commands" to implement new or proprietary features.

To see how the Hayes command set works, start your terminal software. Most terminal software starts up in *command mode*, meaning that you are in direct communication with your modem. If your software does not start in command mode, switch to it before continuing. See your program's manual for instructions.

In command mode, type **ATZ** and press the Enter key. "OK" should appear on your screen. Here's what happened:

✦ The letters "AT" got your modem's attention. The modem now knows that the next string of characters will be a command for it to perform.

✦ The letter "Z" told your modem to reset itself.

✦ Pressing the Enter key told the modem you were finished issuing commands and to execute the one it received.

✦ After resetting itself, your modem reported back that the reset went OK.

Now let's use AT commands to make your modem dial a phone number. If you are using your modem on a touch-tone line, enter **ATDT** followed by the phone number from which you are calling; call yourself. If your phone number were 555-1234, you could enter

ATDT5551234

or **ATDT555-1234**

or even **AT DT 555 - 1234**

You should get a busy signal, because the modem already has the phone line off-hook when the phone company tries to route the call to your number. Press the (Enter) key again to hang up the phone. Now let's see what you did:

✦ "AT" got the modem's attention

✦ The letter "D" told it to get ready to dial

✦ The letter "T" told the modem to use touch-tones

✦ The phone number to dial followed the letter "T"

✦ Pressing the (Enter) key told the modem to execute all of the commands it had received

If you wanted to dial 9, wait half a second for an outside line, then dial 555-1234, enter **ATDT9~5551234**. The tilde character (~) tells the modem to pause for one half-second before executing the next command. Several tildes in a row give you control over how long the modem pauses. Four tildes (~~~~) equals a pause of two seconds.

The preceding paragraph shows how dialing prefixes are constructed. If you create a dialing prefix consisting of ATDT9~~ the modem will get an outside line for you before dialing any number in your dialing directory to which that prefix is assigned.

Here are a few tricks to practice with your modem. Do not hesitate to experiment with these commands. None of them dial out to anywhere or permanently change your modem's configuration.

NOTE: When entering the following commands, remember to have your terminal program in command mode, and *always put the letters "AT" before the rest of each command.*

Command	Function
A/	Causes modem to repeat the last command it received
H0	Hangs up phone (disconnects)
H1	Picks up phone (creates busy signal)
I	Modem displays modem product code
L1	Sets modem's speaker volume "low"
L2	Sets modem's speaker volume "medium"
L3	Sets modem's speaker volume "loudest"
M0	Turns modem speaker off, all the time
M1	Leaves speaker on while dialing, turns off when connection made
M2	Leaves speaker on, all the time

Modem Initialization Strings

An *initialization string* is a set of AT commands stored in your terminal software that the software sends to your modem whenever you start up the software. Just as the MS-DOS commands found in your computer's AUTOEXEC.BAT file automatically set your computer's environment to your liking when you turn on the computer, the AT commands in an initialization string make sure your modem is set up the way you prefer each time you start the terminal software.

You do not need an initialization string in order to run your terminal program and use your modem. If no initialization string is sent to the modem, the modem usually will start in the same condition it was in when you last turned off its power. But initialization strings make *sure* your modem is set the way you want it, and provide a convenient way to customize those settings.

A typical initialization string might look like this:

```
AT S0=0 M1 V1 S7=45 ^M
```

✦ *AT* gets the modem's attention

✦ *S0=0* tells the modem to go into "originate" mode, that is, get ready to make an outgoing phone call

+ *M1* turns the speaker on until a connection is made, allowing you to audibly monitor the call's progress

+ *V1* tells the modem to provide results of its actions in words (*V0* would provide terse, one-digit number results)

+ *S7=45* tells the modem to wait 45 seconds after dialing to get a connection before hanging up

Most terminal software comes with a default initialization string very much like the preceding example. If it works, do not tinker with it. If it does not work, see Appendix B and read your modem's manual carefully before changing the initialization string.

Storing Initialization Strings in the Modem's Memory

The *&Wn* command is so useful it should be part of the "basic" Hayes command set; most modems recognize it. The command *AT&W* will cause the modem to save its current configuration in a memory location inside the modem which you may call *user profile 0*. *AT&W1* will store the current configuration in user profile 1. Many modems can store four to ten user profiles. Some modems' manuals refer to user profiles as *NVRAM* locations (NonVolatile Random Access Memory, meaning the data in NVRAM is not lost when the modem's power is turned off).

Many people use the initialization string ATZ in their terminal software. It tells the modem, "Clear your head, and reset everything to what is stored in user profile 0." This trick simply reduces the time it takes to reset your modem. It is faster for a modem to listen to one ATZ command and execute it than to perform a whole series of commands. Of course, you must first program your modem the way you want it and then save the settings using the AT&W command.

NOTE: If you get confused while programming your modem, the command *AT&F* will reset everything to the modem's factory default settings. You can then start over from scratch, reading the manual to see how everything is set before you change anything.

The AT command set gives you complete control over dozens of aspects of your modem's behavior. If you want to be on such intimate terms with your modem, study the basic AT commands and the complete command set documented in your modem's manual.

Depending on your unique circumstances, configuring your software to work with your modem can be as simple as installing the software and picking a COM port. But if things are not that simple for you, a good command of software configuration options will save many hours of frustration.

CHAPTER

7

MAKING YOUR FIRST MODEM CALL: BULLETIN BOARD SYSTEMS

This chapter offers key information on how to make a call to an online service. Before making your first modem call, run through the following checklist.

✦ Phone line is plugged into modem's *line* jack and wall jack

✦ Modem power is turned on (this applies to external modems only; internal modems get power from your computer)

✦ Terminal software is loaded and properly configured

✦ You have the phone number of the online service you want to call

Oops! Looks like we forgot something; to paraphrase the theme from the movie *Ghostbusters*, "*Where* ya' gonna' call?"

I recommend you start with local *Bulletin Board Systems* (BBSs). A BBS is a computer (usually a desktop PC like your own) that is equipped and programmed for general online functions: public and private e-mail, file transfers, data retrieval, and interactive chat (live teleconferencing). Most BBSs are operated as hobbies or very small businesses, by one or two enthusiastic and knowledgeable *sysops* (pronounced "Siss-op," short for SYStem OPerator).

The complete but relatively simple capabilities of a BBS, and the personal attention of its sysop(s), provide an ideal introduction to the online world. The major commercial online services—CompuServe, Prodigy, GEnie, America Online, and others—are very useful as you'll see in Chapter 8, but can be overwhelming in their content *and* limited in their potential to teach you the finer points of telecomputing.

This chapter reveals the origin, technical capabilities, and culture of BBSland. You will learn where to find BBSs (which can focus on any topic from "Star Trek" to scuba diving); how to introduce yourself to the BBS community; how to be a welcomed guest instead of a nameless "user"; and how to quickly evaluate a given BBS and decide if it is worth your financial support.

NOTE: The Bonus Disk offered by mail to readers of this book comes with thousands of up-to-date BBS listings: names, phone numbers, and specialties. The disk even includes a handy utility for converting these text files into dialing directories for Procomm, Telix, Qmodem, Crosstalk, and other popular terminal programs. See the back of the book for more details.

Why Start with a Little Bitty BBS?

Way back in 1985, my first experience with a modem was on Western Union's EasyLink data retrieval service (since purchased by AT&T). It looked like a wonderful deal: only $0.08 per minute for connect time, no charge if a search came up empty, and only $8.00 for each record I chose to retrieve.

One month after signing up, I got a bill for over $1,200. I pulled the plug on that modem faster than you would sweep a burning cigarette from your lap!

Six months later, a friend gave me a BBS phone number over my strenuous protests that I didn't need a second mortgage. He insisted this local BBS cost nothing. I found that hard to believe, but I called anyway.

The experience was like reading for the first time. So much to do, so much to learn, and it all made perfect sense! I used up my first 30-minute visitor's allotment in one call, and came back for more the next day and every day for a week. My phone bill and credit cards remained blissfully ignorant of my newfound hobby.

Then a message popped up form nowhere: "Sysop breaking in to chat." Here was the person who *created* this marvel, taking time to ask me how I liked his brainchild, and if he could be of any help—at 11:00 P.M.! Quite a difference between this and EasyLink's customer service department, which delighted in putting callers through six voicemail menus and limiting calls to bankers' hours.

So began a long and exciting love affair with BBSs. I have since met dozens of sysops face to face, attended their business and social affairs, communed with all kinds of people worldwide, and generally had the time of my life. A local BBS is the least expensive, most enjoyable way to explore the online world for the first time or the 10,000th time.

A Short History and Overview of BBSland

It all started (like most things) in someone's bedroom, back in January of 1978. Ward Christenson and Randy Suess, snowbound by a Chicago blizzard, wrote the first BBS software so they and their computer club buddies could swap messages without venturing out to the club's headquarters. The initial design was intended to mimic the cork bulletin board at the club, where members posted notes asking for help, offering items for sale or swap, and so on. It wasn't long before members asked for file-transfer capability, so Christenson wrote Xmodem and put it in the *public domain* (meaning anyone could freely use and modify Christenson's creation).

NOTE: The mother of all BBSs, Christenson's CBBS, is still in operation. You can say hello to the Founding Fathers of the Network Nation by logging on at 312-545-8086.

The State of the BBS Nation

According to Jack Rickard, "Editor Rotundus" of *Boardwatch* magazine, there are over 42,000 publicly available BBSs in the U.S. These are just the boards that publicize their phone numbers. BBS software manufacturers indicate that another 100,000-plus private systems exist. (These are usually maintained by corporations for internal communication and customer service and are not publicized or are restricted to authorized callers.)

Major metropolitan areas typically have hundreds of BBSs in each local calling area. It costs nothing to connect with a local BBS, though you may have to pay the sysop something for full access to his or her infobusiness.

Free Versus Practically Free

In the early years of BBSing, most boards were one-line, part-time hobbies. Few sysops charged for access, although many required callers to contribute quotas of messages or uploaded files to keep the online community active. Some sysops requested voluntary donations to help pay for the phone line(s) and improvements to the system's hardware and software. When a hard drive crashed or a modem gave up the ghost, it was customary (and still is) to "pass the hat" among callers to raise funds for essential replacements.

Thousands of BBSs still offer free access (though long-distance callers must pay the phone company). Some free-to-caller BBSs are funded by advertisers or corporate sponsors. Many are run by businesses, in which case expenses are partially footed by the IRS. Customer support and product marketing BBSs are typically free to callers.

Federal, state, and local governments are rapidly joining the BBS fold. Some charge modest fees for access, but most charge nothing.

Nonprofit associations often include free BBS services in membership benefits. Nonprofits sometimes charge nonmembers for access to a BBS; many do not allow nonmembers online, or limit nonmembers to a selection of public message and file areas.

Commercial BBSs unabashedly charge for full access; they are in business, trying to earn a profit. But many commercial BBSs offer free trial memberships, giving callers a chance to taste and (they hope) get hooked on the sysops' wares.

When fees are charged, they fall typically between $10 and $120 per year. The average commercial BBS charges little more for a year's full access than you might pay for a magazine subscription. Most are clear-cut bargains.

Where to Find Local BBS Phone Numbers

The entrance to BBSland is one of those "open secrets." If you find one, you can find them all, because nearly every BBS carries lists of other BBSs in its file libraries. But finding the first entry in your dialing directory can be a challenge. Here are some reliable sources:

Computer User Groups and Clubs   Virtually all maintain a list of BBSs of interest to members. Many run their own BBSs, which are generally open to nonmembers.

Computer Dealers   Many retailers offer BBS lists over the counter to draw customers into their stores. A growing number of dealers maintain support and sales BBSs.

The Reference Desk at Your Local Library   Libraries have embraced BBS technology with enthusiasm. From my desk in Denver, I can search the catalogs and full-text archives of every public library in the state. I can even connect to Harvard University's card catalog and dozens of other libraries nationwide. And it's all FREE! Your local reference librarian should be able to give you a couple of BBS numbers to call. At the very least, one or more of the following publications should be on your library's shelves.

7

✦ *Computer Shopper* A phonebook-sized catalog of computer equipment and software, *Computer Shopper* (and its local counterparts) is available almost everywhere computer magazines are sold (even my supermarket carries it). Their BBS list is so huge, only half of it is published each issue (and the other half is published in the next issue). The boards are all verified every two months, to make sure they are still in operation.

✦ *Boardwatch* The online cosmopolitan's preferred reading, *Boardwatch* magazine covers the unusual, creative, and profitable examples of BBSs; political and legal developments affecting modemers; Internet (see Chapter 10); Macintosh BBSing; the international BBS scene; and product reviews for callers and sysops. Each issue features hundreds of BBS listings. For a sample copy, call 303-973-6038 (voice), or log on to Boardwatch's BBS: 303-973-4222.

✦ *The Yellow Pages* U.S. West and Ameritech are among the phone companies whose directories include BBS entries under "Computers—Bulletin Board Systems." Other categories to check include computer dealers' ads, "Information Retrieval Services," and "Electronic Mail Services."

Toll-Free 1-800 BBSs

If none of these sources is locally available to you, call a toll-free BBS. Search their file areas for the keyword "list" and you will almost certainly find one or more national BBS lists to get you started. (See the section in this chapter on "Browsing File Libraries and Downloading Files" to learn how to search for files.)

BBS Name/Sponsor	Modem Phone Number
Dial-JAN BBS/Job Accommodation Network	800-342-5526
Florida Recycling Marketing System	800-348-1239
Online with Hayes	800-874-2937
OERI BBS/U.S. Dept. of Education	800-222-4922
SBA Online/Small Business Administration	800-859-4636

Dialing a BBS for the First Time

The first time you use your modem is an exciting, sometimes anxious moment. Relax! There is nothing you can do that will hurt you, your computer, or the computer you are calling. Take the steps described in this section one by one, and you will thoroughly enjoy your first modem call.

Terminal and Communication Settings for Calling a BBS

The following terminal software settings will usually work just fine on any BBS:

✦ 8-N-1 (Eight data bits, no parity, one stop bit).

✦ ANSI/BBS or VT100 terminal emulation.

✦ Auto-baud: Set it ON, unless you are using a v.42 or v.42bis data-compressing modem. Auto-baud, you remember, causes your terminal software to automatically switch its port speed (software-to-serial port speed) to match the modem's actual connect speed (modem-to-modem over the phone line).

✦ Local echo: Turn it OFF. The BBS will echo the characters you type back to you. If your terminal software also echoes back characters, tthheeyy wwiill llookk lliikkee tthhiiss....

✦ Line Feeds: Turn them OFF. The BBS will add LF characters to each line it echoes back to you. If your terminal software also adds LF characters, everything you see will be double-spaced.

✦ Session Log: Optional, but a good idea. Your first visit to a BBS will provide a lot of information about how it works, where to find things, and whether it's worth calling back. Capturing your entire session to disk lets you review all the information at a later time, after disconnecting from the BBS.

Manually Dialing a Phone Number

When loaded, most terminal software starts up in command mode, meaning you are in direct communication with your modem and can simply type commands to it. Figure 7-1 shows Procomm's start-up screen, which defaults to command mode. Notice the following exchange between your terminal software and the modem:

```
ATZ

OK
```

When you are in command mode, everything you or your terminal software sends to the modem is echoed back to the screen, followed by the modem's acknowledgment or result code response. In the example above, Procomm sent the initialization command ATZ to the modem. The modem reset and told Procomm everything was "OK."

Now try calling one of the BBS phone numbers listed in this book, or one that you have found on your own. For instance, to dial the *Boardwatch* BBS

7

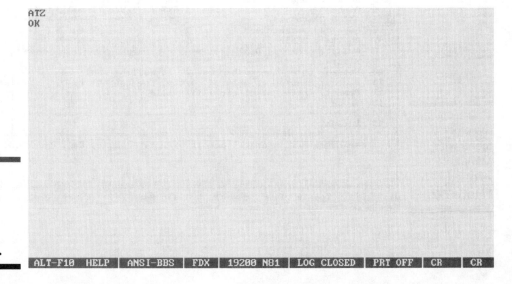

Procomm
terminal
software in
command
mode
Figure 7-1.

using a touch-tone phone just type the following commands and press the
(Enter) key at the end of the line:

```
AT DT 1-303-973-4222
```

NOTE: This example assumes you are making a long-distance call. The
hyphens and spaces in the command are unnecessary; you could have
typed ATDT13039734222, but punctuation makes it easier to check for
mistakes before pressing the (Enter) key.

Most terminal programs have a manual-dial function built in, so you can
dial numbers that are not already in your dialing directory without having to
remember and enter the AT commands. Figure 7-2 shows Telix's dialing
directory menu which allows you to perform this function.

Telix, Procomm, and many other terminal programs let you enter a single
keystroke that represents one of your dialing prefixes, saving you the trouble
of entering the prefix when manually dialing a number.

```
┤ Dialing Directory ├
            Name                  Number      Line Format     Script
   1  Adnet Online             1-317-579-6934  38400 E·7·1
   2  Advanced Micro/Bevins    1-209-222-0227  38400 N·8·1
   3  Advanced System TBBS     1-702-334-3317  38400 N·8·1
   4  Alpha 4                  1-617-229-2915  38400 N·8·1    alpha4
   5  AMCOM-Cleveland          1-216-526-9490  38400 N·8·1
   6  American Databankers     1-918-251-8204  38400 N·8·1
   7  Aquila v.32bis           1-708-820-8365  38400 N·8·1
   8  Assn. ┤ Manual Dial ├
   9  Blazin
  10  Botnay  Enter the number below. It will be sent out
  11  Boardw  exactly as entered, except for Long Distance      ardwat
  12  Braint  Codes, which are still valid.
  13  Bruce
  14  Busine ▶
  15  Busine

      Mark/Unmark with Space. Scroll with ↑, ↓, Home, End, PgUp, and PgDn.


Dial  List  Toggle  Find  Manual  Redial  Add  Edit  Clear  Unmark  Other  eXit
Type a number to be dialed as entered
```

Telix's dialing
directory
menu with
Manual
selected
Figure 7-2.

What Should Happen When the Modem Dials a Number

When you press the (Enter) key to send the dialing command and phone number to your modem, the modem will take the phone line off-hook (just as you take the phone off the hook when you lift the handset), wait for a dial tone, dial the phone number, and wait for another modem to answer. The amount of time the modem waits for an answer is determined by the modem's S7 status register (see Chapter 6). You will hear the following through the modem's speaker (if you turned the speaker on with the AT M1 command):

✦ A click as the modem takes the line off-hook

✦ A dial tone, just like the one you hear when you lift the handset of a telephone

✦ Very rapid tones (as from a touch-tone phone) or pulse/rotary clicks as the number is dialed

✦ One or more rings as the call goes through and the modem waits for something to answer

✦ Another click as the modem on the other end answers

✦ High-pitched squeals as the two modems begin their *handshaking* routine, adjusting to each other's speeds and the line conditions, establishing communication protocols, and so on

7

NOTE: The rather obnoxious handshaking noises should last no more than 5 to 15 seconds. The noise stops once the modems establish a connection.

If you have an external modem, its front-panel lights will change when you firmly connect. If round, colored lights are used on your modem, the one labeled CD (Carrier Detected) will light up. Alphanumeric displays, like those appearing on Supra models of modems, for example, will tell you "CD" or "CARRIER" in so many words. Either way, it means you have a solid connection.

Congratulations! You are connected to your first BBS!

NOTE: Things will go exactly as described in the preceding paragraphs about 99 percent of the time. See Appendix B if your modem does not act as predicted.

Logging On: Exchanging Introductions with Your Host

In any first-time meeting, there may be an awkward silent moment in which neither party makes the first move to introduce themselves. Most BBSs take the initiative; an introductory menu should appear on your screen almost as soon as you are connected; Figure 7-3 shows a typical welcoming screen.

A minority of BBSs just sit there, waiting for you to press the (Enter) key or the (Esc) key to indicate "I'm here; is anyone there?" If you do not get a welcoming menu of some kind from the BBS after three or four seconds, press the (Esc) key twice. Wait for about ten seconds; do not "lean on" the (Esc) key or you may lose your connection. If you still don't get some sort of reaction from your "host," disconnect and try again. You may have just gotten a bad connection.

```
WILDCAT! Copyright (c) 87,93 Mustang Software, Inc.  All Rights Reserved.
Registration Number: 91-2914.  Version: 3.60S (SINGLE-LINE).  Node: 1.

Connected at 9600 bps. ANSI detected.


                        Welcome to GISnet!

              40° 01 05 N - 105° 14 11 W
              Boulder, Colorado USA



What is your first name?
```

A typical BBS "welcome" screen
Figure 7-3.

```
Alt-Z for Help | ANSI-BBS | 38400·N81 FDX |        |    |        | Online 00:00
```

What Most BBSs Will Want to Know About You

Most BBSs keep track of the people who call by recording unique identifiers in a *userlog* database. The minimum information you can expect to be asked is your name and your password.

NOTE: A password serves the same purpose on a BBS as a Personal Identification Number does for your ATM card: it keeps unauthorized people from using your account. Future calls to the same BBS will probably require that you enter your password as well as your name to gain admittance; keep close track of which password(s) you use and the BBSs on which you use them.

Some BBSs insist you use your real name; others don't care what or who you call yourself. The latter type of BBS allows the use of aliases, fictitious names by which users are known to each other in e-mail, chat, and anywhere else a personal name appears.

Often sysops who allow aliases on their BBSs will demand your real name for their own records; don't argue about it. You won't slip a fake name past most sysops, and they are fanatically devoted to keeping their users' real identities confidential.

Registration: How Much Should You Tell a Stranger?

Some sysops want to know much more than your name and password. Common and socially acceptable questions include:

+ The city and state from which you are calling
+ The type of computer you use
+ The make and model of modem
+ The name of your terminal software
+ Your mailing address
+ Your day and/or evening telephone numbers

Many people feel uncomfortable about giving a stranger their home or office telephone numbers. Usually the question is asked for your protection and to

7

give you better service. Many sysops conscientiously call everyone who logs on to their BBS at least once, to verify their location and offer personal assistance in using the BBS. Verification is a responsible practice that discourages abusive callers, keeps minors off of adult-oriented BBSs, and generally shows the sysop's personal interest in your satisfaction.

NOTE: Some registration routines get overly personal or just impossible to honestly answer ("What are you looking for on this BBS?" is one example; this is your first call, so how would you know what to look for?) Others are interminably long, interspersed with screen after screen of rules and regulations. See the section telling you "How to Evaluate a BBS in One Call," later in this chapter, for more information about what to do in such cases.

Mail-In Registration: "They Want My Driver's License?"

Most adult-oriented BBSs require registration by mail. You may receive a paper contract from the sysop, which you must sign and return with a copy of your driver's license or other official identification proving that you are 18 years of age or older.

Other BBSs may require mail-in registration for other reasons. The sysop may not have time to call every new visitor, but still wants proof that you are who you claim to be. Some BBSs do not allow full access until you mail in a check.

If mail-in registration seems woefully inefficient, you are already becoming a modem fanatic, devoted to eliminating paper waste whenever possible. Congratulations!

Immediate Call-Back Verification

The ultimate in customer service may be *call-back verification*: The BBS immediately calls your modem to verify your location, and automatically upgrades the privileges you have on the BBS.

You need to know how to answer such a call. The Hayes AT command *AT A* tells your modem to answer incoming calls instead of placing outgoing calls. In a typical call-back verification, you provide the phone number for the BBS to call back, and the BBS will disconnect. Within 15 to 30 seconds, your phone will ring with the BBS' return call. When the phone rings, send the AT A command to your modem, and it will answer the phone.

Typically, the BBS will send a message like, "This is XYZ BBS calling Joe User. Please enter your password, Joe..." Enter the password you chose when you logged on. If it matches the one the BBS stored, you will get another message telling you that your account has been verified, your access level has been upgraded (more things you can do, more time allowed), and you can call the BBS anytime you want. Then the BBS will disconnect.

NOTE: Call-back verification requires a phone number that goes directly to your modem. Home phones and other single-line phone situations are fine. But if you give the BBS your company's main phone number, your receptionist may be startled to hear from a modem, and the modem cannot tell a human what extension it needs. Call-back verification is risky when you are calling from a multiline phone system. There is no way your modem can tell which ringing line is a modem calling back. The AT A command will send a handshaking squeal to anyone—even your boss!

How to Evaluate a BBS in One Call

So many boards, so little time! Callers do not have to put up with rude, sloppy, or unreliable BBSs. Especially if you are being asked to "contribute" money to the BBS, you have every right to expect certain standards of customer service. The following guidelines will help you decide if a BBS is worth a second call.

7

Sysop's Attitude

What do the registration questions and new-user bulletins tell you about the sysop's personality? Is he/she a good host or a sandbox bully? An open, generous person or a paranoid? Occasionally, you will wonder why a sysop invites anyone to call, given all the suspicion and disregard for callers' time and feelings displayed in the opening screens. Don't take offense; just hang up and keep looking for a pleasant place to spend your online time.

System Design

Is the BBS reliably available and easy to use? If you get a busy signal nine out of ten calls, the sysop is not providing enough phone lines for his or her customers. Worse yet is the BBS whose menu options are labeled according to some arcane scheme known only to the sysop: "Abort" means "Return to Main Menu," "!" means "Goodbye," and so on. Cheap, low-speed modems that require you to make several calls to establish a good connection are another sign of an inferior BBS.

Message Areas

Does the BBS carry electronic conversations on the topics that most interest you? Meeting other people who share your interests is the most entertaining thing you can do on a BBS. With your session log file open, list all the message areas available. If you see one you really like, scan the subject headers of the messages in that area. Are there lots of messages? Are the dates on the messages recent? Is this a party or a funeral?

File Areas

Almost all BBSs have libraries of shareware and public domain programs, text files full of information, digitized photos or computer-generated images. Use the file area's keyword search feature to see how many files match your interests, such as "desktop publishing," "Lotus," "modem," and so on. Use the search-by-date feature to find out how often new files are added to the system.

Cost

Considering all the factors just given, is this BBS worth the price the sysop charges *and* the price of "getting there?" Long-distance calls are a semi-invisible cost of BBSing; you don't know what you owe until the monthly phone bill arrives. A mere $20 per year for three hours per day of access to a multiline BBS may seem like quite a bargain, but the phone bill can look like a mortgage payment if you actually use all of the time you buy.

Basic BBSing Skills

Your calls to BBSs will be more fun and less time-consuming and money-consuming if you practice a few basic skills on a local BBS before venturing out into the long-distance universe. Just as with driving a car, some of these skills take a good deal of practice; others quickly become second nature. Spend some online time experimenting with each of the options discussed in this section until you feel comfortable and fluent in them.

Changing User Preferences

Just as you can customize your terminal software to suit your tastes, most BBSs provide a way to let callers customize how screens appear. You will often find an option on a BBS' main menu labeled "Utilities," "Your Settings," "Your Preferences," or something similar. The help files provided for new

Payment Methods

If you subscribe to a BBS, you will find there are three common ways to pay for it: credit cards, check or money order, and 900 number billing. Each has its pros and cons, as the following explains.

Credit Cards   Credit cards are convenient and safe. If you are not satisfied with the service you receive, you can write to the credit card company and ask that the charges be removed from your account; they will be, with few or no questions from the card company. This procedure does not eliminate any legal debt you may owe the sysop, but it puts your money back in your pocket until the dispute is resolved.

Check or Money Order   Checks and money orders are inefficient and time-consuming, like mail-in registrations, but some people feel more secure sending a check than giving their credit card numbers to strangers online (as if they don't give the number to strangers in stores!).

1-900 Billing   When you dial a BBS number that begins with 1-900, the sysop's charges will show up on your regular monthly phone bill. The usual 1-900 BBS charges by the minute you spend connected (about $0.30 to $1.00 per minute in most cases). Recent innovations in 1-900 technology allow you to call a 1-900 number with your modem, download a "credit authorization code" good for a fixed amount of money, then call the BBS on a normal phone number and enter that code to obtain the amount of access you purchased. The advantage is that you get more BBSing for your buck. You spend only seconds on the 1-900 number, minimizing the 1-900 service provider's $0.25- to $0.30-per-minute charge in addition to the sysop's charges. Charges for 1-900 service can be challenged and removed from your phone bill, as they can with credit card charges. No phone company will cut off your basic phone service for failure to pay 1-900 charges.

7

users should direct you to the right area of a BBS in which to change your preferences. Figure 7-4 shows a typical user preferences configuration screen.

ANSI Color/Cursor Control and IBM Graphics Characters

If you are a steak-and-potatoes kind of person, fancy colors and graphics may not add much to your enjoyment of a BBS. ANSI color/cursor control

```
                  Change User Profile:

A - Set ANSI codes On/Off      G - Set IBM Graphics On/Off
W - Set Terminal Width         T - Set New Terminal Type
L - Set Line Feeds On/Off      C - Set Lower Case On/Off
N - Set # of Nulls             M - Set Message Base Defaults
U - Set File Upload Protocol   D - Set File Download Protocol
P - Set Page Pause (-more-)    S - Show Current Settings

Type Selection or ? for help, <CR> to exit:



   Unregistered  |  ANSI-BBS  |  38400·N81 FDX  |       |      |        | Online 00:00
```

BBS user preferences configuration screen

Figure 7-4.

codes add extra invisible characters to each screenful of data that comes to you, making menu displays somewhat slower than they are without ANSI. If you call a BBS at 2400 bps, you might want to turn off ANSI to gain a bit of efficiency.

Many online games require ANSI to control the movement of animated graphics. If you have ANSI toggled off, such games will inform you that you cannot play them until ANSI is turned on.

Leave IBM graphics characters turned on if your terminal software can display them. Unlike ANSI, graphics characters do not add any invisible overhead to data transmission, so you won't gain any speed by turning graphics off. The boxes, borders, and shadings that graphics provide make a BBS menu more readable.

Page Length, Page Pause, and Nonstop Scrolling

Each screenful of information your monitor can display may be considered a "page." The standard page length is 24 lines. If you set your page length to 24 lines, and turn on the "pause at end of each page" option, the BBS will stop displaying a menu, text file, file directory, or other listing at the number of lines you set for page length.

If you have set a page length shorter than the length the sysop used when designing menus, part of each page will appear chopped off. If this happens, you must press the (Enter) key to make the rest appear, which means unnecessary labor from you. Change your page length to match the length the sysop recommends.

If page length is set longer than the number of lines that will fit on your screen at one time, the top few lines will scroll off the top of your screen. Change your page length to a smaller value.

Nonstop scrolling ignores page length when displaying menus, text files, and so on. This option is desirable when you use session logging to quickly capture lengthy help files, file library directories, and other long blocks of text that you do not want to stop and read while connected to the BBS.

Another term for nonstop scrolling that you will often encounter is "page pause." If page pausing is turned off, you have in effect turned nonstop scrolling on.

NOTE: Well-designed BBSs assume each menu should be no more than 23 or 24 lines long, so they will always fit on a standard caller's screen. You can turn on nonstop scrolling on such BBSs and enjoy the benefits without losing the top few lines of each menu.

Screen Width or Characters Per Line

Either of these terms is used to describe how many characters should be displayed from left to right across the screen before words start wrapping around to the next line. The standard screen width is 80 characters, and most BBS menus are designed to be viewed at this width. If menus look "broken up," double-check your screen width and adjust it if necessary.

Default File-Transfer Protocols

Just as you can set a default file-transfer protocol in your terminal software's dialing directory entry for a given BBS, the BBS can "remember" which protocol you prefer to use from one call to the next. Setting a default protocol saves time and keystrokes online, because you do not have to select a protocol each time you transfer a file.

Password Change

You can change the password associated with your name on each BBS. It is rarely necessary to do so, but if your password somehow gets into the wrong hands, it is nice to be able to change it immediately.

Hot Key Menus

Hot keys execute commands immediately when pressed. Some BBS software, notably TBBS and Wildcat!, constantly monitors your connection to see if you have pressed a key. If a keystroke is detected while a menu is being displayed, and the key you pressed is one of the menu selections, the BBS will instantly stop sending the rest of the menu and execute your command.

7

This hot key feature saves frequent callers a lot of time, especially at 2400-bps speeds. You don't have to wait for a whole menu to unscroll before executing a command.

Browsing File Libraries and Downloading Files

Most BBSs collect hundreds or thousands of shareware, public domain, and informative text files, and make them available for callers to download. Finding the files you want can be time-consuming (and costly if you call long distance or otherwise pay by the minute). The following sections give some techniques used by experienced "file freaks" to minimize these costs.

Downloading Compressed File Directories

Many sysops encourage callers to download a directory of all the files on their BBSs and browse it offline (after they disconnect). Sysops don't want you tying up their phone lines for half an hour while you browse through file descriptions. Downloadable file catalogs are generally updated daily.

Usually, a file catalog will be offered in archived (compressed) form, greatly reducing its size and the time it takes to download it. You will need the "unpacking" utility for the compression method used on the file. Common compression methods generally correspond to the file's extension:

+ *.ZIP = PKZIP/PKUNZIP

+ *.ARJ = ARJ.EXE (used to pack and unpack)

+ *.ARC = ARC/XARC

+ *.LZH = LHARC (used to pack and unpack)

NOTE: The most recent version of PKZIP/PKUNZIP is 2.04, but many sysops still use v1.10 because it is compatible with their QWK mail programs; see the section later in this chapter on "Saving Time and Money with Offline Message Management." *Get both versions of PKZIP/PKUNZIP and keep them handy!* Version 2.04 creates smaller compressed files, but these cannot be uncompressed by version 1.10 of PKUNZIP. Most offline mail readers require that you have PKUNZIP version 1.10.

Searching for Files Online by Keyword

You can enter a word, partial word, or more than one word that describes the type of file you are seeking, or part of a file's name if you happen to know it. The BBS will rapidly search its file list and show you the files (and their descriptions) that include your keywords. Figure 7-5 shows an example of the results such a search can produce.

```
Type P to Pause S to Stop listing

>>> Selection string = list

   ALLFILES.EXE    458953    5/05/93   List of All File Bank Files
   ASTFILES.EXE     20776    5/05/93   List of All Astronomy Files
   BBSFILES.EXE     59843    5/05/93   List of All BBS-Support Files
   CIAFILES.EXE     15030    4/09/93   List of All CIA Country Files
   GRAFILES.EXE     30978    5/05/93   List of All Graphics & Other Amusements
   IBMFILES.EXE    242382    5/05/93   List of All IBM Compatible Files
   MUFFILES.EXE     14054    5/05/93   List of All MUFON Files
   PRGFILES.EXE     72574    5/05/93   List of All Programming Files
   SIGFILES.EXE     51354    1/01/93   List of All PC-SIG Library Files
   TXTFILES.EXE     22168    5/05/93   List of All Text Files
   UTLFILES.EXE     82798    5/05/93   List of All Utility Files
   WINFILES.EXE     26745    5/05/93   List of All Windows Files
   WRDFILES.EXE     19454    5/05/93   List of All Word Processing/Desktop Files
   BUSFILES.EXE     29079    5/05/93   List of All Business & Finance Files
   EDUFILES.EXE     14204    5/05/93   List of All Educational/Science/Medical Files
   HOMFILES.EXE     16306    5/05/93   List of All Home, Sports, Bible, Etc. Files
   GAMFILES.EXE     37541    5/05/93   List of All Games, MIDI & Music Files
   RADFILES.EXE     13387    5/05/93   List of All Radio & Electronics Files
   ALLFILES.TXT   1338194    5/05/93   List of All File Bank Files
-More-
 Alt-Z for Help | ANSI-BBS | 38400·N81 FDX |       |      |         | Online 00:02
```

Searching for
the keyword
"list" in a BBS'
file areas
Figure 7-5.

New Files and Date Searches

A BBS remembers when you last called. Often you can press a single key to list only files that have been added to the directory since your last call. A common variation on this option allows you to enter a starting date, and the BBS will list only files that have been added on or since that date.

Flagging Files for Later Downloading

Some BBS programs, including PC Board, WildCat!, and The Major BBS, offer the option to flag or tag a file when you see it, and then continue browsing the file listings. When you finish browsing, you can download all of your flagged files with one command. Flagging is very convenient because you do not have to jot down filenames as you browse, and you do not have to enter filenames one at a time to download them.

How to Download Files

Once you know what you want, you must tell the BBS how to send it to you, and tell your terminal software how to receive it. Figure 7-6 shows an example of how downloading looks online. The step-by-step procedure is as follows:

✦ Select the Download option on the BBS

✦ Enter the name of a file you wish to download

✦ Tell the BBS which file-transfer protocol to use

✦ Tell your terminal software which protocol to use

7

```
D

Enter up to 5 files. Press [ENTER] alone to stop.

                           Bytes        Time     Total Bytes   Total Time
                        ------------  ----------  ------------  ----------
File # 1? allfiles.zip      18,670        0.4        18,670        0.4
File # 2?

Automatically logoff after last download is completed? [N]
Please select a protocol:

[A] Ascii        [X] Xmodem        [C] Xmodem/CRC    [O] Xmodem1K
[Y] Ymodem       [Z] Zmodem        [K] Kermit

Select [A X C O Y Z K] ? [ ]




Alt-Z for Help | ANSI-BBS | 38400·N81 FDX |         |        | Online 00:01
```

BBS download
option and
file-transfer
protocol
Figure 7-6.

NOTE: You can skip the last two steps if you have specified Zmodem as the default protocol in *both* your BBS user preferences and in your terminal software's dialing directory entry for the BBS. The file transfer will automatically begin when you tell the BBS which file you want to send.

Zmodem, Ymodem-batch, Kermit, and other fairly recent file-transfer protocols allow batch downloads, meaning you can enter several filenames in one download operation, and all will be sent back to back. Xmodem and plain Ymodem require you to repeat the steps just outlined for every single file you want to download.

Using E-Mail and Public Message Areas

Writing messages to other BBS callers and reading what others have written constitute the joy of BBSing for many callers. Many friendships, business relationships, and even marriages have started online. Here are some tips on making the most of private e-mail and public message areas.

Searching for Interesting Topics and People

Most BBSs let you enter keywords that describe subjects in which you are interested. See Figure 7-7. Only messages whose subject headers contain those words will be displayed. You can also tell the BBS to check the "From" or "To" parts of each message header for the name or partial name of someone whose message(s) you want to find (including messages to or from you).

```
Type P to pause, S to stop, N to skip to next msg

Read Electronic Mail:
<I>n Box
<O>ut Box
<B>oth In and Out Boxes
<A>bort Reading Mail

Which One? B

<F>orward or <R>everse Multiple
<N>ew Messages
<M>arked Messages
<S>elective Retrieval
<I>ndividual Message(s)
<A>bort Retrieve

Which One?
```

```
Unregistered  |  ANSI-BBS  |  38400-N81 FDX  |    |    |           |  Online 00:00
```

TBBS systems provide many ways to search and read messages
Figure 7-7.

NOTE: The Major BBS extends keyword search capability to the full text of each message's body. A full-text search of this kind can take much, much longer than a search of header fields only, but it can locate messages you might otherwise have missed.

7

Following Threads of Conversation

The subject header of each message provides a *connector* between different messages, making it possible to follow a thread of conversation forward or backward by displaying only messages that have the same subject header. (Figure 7-8 shows the "Always follow" thread option.)

Unfortunately, people often neglect to change the subject header when changing the subject in their replies to a thread. You will often find messages in a thread that have nothing to do with the thread's subjects. No one has ever persuaded such people to change their bad habits; don't aggravate yourself or other callers by trying.

Writing Your Own Messages

When you decide to join the party and contribute to the conversation, select the option for entering a new message. This option may be labeled "Write," "Post," "Enter," or some other variation on the idea of contributing your two cents' worth.

The BBS automatically assumes the message is from you, so there is no need to enter your own name in the From field. The first thing you will usually

```
Type P to pause, S to stop, N to skip to next msg

<F>orward Read All
<R>everse Read All
<N>ew Messages Only
<M>arked Messages Only
<S>elect/Search for Specific Messages
<I>ndividual Message(s) by number.
<A>bort Retrieve

Which One? F

Pause after each msg(Y/N)? N

For reply chains:
<1> Ask on Each
<2> Always follow
<3> Never follow
<?> for help

Which one?

 Unregistered  | ANSI-BBS | 38400·N81 FDX |       |   |        | Online 00:00
```

Reply chains
let you follow
BBS
conversations
Figure 7-8.

have to enter is the addressee's name, in the To field. (See Figure 7-9.) The name can always be the specific name of another user, but there are two commonly used generic names you should know:

✦ *Sysop* Putting the word "Sysop" in the To field will generally send the message to the operator(s) of the BBS. Because "Sysop" identifies a unique person or group of people who share an electronic mailbox, you can use this name for private e-mail as well as public messages.

✦ *All* Putting the word "All" in the To field is often an acceptable way to address public messages to every other caller. "All" is *never* acceptable as an address in a private e-mail message! The BBS will not know which specific individual is supposed to receive the e-mail; it will go undelivered or be rejected out of hand.

The subject of your message should be specific and contain keywords that you would find if you were looking for messages on this subject. (See Figure 7-9.) Avoid vague subjects like "Question for All." If you have a question about using macros in WordPerfect 5.1, for example, a good subject would be "Using Macros in WordPerfect 5.1."

Attaching Files to Messages
Some BBS software, including TBBS and WildCat!, let you combine message and file-transfer functions in a very handy way. You can write a message, then upload a file that is "attached to" or "enclosed with" that message.

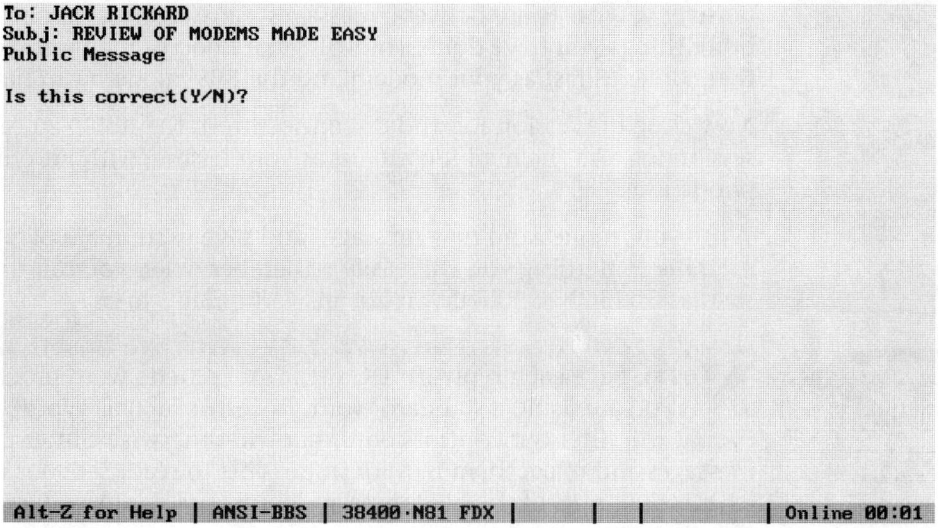

```
To: JACK RICKARD
Subj: REVIEW OF MODEMS MADE EASY
Public Message

Is this correct(Y/N)?
```

```
Alt-Z for Help | ANSI-BBS | 38400·N81 FDX |      |    |           | Online 00:01
```

Addressing a BBS e-mail message
Figure 7-9.

Anyone who reads your message can press a single key to download the attached file. Many people use this cover letter/package technique to send files through private e-mail or post files for everyone to download in public message areas. The file-attachment method saves you the trouble of telling someone about a file in a message, switching to the file areas, and uploading the file.

Saving Time and Money with Offline Message Management

Reading and answering messages is very time-consuming; at long-distance prices, it also can be expensive. Many BBSs limit the amount of time you can tie up one of their phone lines on a single call, so you may be disconnected in the middle of reading or writing a message (adequate warning is usually given). The following sections give two ways of conserving time and money spent on messages.

Log Mail Nonstop, Manually Upload Replies

Before you go into the message areas, stop at the user preferences menu and turn off page pause (or turn on nonstop scrolling, if the BBS calls this feature by that name). Go to the message area and get ready to read mail. But first, open a session log file and name it something like IN-MAIL.LOG.

Many BBSs let you display all messages without having to stop at the end of each message to reply. Choose this option. It may be "Nonstop scrolling" (answer yes) or "Pause between messages" (answer no). Combined with the other things you have done, you will get a flood of mail into your session log that comes as fast as your modem and the BBS' modem can handle it.

Now close the session log and disconnect from the BBS. You can read the session log and the mail it contains at your leisure, without tying up a phone line.

Write your replies and new messages and save each in a separate file. Name each file something you will easily remember when you call the BBS again, such as BILLJONES.REP if you are answering Bill's message.

NOTE: Save each reply in "DOS text" or "generic word processor" format, if you are using a standard word processor such as WordPerfect. Either format will filter out control codes that will otherwise clutter up your messages and make them hard or impossible to read. Set your margins within the limits of the BBS' message "forms," so words will wrap to the next line where you intend them to.

Now call the BBS again. Go to the message areas and select the option to write a new message. Enter the name of the person to whom you want your first message delivered. If you want your reply added to a thread, enter the same subject as the message to which you are replying.

At this point, the BBS will be ready to accept the body of your message, which is in the file you wrote offline. Some BBSs offer the option to upload a message prepared offline using an error-correcting file-transfer protocol such as Xmodem, Zmodem, and so on. But others will just put you into the message editor and expect you to start typing.

The file you wrote offline will do the "typing" for you. If you are at line 1 of the message editor, select your terminal software's Upload option and choose the ASCII protocol. Upload the file containing the body of the message you want to send. It will appear line by line on the screen, as if a very fast typist were entering it. When the file upload is finished, end your message with the Save command, or choose the Edit command to make any changes or additions to your uploaded message.

Repeat this addressing and uploading process for each file written offline. This technique saves online time and money, but it is obviously tedious. Fortunately, there is a better way.

QWK Offline Mail Management—the Easy Way

Thousands of BBSs and millions of callers have adopted the *QWK offline mail handling standard*, which effectively automates all of the tedious steps described in the preceding section. You need a QWK-compatible mail-reader program to take advantage of this welcome innovation. The BBS you call must be running a QWK-compatible mail-management program such as TomCat! (WildCat!'s BBS) or QSO (TBBS boards). Look in the BBS' bulletins and message areas for notices of what offline mail system, if any, is available.

A QWK-compatible BBS lets you specify which of many message areas interest you; the number of messages you want to collect in any one session (to conserve connect time); whether you want to automatically conduct a new-files search and receive the results; whether new bulletins and other news should be included in your mail run; and other options depending on the specific QWK program the BBS uses. Figure 7-10 shows an example of one QWK mailer's configuration options.

Once you select your preferences, just press the "Download QWK packet" option (or its equivalent, depending on the QWK system the BBS uses) and watch things fly. In just 30 seconds to a couple of minutes, depending on how many messages must be searched, the QWK program will create a custom mail packet just for you. Generally, the mail packet will be compressed using one of the archiving utilities such as PKZIP to save downloading time.

Download the mail packet using one of the file-transfer protocols. Often a QWK program can be configured to search, pack, compress, download the packet to you using Zmodem, and automatically disconnect you when the whole process is over. You can start a QWK mail run and go do something else.

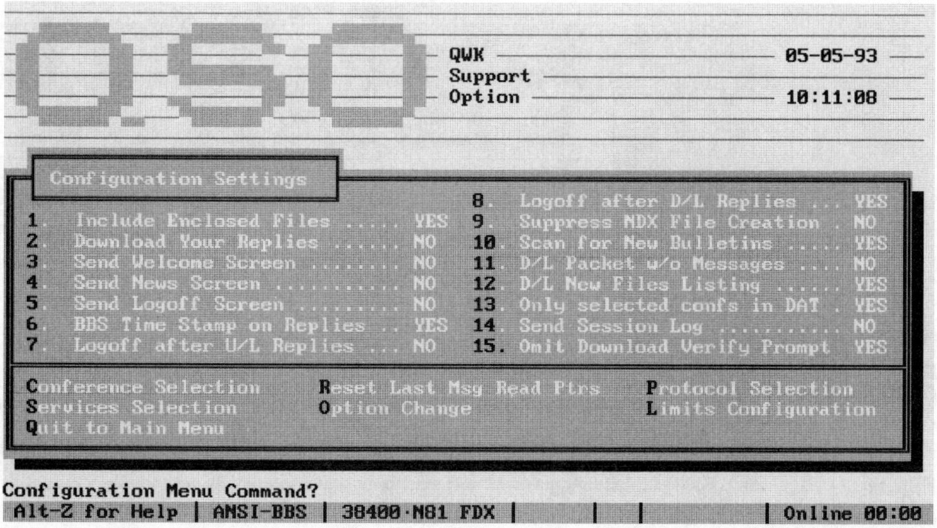

7

One of QWK mailer's configuration options

Figure 7-10.

After you receive your QWK mail packet, you will use one of the two dozen or so *offline mail readers* to open the packet, sort the messages, and write replies and new messages offline. Effectively, a QWK mail reader puts the BBS message functions on your desk; things look and work much the same as if you were online. Figure 7-11 shows one example of a QWK mail reader.

After writing replies and new messages, you will save them in a QWK-compatible *reply packet*, which generally ends with the extension *.REP. Most QWK mail readers handle this function with very little effort on your part.

Now call the BBS and upload your REP packet to the QWK mail processor. It unpacks your replies and adds them to the appropriate message areas and subject threads.

QWK mail may be the most important innovation in BBS technology since Ward Christenson wrote the first file-transfer protocol, Xmodem. The capacity of a BBS, measured in terms of the number of callers it can handle in a given period of time, is enormously increased when each caller spends just a couple of minutes in the message areas per call.

Obviously, you benefit too. You spend less time online, find messages of interest automatically, get fewer busy signals from your favorite BBS, and keep a permanent record of all your correspondence in the offline reader's database.

— SPEED READ Ver. 1.20 —

eSoft Support Board — Aurora, CO

Area	Total Msgs.	Keep Old	Last Packet	Unread	Description
0	1	0	1	0	Replies
0	84	100	2	0	Personal
0	0	500	0	0	QSO-INFO
1	87	500	0	0	NEWFEATURE
2	129	500	14	95	LOUNGE
3	349	500	12	121	TBBS
4	108	500	4	46	TDBS
20	21	500	0	0	EMAIL

Welcome   News   Bulletins   Files   Goodbye   F10-Picklist

Phil Becker, Sysop

Speed Read, one example of a QWK mail reader **Figure 7-11.**

"Doors" to Online Games, Databases, and Other Programs

A *door* or *Doorway* program, in BBS terms, is a program that can be run by temporarily exiting from the BBS software while maintaining your modem connection. The BBS software effectively "steps aside" and allows you to communicate directly with another program that ordinarily would not communicate through a modem.

Doors can be just about anything: Games, order-entry systems, registration questionnaires, call-back verifiers, lookup databases, and so on. Door programs are often written by professional software developers and sold to BBS sysops as a means of enhancing a BBS.

"Chatting" with Other Users in Real Time

A *multiline BBS*—one that can have callers on more than one phone line at the same time—frequently offers simultaneous callers the option of typing messages back and forth to each other while they are connected. This type of *chatting* (also known as teleconferencing) is a very popular activity; some BBSs are devoted almost entirely to chatting users. Figure 7-12 shows a sample chat session between the author and his literary agent. Some large BBSs often have between 4 and 15 people in various "chat lounges," shooting the breeze over their modems. If you would rather have a live conversation than an e-mail correspondence, chat may interest you.

7

```
Hi, Nick, how is So. Calif. today?

Very nice but slightly smoggy.  Lots of line noise here last night.  The marsh
marshins must have been active...

Your spelling of Martians is going to be read by millions of people (hopefully
(hopefully).  How is Patti doing?

Fine.  She is taking David, to school right now.  I'll tell her you inquired.

Good; she's been real sweet whenever I call.  Well, I guess I'll say byebye

wait... tell your readers if they want a good telecom book to Get Dvorak's Gui
Guide to PC Telecommunications by John C. Dvorak and Nick Anis [grin]

I've plugged that book several times in Modems Made Easy.  Have FUN!

ttulater


Sysop CHAT ended at 09:33

↑ ↓ PgUp PgDn - scroll      Home - beginning      End - end
F - find text      I - screen image      Shift-PrtSc - print screen      ESC - exit
```

A sample chat session

Figure 7-12.

Etiquette and Customs of BBS Society

BBSland and its citizens, like any other unique culture, have over time formed certain customs and unspoken rules. If you traveled to a foreign country, you would be well advised to at least briefly study its local customs in order to be a welcome guest. The same is true in online society. Here are some simple do's and don'ts.

Read the Instructions

Sysops are chronically vexed by lazy callers who refuse to read the carefully crafted help files and instruction manuals provided online. Be considerate of your host's time, and learn what you can on your own before asking where to find or how to do something.

Give and You Will Receive

Guests who show up empty-handed, who hang back along the walls and contribute nothing, are unwelcome at most social gatherings. Upload files you find useful, instead of just downloading from the BBS. Write messages to other callers; try to be helpful, or at least amusing. Often sysops impose upload/download quotas that require you to send one file for every few you download. The amount of time and access privileges you receive may be tied to your participation in message areas. The point should be quite clear: Be a contributing member of the BBS society, not just a leech.

Think Twice Before You Reply

Visual and audible cues about the meaning of your words are unavailable in electronic messages. Words that "sound" inoffensive as you write them may be misconstrued when read. You will often read something that rubs you the wrong way; don't blast back a scathing reply. Politely inquire of the writer if what you think you read is what they really meant; often the message will be clarified and hurt feelings avoided.

Avoid Hanging Up on Your Host

Don't just break your connection when you save a message or finish downloading a file. The Goodbye option on every BBS serves important housekeeping functions that may be disrupted by a rude, abrupt disconnection.

DON'T TYPE TOO "LOUD"

Entering messages in uppercase letters makes it appear to other people that you are "shouting." Use uppercase sparingly, and only to emphasize a politely phrased point.

BBSing Can Be Infinitely Rewarding—and Addictive

The term "modem maniac" was first used on a BBS to describe callers who seemed to spend their lives online. "Modem widow" is equivalent to "golf widow," but a greater tragedy since BBSing is a year-round "vice." My own BBS-related long-distance bill is consistently larger than most people's car payments.

Many modem users begin in BBSland and never find a good reason to leave it. While there are tens of thousands of BBSs and millions of fellow modem users available through them, you are well-advised to keep expanding your online horizons. The rest of this book points the way to entire universes "beyond BBSland."

CHAPTER

8

INFORMATION CARRIERS: MALLS FULL OF INFOBOUTIQUES

This chapter explores some of the major information carriers, *huge electronic "shopping malls" in which many different information entrepreneurs display their wares. With just one phone call you can search thousands of databases, send e-mail to anyone (even if the addressee has no modem), download gigabytes of files, do your banking, book airline reservations, and buy anything from a new* computer to a box of gourmet chocolates. This chapter first looks at general factors that you should consider when selecting an information carrier; the second half of the chapter focuses on what the various carriers offer.

The Advantages of Using Information Carriers

Information carriers cost a *lot* of money compared to a $20-a-year BBS. But they offer some advantages rarely or never found in BBSland:

✦ *Local Access Nationwide* Most information carriers give you a choice of several hundred phone numbers in all major metropolitan areas (and some pretty minor ones). If you spend hours every month calling long-distance BBSs, online carriers can save you a bundle of money.

✦ *Virtually No Busy Signals* Each *access node* (group of modems connected to a phone number) that an information carrier provides is usually well-supplied with modems. A popular BBS may be busy for hours, usually when you *know* it has the mail or files you need right now. Most information carriers earn money by the minute, from you or from the infoboutique you are calling on the carrier. So the carriers are pretty careful to maintain an adequate number of modems.

✦ *Cross-Media Electronic Mail* Many information carriers provide a wealth of communication options far beyond those found on BBSs. With the right information carrier, you can send a message to anyone who has a modem, a fax machine, or even just a mailbox. You can also address e-mail to people who use information carriers other than the one you use; your message and their reply will be forwarded across the boundaries of the electronic kingdoms.

✦ *Millions of Callers* Because information carriers offer so many services, and are heavily marketed, they attract millions of modem users. You will find more of everything: message areas, databases, files—but most of all, more *people* with whom to share your online adventure.

The huge audiences that use information carriers also attract information vendors who would not bother linking up with a small BBS. Banks, major department stores, newswire services, and other mass-market merchants provide a wealth of shopping, services, and information found only on large carriers, with a much higher level of convenience than can be found on local BBSs. Many software companies provide online support through information carriers, mainly to avoid the burden of running their own BBS.

Information carriers often act as teleconference centers, hosting online conventions and workshops. Industry leaders, celebrities, and organizations host scheduled teleconferences in which hundreds of callers can ask questions of leading experts on subjects ranging from Unix programming to baby care.

Information carriers are huge, diverse, active places in which to live the online life.

Choosing and Using an Information Carrier

There are some important factors to consider when choosing an information carrier. In many ways, the process is like choosing a major city in which to live. Some characteristics of city life are vitally important to some people, while the same factors may not matter at all to other people.

The Cost of Living Online

Information carriers compete on prices as fiercely as airlines compete on fares—and the "special offers" can be just as tricky. Most information carriers now offer basic accounts—with access through a local phone number—for less than $10 per month. But you need to make sure you can get what you really want for that price before signing up. The following lists some of the common "gotchas" to consider when choosing a budget account.

Restricted Calling Hours

"Unlimited connect time" for one monthly fee usually means the information carrier limits your calls to certain hours and days. If you think you'll need to log on during prime business hours, the prime-time connect fee should be your primary cost concern.

8

Surcharges for High-Speed Connections

Many information carriers still charge much more for use of 9600-bps modems than they do for 2400-bps connections. A fast connection may cost an additional $0.25 per minute compared to free low-speed time. If there is any difference between the cost of 9600- and 2400-bps access, the latter should be less than one-quarter of the former, giving you an incentive to efficiently use the high-speed lines. (See Chapter 13 for more information.)

Extended Services

Flat-rate basic accounts are lures used to expose you to attractive online services that cost more money. This practice is not as deceptive as it may seem. Your local shopping mall doesn't charge you to park your car. The mall owner makes money by enticing you into the stores, hoping you will spend money there so the owner can get a percentage. This is a perfectly normal and acceptable business practice. Just be sure you know the cost of accessing the services you really want before signing on with an information carrier that offers extended services.

Heavy-User Surcharges

The flat monthly fee may not cover all of your online activity. Many carriers allot you a certain number of messages per month and then charge for each message sent once you exceed your allotment. Some carriers charge extra for individual messages that are longer than a specified size limit. File transfers of more than a few thousand bytes often cost more. Few carriers charge for extra connect time; the mall owner *wants* you to stay and shop as long as you wish.

Special Software Requirements

Some information carriers, such as Prodigy, require purchase of custom software that you use only to connect to them. Most of these carriers make it up to you by giving full credit for the cost of the software toward connect time and extended services use. But remember that custom software takes up space on your hard drive, often over 1M, and it cannot be used for anything else.

Taking Advantage of Starter Kits

Because they offer so much and price things so confusingly, information carriers find they attract more customers by offering free trial offers. These starter kits generally include one to five hours of free connect time, credits you can spend in sampling extended services, and detailed guides to everything available.

Starter kits are often bundled with modems. Do not throw away all of those brochures that come with your modem; many are worth money when exploring information carriers. You'll find CompuServe starter kits in virtually every modem package; a $25 to $40 credit is yours for the asking.

Experienced modem users often accumulate several starter kits for one information carrier. You can set up another trial account and extend your free use of any carrier.

The rest of the chapter looks at individual information carriers.

CompuServe: The Biggest and Busiest

CompuServe is the largest information carrier, boasting well over 1.5 million members. The company's full name is often abbreviated as *CIS*. (Some people spell it CI$ or Compu$erve in reference to its connect charges.) Now owned by H&R Block, the tax-preparation company, CompuServe provides

24-hour access through local phone numbers in hundreds of cities worldwide.

To sample CompuServe free of charge, call their customer service department at 1-800-848-8990 (614-457-8600 if you are in Ohio) and ask for a local access number. If you cannot get an access number in your area, CompuServe may not be the right choice for you; long-distance calling charges will dramatically inflate your bill.

NOTE: Before using your terminal software to dial the CompuServe access number, make sure your communication parameters are set to *seven* data bits, *even* parity, and one stop bit (7-E-1).

When you connect to the access number, follow these steps:

1. Press the (Enter) key once; that should bring up the Host Name prompt shown in Figure 8-1.
2. Enter **CIS** in response to the Host Name prompt, and press the (Enter) key.
3. Enter **77770,101** when asked for user ID and press the (Enter) key.
4. Enter **FREE-DEMO** when asked for your password and press the (Enter) key. It doesn't matter if you type the password in uppercase or lowercase letters. For security reasons the password will not appear on your screen.

Congratulations! You are now on CompuServe! A welcoming message like the one shown in Figure 8-1 will be displayed one page at a time. When you see the "Press <CR> for more" prompt at the bottom of your screen, press the (Enter) key to move on to the next page.

NOTE: <CR> means carriage return, a common term for the (Enter) key in the online world.

Cruising CompuServe's Demo

Beyond Figure 8-1's welcome screen lies the menu shown in Figure 8-2. Option 1 displays a paragraph or so about each major category of service CompuServe offers, with the option to view more detailed information about a service if it interests you. See Figure 8-3 for an example of this quick tour.

```
Host Name:  CIS
User ID: 77770,101
Password:

CompuServe

Welcome to the CompuServe Sampler - a FREE online preview of the world's
largest information service.

We've prepared this sampler to give you an idea of the services available.
Keep in mind that this is a just a sample of the services you'll find on the
CompuServe Information Service. Also, our free software enhances the look and
feel of the service beyond what you will see here.

Some tips to help you get started:

  - When you see a menu (list) of items, enter the number next to the choice you
    want.  (That is, type the number and then Press <CR> for more !

  - To get back to a previous menu, enter M.

  - To return to the beginning of this sampler, enter T.

  - To leave and disconnect from CompuServe, enter OFF or BYE.

Remember, CompuServe is more than just information, it's people connecting with
people.  With more than 1,700 services and 900,000 members, we're sure you'll
find more of the services *and* people you want on CompuServe.

This online preview does NOT show how most of our new members use CompuServe.
We now have special software for IBM and Macintosh that revolutionizes the way
members use CompuServe.  It includes communications software, a graphic interface
and pull-down menus. The software comes FREE with a Membership Kit purchase.

To join you'll need a CompuServe Membership Kit.  To find out more on how to
join or to purchase a membership kit, select "How to become a Member" from the
next menu.  Be sure to check for this month's special offer too!

Or call us at 800-848-8199.

Press <CR> for more !
```

The
CompuServe
demo logon
screen
Figure 8-1.

```
CompuServe                DEM-1

 1 Tour of the Service
 2 Sample Menus of the Service
 3 Find a Topic
 4 What's New

 5 How to Become a Member
   * Free Information and Special Offers *

Last page, enter choice !1
```

The
CompuServe
demo system
main menu
Figure 8-2.

```
CompuServe              TOR-127

COMMUNICATIONS/BULLETIN BOARDS contains the CompuServe Mail service (basic),
a "real-time" CB Simulator (+), CLASSIFIEDS (basic), many discussion forums (+),
clubs and special interest groups, and a FEEDBACK feature that lets you leave
messages for Customer Service. GO COMMUNICATE takes you to this section.


  1 More on COMMUNICATIONS/
      BULLETIN BOARDS
  2 Continue the Tour
  3 Exit to TOP Menu

Enter choice or <CR> for more !
```

A typical
CompuServe
tour screen
Figure 8-3.

NOTE: Each screen has a name, such as DEM-1 and TOR-127 in the upper-right corners of Figures 8-2 and 8-3. If you know the name of a screen, you can quickly jump right to it from any other screen; just enter **GO DEM-1** at any "enter choice" prompt to jump to the demo's main menu.

The other demo options are self-explanatory. Take your time; the visit costs you nothing. There are over 1,700 services available on CompuServe. Call the demo service as often as you wish to find the services that interest you.

Ending Your CompuServe Tour

8

Enter **BYE** or **OFF** at any prompt to get out of CompuServe. You will still be connected to the mainframe computer; just tell your terminal software to hang up the phone (usually by pressing the Alt-H key combination). You will not offend or confuse the mainframe.

CompuServe Pricing Plans

The Basic Services offered by CompuServe at about $9 per month include unlimited connect time day or night, up to 60 three-page messages at no additional charge, and a host of news, reference, shopping, entertainment, travel, and member support services. The last category even includes Practice Areas where you can become familiar with CompuServe's uploading and downloading techniques, message addressing, menu navigation, chatting, and other procedures, before venturing into the pricier Enhanced Services areas.

Many infoboutiques on CompuServe cost extra. These Enhanced Services are clearly marked with a ($) symbol, so you know before you select an option whether it is going to cost you more money.

File transfers on CompuServe can cost extra if you are sending (uploading) a file or downloading one from an Enhanced Service area. For example, sending a 98K file containing two chapters for this book and their artwork cost an additional $2.00. Receiving (downloading) a file sent to you by another member costs nothing; it is part of your Basic Service electronic mailbox.

Overall, CompuServe is a good value for anyone who wants a nationally known online address used by millions of callers per year. The Enhanced Services are expensive, but you can minimize connect-time charges in these areas by using offline search-preparation software to automate your sessions on CompuServe. See Chapter 13 for more information.

GEnie: The Night Owl's Bargain

GEnie is General Electric Information Services' answer to CompuServe. For about $5 per month for Basic Service, GEnie costs less than CompuServe and delivers at least as much—*if* you call at night (6:00 p.m. to 8:00 a.m. your time) or on weekends, and only at 2400 bps.

NOTE: If you call GEnie at 9600 bps, you will pay $18.00 per hour during non-prime time hours (nights and weekends) or $24.50 per hour during prime time.

Basic Service on GEnie gives you unlimited electronic mail as opposed to the "excess mail" fees charged by CompuServe, Prodigy, and other carriers. Many (though not nearly all) of GEnie's Round Tables are included in Basic Service. *Round Tables* are GEnie's name for bulletin boards; CIS calls them *Forums*, and charges extra for access to any Forum.

GEnie's online research features (news, financial data, encyclopedia, other full-text databases) are not quite as extensive as CompuServe's, but are broader and more useful than any *other* information carrier's database selection.

The biggest flaw in GEnie is its antiquated, text-only interface. GEnie is great for heavy readers, good for chatting with other users, and perfect for researchers capturing rows of numbers. But online games just don't look the same in TTY 7-E-1 mode.

If you like smaller communities instead of huge cities, you will find GEnie very comfortable. GEnie's membership base is counted in the hundreds of thousands versus CompuServe's and Prodigy's million-plus; so GEnie gives you ample opportunity to meet plenty of new people, but doesn't present an overwhelming faceless mob.

GEnie used to offer an extensive demo account like CompuServe's, but as of this writing you can view only an online description of services, fees, and restrictions before being asked how you want to pay for your choice of service. Apparently, the folks at GEnie think their 30-day money-back guarantee relieves them of the responsibility to fully demonstrate their wares to shoppers; if you agree, it will only cost $4.95 to get a full taste of GEnie.

Logging On to GEnie

To log on to GEnie, follow these steps:

1. Set your communication parameters to 7-E-1.
2. Turn on local echo in your terminal software; GEnie does not echo what you type back to you, so your software must display what you type on your screen. If you don't turn on local echo, nothing you type will appear on your screen, even though the GEnie menus will appear.
3. Dial 1-800-638-8369 and wait for a connection.
4. Enter **HHH** as soon as you are connected; there will be no prompt from GEnie until you do so.
5. At the prompt U#=, enter **XJM11701,GENIE** and press ⌷Enter⌷.

The first screen you see will be the narrow one shown in Figure 8-4. Things will "spread out" to fill the width of your screen after you tell GEnie how many characters wide your screen is.

All you will get from GEnie is a text file display detailing service options, pricing, and hours when Basic Services are available. Then you will be asked for your name, address, and telephone numbers. Finally, you will be asked how you want to pay for your GEnie subscription.

Logging Off of GEnie

Interestingly enough, the only way to exit GEnie without subscribing is by hanging up the phone line from your end. Go ahead and do so. Some

8

Logging on to GEnie's free sample system
Figure 8-4.

```
U#=

 *** WELCOME TO GEnie [R] ***

GEnie, the information service
for micro-computer enthusiasts
and professionals...like you!


Screen width in characters
Example:  75  ?
```

high-pressure sales rep must be responsible for this "assumed close." Shoppers are free to walk away.

Delphi: Best Buy for Business Use

Delphi, founded in 1981, is noted for its innovative low pricing; it was the first information carrier to offer 2400-bps access with no surcharges for "high-speed" access. Its laid-back, almost Bohemian atmosphere is a distinctively BBS-like trait. If you are looking for something completely different online, do not pass up Delphi.

At this writing, Delphi is offering five free hours of evening and weekend connect time to new subscribers. After your free trial, you can continue using Delphi for as little as $1 per hour. It just doesn't get much cheaper on information carriers.

Signing Up for Five Free Hours on Delphi

Use your modem to dial 1-800-365-4636, communication settings 8-N-1 (8 data bits, no parity, 1 stop bit). When you connect, press the (Enter) key. Be patient; it may be two or three seconds before the opening menu appears.

Enter **JOINDELPHI** when prompted for your password. You will be invited to enter your name, address, and phone number. Then you will select your own User Name, the one-word name by which you will be known to other Delphi members. Delphi even suggests several possible user names for you, based on your real name: john, johns, jsmith, and so on.

To subscribe to Delphi and get your free hours, you will have to enter a major credit card number to cover future bills, if any. Then you will choose your own password.

Once your account is set up, Delphi will offer one or more local access phone numbers to you; select one. Using this number during non-prime times costs you nothing in long-distance telephone expense; Delphi effectively becomes a local phone call away! Only Delphi's low connect-time charges will apply after your free trial hours.

The last page Delphi shows you includes your own User Name, password, local access number, and other customized instructions for logging on again. Just press the (Prt Sc) key on your keyboard to print a copy, or review the instructions later if you logged your session to a disk file.

Financial Market Reports and Services

Despite its generally beatnik reputation, Delphi is a business person's secret weapon. The selection of news, financial, and research services is second to none. See Figure 8-5 for a glance at business and personal financial tools available to Delphi members.

Delphi provides continuous stock quotes and mutual fund updates for NYSE, American, and NASDAQ stocks. Quotes of specific stock and commodity prices are delayed 15 minutes. But MarketPulse, an exclusive Delphi service, provides real-time updates of overall markets, including the current Dow Jones Industrial Average, the most active stocks, largest advances and declines, and biggest percentage gains/losses. Note in Figure 8-5 that MarketPulse carries a $0.50 surcharge per peek.

Trendvest is a financial portfolio and stock analysis service that Delphi members can use to manage and manipulate their money. Newsletters such as Donaghue's Money Fund Report provide weekly rates for CDs, money funds, and other financial instruments.

General Member Services

Delphi has plenty of everything modem maniacs want: files to download, message areas on hundreds of topics, public bulletin board subsystems, shopping services, games (all text-oriented), and yes, "It's got an encyclopedia." In fact, the very first online encyclopedia appeared on Delphi in 1981. Figure 8-6 shows Delphi's Main Menu; you get the idea.

Delphi: A City of Creative Opposites

8

The ancient Greek city of Delphi was acclaimed as the center of the universe and the home of the world's most famous oracle. (The oracle was famous for giving prophecies so ambiguous and vague that they could never be proven wrong.) Delphi was also the earthly hangout for creative but opposing gods: Apollo the Rational and Dionysius the Party Boy, for example.

A Delphi business services menu
Figure 8-5.

```
Business and Finance Menu:

UPI Business News                    PR Newswire - Press Releases
Business Wire - Press Releases       RateGram CD Reports
Commodity Quotes                     Register of Public Corporations

Dow Jones Averages                   SOS - Stock & Options Advisors
Financial and Commodity News         Stock Quotes
Forum                                Translation Services
Futures Focus                        Trendvest Market & Mutual Fund Ratings
MarketPulse ($0.50)                  HELP
Money Fund Report from Donaghue      EXIT
Mortgage Calculator

BUSINESS>Which service?
```

```
MAIN Menu:

Business and Finance      News, Weather, and Sports
Computing Groups          Reference and Education
Conference                Shopping
Entertainment and Games   Travel and Leisure
Groups and Clubs          Using DELPHI
Internet Services         Workspace
Mail                      HELP
Member Directory          EXIT
```

The Delphi
main menu
Figure 8-6.

The modern, online Delphi is equally cosmopolitan. Delphi is a marvelous place to meet people of vastly different intellectual, career, and social backgrounds. Celebrated authors, scientists, business leaders, and artists lurk everywhere—and online, they're all "just folks."

Prodigy: The Information Carrier Everyone Knows

No one has done more to raise the public's consciousness about modems and online services than the folks at Prodigy(sm). Two master marketers, Sears and IBM, teamed up to create the online mall to end them all. The project cost nearly $800 million and 600 *centuries* of programmers' time before Prodigy ever went online. No one will say what has been spent on advertising and selling the finished product. But if you have never seen a Prodigy TV commercial, print advertisement, or direct-mail flyer, you must have been out of this solar system since 1988.

Pretty Pictures, Pretty Slowly

Prodigy is different from most other information carriers in that it is not a text-based system to which you can log on with your general-purpose terminal program. Prodigy screens, menus, and so on are all graphic images, composed of dots like a fax image. You need custom software, provided in the Prodigy membership kit, to log on.

You also need a fair amount of patience, if you log on at 2400 bps. Those graphics images take much longer to transmit to your screen than standard ASCII text characters. It is not unusual to stare at the "Working..." prompt for 20 to 30 seconds while Prodigy changes pages.

The graphical interface is great for nontypists. Most people use a mouse with Prodigy, pointing and clicking their way through menus, message headers, and other options.

The "Shop 'Til You Drop" Carrier

Almost every Prodigy screen carries an advertisement teaser; see Figure 8-7 for an example. Selecting one of these teasers provides detailed product and ordering information. If you wish, you can view one or more screens full of information about an offer, and order right on the spot before returning to where you were.

Prodigy's shopping services include J.C. Penney and Sears catalogs, travel services, specialty items such as gourmet chocolates and flowers, and other consumer/home oriented wares. Computer and business merchants are well represented, but the emphasis on Prodigy is the home and family market.

Basic Services and Prices

For about $15 per month, Prodigy provides local access phone numbers and unlimited connect time. At no additional cost, you can send up to 30 e-mail messages per month (the Bulletin Boards are Prodigy's most heavily used areas), search Consumer Reports databases, book airline tickets, read over 30 nationally known news and opinion columns, play games, read newswire reports, and of course shop in the Mall.

Prodigy gives special emphasis to child education. School-aged children can access an interactive *Weekly Reader,* which includes Story World, a great way to encourage kids to develop creative writing skills. Kids select a story, read what's been written so far, then contribute their own paragraph(s) to the plot. There is a SmartKids Quiz, where correct answers yield various prizes and recognition. Children even have their own Bulletin Board, called The CLUB.

8

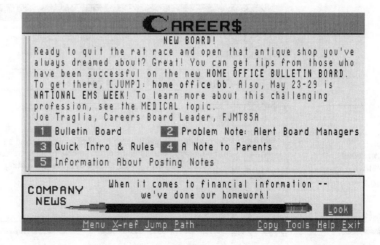

Prodigy
advertisement
teaser
Figure 8-7.

Getting Started on Prodigy

You can buy membership kits for about $40 in most computer stores, and of course in Sears department stores. Get detailed information about Prodigy services by calling 1-800-822-6922, ext. 205.

Tɪᴘ: Don't buy a membership kit directly from Prodigy; the kits are steeply discounted at all resellers.

America Online: Prodigy's Biggest Challenger

America Online is a visually exciting alternative to Prodigy. Founded in 1989, AOL has over 200,000 members. Custom software is required, and is available for MS-DOS, Windows, Macintosh, and Apple II-class computers.

AOL's basic service costs about $8 per month, but it includes only two hours of online time. Additional time costs $0.10 per minute, but that includes access through hundreds of local access nodes.

Files, databases, and shopping are well represented on AOL, but the big story here is user interaction. AOL members are heavily into bulletin boards, private e-mail, and especially live chat (which can use up your free time very quickly). The graphical interface is clean and efficient. Figure 8-8 shows how simple it is to enter an electronic message.

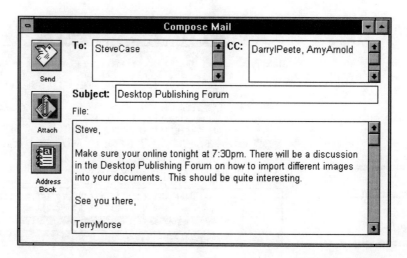

Sending mail
on America
Online
Figure 8-8.

How to Access America Online

AOL startup kits are better than free; they come with ten hours of free connect time as of this writing. To order a startup kit, call 1-800-827-6364 or (in Virginia) 703-448-8700. AOL Customer service keeps interesting hours: noon till 11 p.m. EST. You can leave your order information on a voicemail system, and your order will be shipped within 24 hours.

Information Carriers Offer Simplicity, Variety

The convenience of making just one call to access thousands of different services, learning just one way of doing things online, and paying just one bill per month is the primary advantage of using an information carrier. Local access numbers are another advantage, though many BBSs are now hooking into these nationwide networks too.

The downside of information carriers is that you learn just one way of doing things. I have seen questions on Prodigy from members who wanted to know how to use their Prodigy software to call a local BBS; you can't. The obviously arrested development of this Prodigy member's online abilities saddens me. I hope that you continue to learn new ways to benefit from being online. I have great hopes that the things users will be able to do online will just continue to expand.

8

CHAPTER

9

ELECTRONIC MAIL AND FAX SERVICES

Your primary interest in modems may be sending messages and "packages" that you currently send through the U.S. Postal Service (called "snail-mail" by the modem-wise) or through private express couriers such as Federal Express. If so, you are not alone. International Data Corp. estimates that the number of electronic mail users will skyrocket from 15 million in 1990 to over 45 million in 1993. Basic electronic mail services are extremely useful and generally inexpensive.

Dvorak's Guide to PC Telecommunications by John Dvorak and Nick Anis (Osborne/McGraw-Hill, 1992) defines *electronic mail* as "the transmission of correspondence such as letters and memos from computer to computer over a network of some sort." Correspondence can include graphics and other types of nontext information, even executable program files such as Lotus 1-2-3. For all intents and purposes, e-mail also includes file-transfer functions.

Who Needs an E-Mail Service?

People who want the convenience and speed of electronic mail but also need the ability to send correspondence anywhere, not just to other modem users, are prime customers for dedicated e-mail services. Whereas BBSs and information carriers have (until quite recently) confined themselves and their users to the modem-owning population, e-mail services have long emphasized universal delivery. Here are some examples of how e-mail exceeds the reach of online-only services:

✦ *Instant Letters* Correspondence delivered in seconds to any other subscriber in the world; what most people think of when they think of e-mail.

✦ *Overnight Letters* Laser-printed copies of your messages can be hand-delivered by noon the next business day, for less than the cost of traditional couriers. Your message travels via modem most of the way; hand-delivery finishes the process in the addressee's city.

✦ *Expedited U. S. Mail* Your e-mail flies to a printing center nearest your addressee, where it is printed and sent on by First Class Mail. Coast-to-coast and international users can shave days off delivery times, and still reach correspondents who are not e-mail users.

✦ *Fax Dispatch* If you don't have a fax machine or a fax-data modem, you might drive to the local mailbox-rental service and pay to use their fax machine. But if you have e-mail service, you need never leave your desk to send a fax. Your e-mail message can be stored and forwarded to any Group III (standard) fax machine in the world.

✦ *Broadcast Fax* You can set up *distribution lists*—lists of names and fax phone numbers of people who should receive copies of any given fax—and store them on an e-mail service's computer. Then, when you want to fax the same memo to 25 offices, you need only transmit it to the e-mail service once, along with the code number of the appropriate distribution list.

✦ *File Transfers* Most e-mail services now support at least the Xmodem and Kermit file-transfer protocols, so sending nontext files is as easy as uploading them to a BBS or CompuServe. MCI Mail also supports the Zmodem protocol, the hands-down choice whenever it is available.

✦ *Bulletin Boards* You can create, maintain, and search electronic bulletin boards. Boards you create give you control over who has access and what appears on the boards. There are many such bulletin boards on MCI Mail, most of them product support or promotional systems.

✦ *Directory Services* You can look up any other subscriber's e-mail address, and just pick an addressee's name from a list of possible matches.

✦ *Return Receipts* When a message you sent is retrieved by the addressee, you get a date/time-stamped receipt in your own electronic mailbox.

✦ *Shared Lists* Distribution lists you post for any MCI Mail user to use, or publish for just a few other users to read. Shared lists might include e-mail addresses for public-contact people in your company, or a private shared list for all of your salespeople.

✦ *Letterhead and Signature Graphics* You can store an electronic image of your letterhead, logo, and even a legal signature on MCI Mail, and append such graphics to messages. When printed, correspondence that uses these types of graphics look more professional and traditional.

✦ *Information Services* Some e-mail services provide access to databases, news services, and other information services that most people think are only available on CompuServe, Prodigy, and other larger information carriers.

Sending Messages Between Different E-Mail Services

9

E-mail service providers are competitors; in the early days of the industry, each service delivered mail only among its own subscribers. But customers' needs for universal delivery systems outweighed the advantages of this "captive audience" approach. Today, you can send e-mail from your service to almost any other.

DASnet: Filling the Inter-System E-Mail Gap

The problem of moving e-mail from one service to another was addressed by DASnet in 1987. DASnet receives mail from one e-mail service, deciphers its address to another service, converts the message to the addressee service's format, and forwards the message on to the addressee. Replies go through the same process on their way back to the original sender.

DASnet interconnectivity is included as a standard feature in many e-mail service packages. DASnet also can be ordered as a separate service, and used with many e-mail services, such as AT&T Mail, BIX, Dialcom Network, Western Union's EasyLink, MCI Mail, SprintMail, and so on.

X.400: The International E-Mail Standard

DASnet's market niche may disappear in the next two years, as an international standard known as *X.400* is adopted by more and more e-mail services and software developers. X.400 is a protocol that defines how electronic mail is addressed, stored, and transmitted. If every vendor adopts X.400, as seems to be the trend, e-mail will truly become a universal medium.

MHS Opens Local Area Networks to E-Mail

Novell, the leading vendor of Local Area Network (LAN) software, developed its own software for sending e-mail from one LAN to another. Novell's MHS (Message Handling System) works just as well over modem links as it does over hardwired networks. E-mail services and information carriers such as CompuServe have seized on this opportunity to extend their universal delivery strategy inside the walls of corporate customers.

I use my CompuServe MHS mail services to submit chapters of this book to my editor at Osborne/McGraw-Hill. Instead of stopping at his CompuServe mailbox, the MHS message is delivered right to Bill's own workstation through Osborne's LAN. I no longer have to call and tell him a chapter's waiting on CompuServe, or wonder if he has picked it up yet.

Linking Information Carriers and E-Mail Services

CompuServe, GEnie, Delphi, and the rest, suffer the same lack of interconnectivity that limits the usefulness of electronic mail services. Information carriers are addressing customer demands for interconnectivity, again at added cost.

If you want to address e-mail to an MCI Mail account from your CompuServe mail utility, just enter this line in the To field of the CompuServe message form (see Figure 9-1):

```
>MCIMAIL:123-456
```

The rightward-pointing arrowhead is necessary; press the Shift key and then type a period to create it. ">MCIMAIL" tells CompuServe you are addressing this message to someone on MCI Mail; the number following the colon is the person's MCI Mail address.

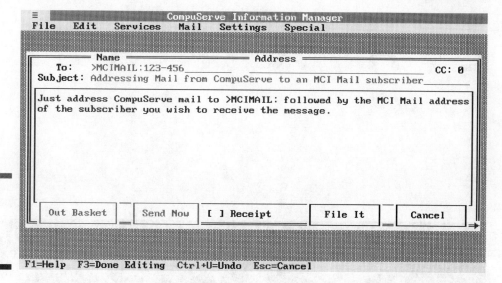

CompuServe
message
addressed to
MCI Mail
Figure 9-1.

Telex: The Original E-Mail Service Is Alive and Well

Telex was established in the 1920s to transmit textual data through a
network of teletypewriters (TTY) or teleprinters. Today, there are still over
two million telex machines in operation worldwide, many in places where
modems and personal computers are uncommon.

Like e-mail fax services, Telex can be used to deliver printed messages to
people who do not have a modem and computer. But anyone with a Telex
typewriter can also *reply* directly to your electronic mailbox. Telex services
are available on most e-mail services, and on many information carriers. The
Delphi information carrier provides a Telex address at no extra charge to its
subscribers.

Universal Electronic Mail Is Almost Here

You can credit MCI Mail, CompuServe, and other e-mail providers with
helping to keep the price of stamps and express couriers down. It is now
usually cheaper and faster to send documents via e-mail to almost any
address on earth.

More than 45 million e-mail users, not counting the millions of information
carrier users and Telex users, are saving literally piles of money and tons of
paper with e-mail. But there is an even more inexpensive way to send e-mail
to even more online penpals. The Internet is free, and the subject of the next
chapter.

CHAPTER

10

INTERNET: THE GLOBAL SUPERCARRIER

This chapter is about the world's biggest online community. If CompuServe's 1 million subscribers and 1,700 infoboutiques awed you, then the Internet may send you into shock. Imagine an information carrier that does all of the following:

✦ Connects you to over 15 million people in 50 countries, on every continent including Antarctica

✦ Gives you access to the files, doors, databases, and message areas of more than 1,500,000 private, corporate, and government computers

✦ Transmits more than 1 *trillion* (1,000,000,000) bytes of data per month

Now imagine that you can dive into this virtually infinite ocean of online adventure with just a local phone call, and swim as far and for as long as you like for free! You can with the Internet. Take a deep breath and get ready to explore the farthest frontier of the online universe.

Your Tax Dollars at Work Online

The Internet began in 1969 as a government-sponsored military computer network, linking corporate and university research centers so that scientists could share computer resources and swap information on secret research projects. This original network was known as DARPAnet (Defense Advanced Research Projects Agency network). Access to DARPAnet was closely restricted to security-cleared defense contractors and researchers.

In the early 1980s, DARPA established a second network, Milnet, to permit unclassified communication among academics and scientists. DARPAnet and Milnet established interconnections, and the whole thing became known as the DARPA Internet.

The scientific and academic community, which traditionally chafes under government constraints, soon formed other, more open networks such as UUCP (linking users of the Unix computer operating system), USENET (User's Network), CSNET (Computer Science Network). These special-interest networks eventually linked up under the Internet umbrella.

The big moment in Internet came in 1986, when the National Science Foundation Network (NSFNET) was established to link scientists and researchers to five supercomputer sites. The myriad of other networks scrambled to link up with these huge, ultra-fast supercomputers, causing NSFNET to replace DARPAnet as the primary internetworking coordinator. (DARPAnet was honorably retired in 1990.) The Internet grew by leaps and bounds under NSFNET's coordination, and continues to grow at the rate of 10 to 15 percent per month.

Today, nobody truly knows how big the Internet is. One estimate (that of Tracy LaQuey, author of *The Internet Companion* and pioneer of The Internet Society) is that it has over 5,000 computer networks worldwide, each of which includes dozens to thousands of individual computer centers and their many users. Suffice it to say that the Internet has quietly grown into the global information superhighway, while commercial carriers such as CompuServe, GEnie, and the rest, fought over market share.

Nonacademic Internet Users

A resource as huge and versatile as the Internet cannot and did not escape the notice of private enterprises and individuals. Under steady pressure from former students who missed their university-sponsored access, and from corporate interests who contribute to research, the once "geeky" Internet opened its intellectually elitist doors. It now includes a rich variety of nonacademic resources and users.

Journalists conduct research on topics ranging from computer science to sports scores. Doctors transmit test results and digitized X-ray images. There are Internet bulletin boards for artists and farmers. Schoolchildren exchange lessons in geography, literature, and language with peers in dozens of countries. Librarians search the catalogs and government archives of libraries across the country for the benefit of local patrons. Business users contact clients and exchange purchase orders; many business cards now carry an Internet e-mail address.

No matter who you are or where you live, *you* can join the Internet global family either through e-mail or a live connection to the Internet. We'll look at the e-mail method first.

Getting E-Mail Access to the Internet

Establishing your own Internet e-mail address is easy and usually free. Gaining full access to file-transfer privileges and interactive connections with distant Internet computers can cost some money and be more challenging, but not much more costly or difficult than your first BBS call.

10

Getting an Internet Mailbox

If you already subscribe to one or more BBSs, information carriers (such as CompuServe and GEnie), or electronic mail services, the odds are good that you can send and receive mail via the Internet. The Internet is firmly established as the most widely used inter-system connectivity solution. Check your existing online accounts first to see if you already have Internet access and how your particular host implements Internet e-mail.

If you do not already use an online service that includes Internet, refer to Appendix A, which lists many. If you cannot find a local Internet host site through the resources listed in Appendix A, try some of the following avenues:

✦ Ask your data processing manager at work if your employer has Internet access and will give you a mailbox.

✦ Call your local reference librarian and ask if Internet mailboxes are available for patrons.

✦ Contact the computer services departments of local elementary and high schools, community colleges, and universities.

✦ Go to local computer user group meetings and ask about Internet connections

✦ Ask your children if they have any electronic pen pals at school. You may be surprised to learn they do, and if you ask nicely they may let you use their Internet accounts, or get one of your own.

NOTE: Beginners are strongly urged to start with an Internet connection through a BBS or information carrier such as CompuServe; addressing Internet mail on such services is usually little different from addressing regular mail. If you really want to dive right into the "raw stuff" of Internet e-mail, first read *The Internet Companion*, by Tracy LaQuey and Jeanne C. Ryer (Addison Wesley, 1993).

Understanding Internet Mail Addressing

Once you obtain an Internet account, you need to become familiar with how Internet messages are addressed. Internet addresses look a little strange at first, but so would your U.S. Postal Service address to someone who had never seen ZIP codes or the phrase "P. O. Box" before. Once you understand a few key concepts of Internet addresses, they are really quite logical and easy to decipher.

An Internet address consists of two parts, separated by an @ symbol (Shift-2 on your keyboard). The part to the right of the @ symbol is the "host name"—the Internet name for the host computer site to which the message will be routed. The second part, to the left of the @ symbol, is the user name, the address of the specific user to whom a message is addressed.

Think of the host name as the street address, city, state, and ZIP code part of a U.S. Postal Service address. The host name gets your letter to the right physical destination. The local name is the like the rest of a paper letter's address, telling the folks who sort letters which specific person (or department) should get your letter. One of my Internet mail addresses looks like this:

```
david.hakala@boardwatch.com
```

When read aloud, this address sounds like "David dot Hakala at Boardwatch dot com." Boardwatch.com refers to *Boardwatch* magazine's BBS, one of my daily online haunts.

You also could reach me on CompuServe via the Internet even if you do not subscribe to CompuServe. My CompuServe mailbox is 74720,3377. The Internet uses periods ("dots") instead of commas or spaces for most punctuation, so an Internet message addressed to my CompuServe mailbox looks like this:

```
74720.3377@compuserve.com
```

My name is unnecessary because any mail delivered to my mailbox number will pop up when I log on to CompuServe.

If you have ever addressed a paper letter to a person or department in a large organization, you may have seen some very long and strange-looking addresses, such as this one:

```
John Smith
MS 6578-PER
MegaCorporation
Box C-128
1 Megacorp Boulevard
Big City, NY 10012-6578
```

You do not need to understand MegaCorp's internal mail routing scheme to send a letter to John Smith; you just have to be careful how you type his address. Similarly, if you run across an Internet address like the following, you just have to write it down exactly as it is spelled to use it—you don't need to understand what each component of it means:

```
wallace%TV60MIN@cunyvm.cuny.edu
```

10

NOTE: The last three or four characters of an Internet address indicate the type of host site to which you are addressing mail. The *.com* in *boardwatch.com* and *compuserve.com* indicate that these are commercial organizations. The *.edu* in *cuny.edu* indicates an educational host site.

E-Mail Lists: Traveling Bulletin Boards

Use the Internet for a while and you will notice people referring to "lists" in which they participate. They are talking about *electronic mailing lists*, topic-oriented collections of messages maintained by a host site administrator and distributed to any number of Internet users who want to receive the collections of messages.

Internet lists are like BBS message areas (CompuServe forums, Prodigy clubs, and so on), in that they provide a focal point for the exchange of *public* messages that any participants can write, read, and answer. Any message you add to a topic's chain of messages will be distributed to all other Internet users on that topic's mailing list. Think of it as passing a memo around the office for people to annotate, except that everyone gets a fresh, up-to-date copy each time a new note is added.

People usually first encounter a list in the form of a group of messages found on a BBS or other subscribing host site. No matter where online you first encounter a list, you can have your own personal copy of the list's messages mailed to any Internet address you like. Joining a list is a relatively simple matter of asking to be put on it.

First, you need to find the list manager, the human being (or computer) who maintains the mailing list and all the messages associated with it. Look for introductory or policy-statement messages from the list manager. Figure 10-1 shows an interesting example of a mailing list message from *clinton-info@campaign92.org*, the computer site that "managed" Bill Clinton's online Presidential campaign.

Second, just write to the list manager and ask to be put on the mailing list. To add boardwatch.com to the Clinton mailing list, Boardwatch's sysop simply sent an Internet message to *clinton-info@campaign92.org* that probably read something like, "Please add the e-mail address *clinton@boardwatch.com* to your *clinton-info@campaign92.org* mailing list."

NOTE: Subscription requests should be kept brief and to the point, because the list managers receive many requests per day. But it is good etiquette to add a complimentary or introductory sentence, such as, "Love your list! Please add my address to it...."

Master Directories of Internet Mailing Lists

You can download a list of Internet e-mail lists maintained by SRI International. The file is over 800K long, and you will have to make a live connection via anonymous FTP to *ftp.nisc.sri.com*. (See the section in this chapter, "Live Connections to the Internet" for instructions on using FTP to download files.)

Appendix A describes other places to get master lists.

Many Internet host sites, including boardwatch.com, subscribed to the Clinton Campaign's Internet mailing list
Figure 10-1.

```
From: Clinton/Gore Transition Server <Clinton-Info@campaign92.org>
Subject: The Campaign Information Service
To: clinton@boardwatch.com
Message-Id: <19930402204236.6.MAIL-SERVER@LEX-LUTHOR.AI.MIT.EDU>


Explanation: Welcome to the 1992 Presidential Campaign Information Service.

This is an automatically generated message, one of many informative
messages that you can request.  This message is an electronic computer
form.  It asks a series of questions to which you can respond.  Each
question has an explanation, some instructions and a list of valid responses.
```

Lists are not the only way to participate in message collections delivered to your mailbox; we haven't even touched on USENET newsgroups or BITNET, two other enormously active list groups. (See Appendix A for contact information.) There are thousands of special-interest e-mail lists on the Internet. Many lists add hundreds of messages per day. Be selective in choosing your lists, or you might spend your whole life reading and answering e-mail.

File Transfers Via Internet E-Mail

Internet e-mail is like MCI Mail and other text-oriented e-mail services (see Chapter 9), in that any nontext file you want to send must first be translated into ASCII text codes. You will need e-mail software that includes Internet-compatible translation utilities if you want to send executable, database, or compressed files via Internet e-mail.

A nontext file must be translated back into its original version at the receiver's end. Errors can creep into a file during either translation process, making this method less reliable than the straightforward file-transfer procedures described in the following section.

Message length limitations are another drawback to sending files via e-mail. Most Internet mail is restricted to messages (or translated files) smaller than 50K. Your message or file may be "returned to sender" or split into two or more messages if you violate this restriction. A nontext file split into two Internet messages will be difficult or impossible to reassemble into anything usable.

10

Live Connections to the Internet

So far we have not ventured outside of the familiar world of BBS and information carrier mailboxes. Everything we have looked at is essentially "mail-order" communication. But you can directly connect to the Internet, and access many thousands of remote computers from your local host site.

To make a live, real-time connection to a remote Internet host site, you need three things (two of which you know how to get or already have):

✦ A modem-equipped computer

✦ Terminal software (the general-purpose kind discussed in Chapter 7 will do)

✦ A full-access user account on an Internet host site (a computer that is constantly connected to the Internet)

A full-access user account lets you use the host's link to the Internet to access other Internet hosts in real time. Such "live" linking lets you transfer files, run door programs, or simply browse the remote computer's disk drives as if you were sitting at its keyboard instead of your own.

Getting a Full-Access User Account

You may be able to get full access to remote computers from the same source that provides your Internet mailbox: your employer, local library, university, and so on. While some generous employers and public institutions provide free full-access user accounts, be prepared to pay for the privilege. Full access is expensive to provide, and ties up the host's phone lines much longer than just sending and receiving e-mail does.

Many universities and other publicly funded institutions charge as little as $1 per hour for full access to the Internet. Commercial Internet access providers, such as PSInet, may charge fees rivaling the Enhanced Services of CompuServe and other information carriers ($8 to $24 per hour in most cases).

Remote Login: Connecting to an Internet Host

Most people will place a phone call to reach their Internet host. If you are using a Local Area Network to connect with an Internet host computer (as you might if your employer provides the Internet host), follow the instructions given by your user account provider.

The same terminal software you use to dial up a BBS will also connect you to an Internet host. Once you connect to the Internet host, the login process is similar to what you might encounter on a BBS, but even simpler. A typical login to an Internet host would include these quick activities:

✦ Setting communication parameters. Many Internet hosts are mainframe computers, using 7-E-1 settings and VT-100 terminal emulation. Read the instructions!

✦ Dialing the host's remote-access phone number.

✦ Entering your *login id*, such as "dhakala".

✦ Entering a password for verification.

That is usually it. Internet hosts tend to be less flashy and welcoming, more down-to-business than BBSs. You will rarely see multiple screens of rules and self-promotion on an Internet host, or encounter the interminable questionnaires some BBS sysops force callers to answer.

On the downside, you may not get much help from your Internet host with menu and directory navigation, host-specific commands, and so on. Internet hosts tend to assume that people logging on know what they are doing. Keep that instruction book handy, and study it before logging on.

Things You Can Do After Logging On

Now that you are effectively in command of what is probably an immense, powerful mainframe computer, what can you do? That depends on your user account's *access privileges*, the information stored on the remote host that tells it how many and what kind of access privileges you have been authorized. Depending on the access privileges you are given (or perhaps purchased), you may be restricted to one or two activities or have the entire run of the place.

Usually, your access privileges will include the ability to search specific databases, run host applications (door programs in BBS terms, as you'll recall from Chapter 7), read/write personal and list mail, maintain your personal file directory(ies), upload files from your computer to the host, and download files from the host.

10

Telnet: Leaping from Your Host to Others

The Internet host to which you directly connect is in turn connected to the entire Internet system. You can use one of the utility programs that reside on your host to make a remote login connection to another Internet host, anywhere in the world. If the site to which you directly connect is a local phone call from you, you can globe-trot around the Internet without paying long-distance charges. Some Internet host sites charge a nominal fee ($1 to $2 per hour) for this service, but many do not.

The program that makes this free leapfrogging possible is called Telnet. You use Telnet just as you might use the MS-DOS COPY command. Whereas the COPY command needs to know the name of the file to copy, Telnet needs to know the Internet address of the remote host site you want it to call. To log on to the NASA Spacelink Internet host, for example, you would first log on to your direct host, and then type this:

```
telnet spacelink.msfc.nasa.gov
```

Now press the ⏎ key. Your host will dial out on another line, and you will go through the same login procedure all over again. But once you log on to the NASA computer, your own host effectively becomes invisible.

Breaking a Telnet Connection

Sometimes novices (and experienced users on unfamiliar turf) have difficulty breaking their connections to a remote host after using Telnet to log in. Seldom are there any convenient, BBS-like menus with options clearly labeled "Goodbye." You have to find the right command for the system you are calling, or guess it, before the remote computer will hang up the phone. Finding the magic "let me go" command can be as frustrating and time-consuming as hunting for an obscure MS-DOS command you desperately need but have rarely or never used.

Always read any instructions that appear onscreen when you first log on to a remote host, and take the time to write down important commands like "how to exit." Do not trust your memory with the exit-word; many online sessions provide an overload of information that often drives "obvious" memories clear out of your head.

NOTE: Simply hanging up *your* phone will break the connection between your computer and your *direct* host, but it is extremely rude to leave your direct host sitting there with a long-distance connection to the NASA Spacelink no one is using. Such inconsiderate and costly behavior might even get your user account canceled.

FTP: The Internet File-Transfer Protocol

Along with the Telnet remote-login utility, most Internet hosts also have a program called FTP (File-Transfer Protocol), that is used to transfer files between computers on the Internet. The word "protocol" is a bit of an understatement; FTP features a number of commands for locating files, moving among directories on the host, and requesting uploads or downloads of specific files. The Zmodem protocol, by contrast, simply determines how a file transfer already in progress is handled.

To start an FTP session with a host to which you are directly connected, just type **ftp** and press the ⏎ key. (Remember that while you are logged onto it, you are giving commands to the *remote* computer, not your own; you do not need the FTP program on your own computer.)

NOTE: You also can tell the remote host to open a file-transfer link to yet another remote host; just type **ftp** *host-name* and press the (Enter) key. (Example: **ftp spacelink.msfc.nasa.gov**) Like Telnet, this command will dial up a remote computer, but you will only be able to use the file-transfer functions of FTP.

Once FTP is active, a number of file-manipulation commands are available to you. Read the documentation of the remote host whose FTP you are using to learn the specific commands available on a given system. Commonly available FTP commands include:

+ *dir* or *ls* to list the files in the current directory
+ *cd* <directoryname> to switch to another directory
+ *cdup* to move one step up the directory-chain "ladder"
+ *pwd* to print the name of the working (current) directory
+ *get* <filename> to download a file from the host to you
+ *put* <filename> to upload a file from you to the host
+ *help* to get a list of available FTP commands
+ *help* <commandname> to get detailed help on a given command
+ *bye* or *quit* to break the file-transfer link and exit

NOTE: Many Internet hosts use the Unix operating system, in which filenames are case sensitive. If you type **README** (uppercase) when the file's name is readme (lowercase) you will *get* nothing.

10

FTP assumes you are transferring a text-only file unless you tell it otherwise. Program, data, and compressed files will suffer damage unless you specify that they should be treated as binary files before you upload or download them. After invoking FTP and *before* you enter **get <filename>** or **put <filename>**, type the word **binary** and press the (Enter) key.

Anonymous FTP: Getting In Without Logging On

Making information widely available is one of the primary purposes of the Internet. If you need a copy of the U.S. Constitution, the Internet philosophy says you should not have to sign up for a user account in order to get it. Anonymous FTP lets anyone download a specific file (or any of a group of files) from an Internet host computer without having a unique login name or password on the host system.

You still need a login name; enter **anonymous** at the logon prompt. This usually can be followed by any password you may dream up, although some systems insist you enter **guest** as your password.

While not every Internet host allows anonymous FTP, over 1,300 known systems do. The gigabytes of information available through anonymous FTP include shareware files, electronic books (try downloading *Zen and the Art of the Internet*), and graphics images.

Internet: The Infinite Voyage

There are many more ways to cruise and use the Internet than can be covered in this chapter. No one, not even the people who administer traffic on the Internet, really knows how many computers and people this marvelous invisible highway links. All we can be sure of is that it is still growing.

Internet: The Complete Reference, is a comprehensive guide to life on the global Information highway, written by Harley Hahn (Osborne/McGraw-Hill, 1993). If you try the Internet and want to learn more about it, look for this excellent reference book in libraries and bookstores.

The next chapter eliminates the middlemen by showing you how to directly connect with anyone with whom you want to swap e-mail or exchange files.

CHAPTER

11

PERSON-TO-PERSON MODEM CALLS

You do not need to call CompuServe, a BBS, MCI Mail, or any other third-party service in order to communicate by modem with friends, relatives, and business colleagues. You can call your online acquaintances direct. All it takes is two modem-equipped computers on either end of a phone line, and at least one person who knows what they are doing. When you finish reading this chapter you will be that expert.

This chapter explains how to use ordinary terminal software to answer a call from another modem, chat with the caller, and transfer files from computer to computer. Then some specialty applications of person-to-person modeming are examined:

✦ *Personal-E Mail*, a recent shareware program, provides an example of easy-to-use no-cost electronic mail. It can remain in memory at all times, so anyone can send you mail or pick up theirs without calling you first to set up things. Personal-E Mail can even distinguish between modem and voice or fax calls and route a non-modem call to an answering machine or fax.

✦ *WizLink* is a remote control program that lets you monitor what someone else is doing on a remote computer and take over control at any time. You can run the remote computer's software, type instructions to the remote user, transfer files, and generally act as if you were sitting next to the remote user. Consultants, technical support reps, and helpful neighborhood computer gurus find it easier to log on instead of traveling to their clients' sites.

✦ *LapLink V* is a high-performance file-transfer program, a favorite of portable computer users, corporate software library managers, and anyone who needs to move files from one place to another. LapLink provides an example of *remote installation*; it can install itself on a remote computer over a phone line. This capability solves the problem of what to do when the remote user does not have the necessary software to make a person-to-person connection.

Finally, we will look at the *host mode* of your terminal software, using Telix's HostPlus module as an example. Host software lets you set up a miniature BBS using your terminal software.

Person-to-person modeming is easier and cheaper than running your own online service. Neither party needs to buy a subscription to an e-mail service, BBS, or information carrier. There are no connect-time surcharges, e-mail postage fees, or other added-value charges to pay, just the price of an ordinary phone call. (See Chapter 13 for some ways to keep the cost of long-distance modeming down.)

Businesses that transmit confidential messages or document files find extra security in person-to-person connections. Data goes directly and only to the addressee, and no copies are stored (even temporarily) on any third party's computer.

You can do anything you want on a private phone call; you are not limited to the functions offered by a third-party service. If your favorite chess game is not on Prodigy, you can play it one-on-one with another competitor. You can start your own private message center on any topic you choose, instead of forcing your special interest into a predefined category on a BBS. There are no time limits or file-transfer byte limits, as are common on BBSs.

Some things simply cannot be done through a third-party service, like remotely controlling a customer's computer to see why they cannot start the software you sold them. (An Internet telnet connection is a form of remote control, but it is unlikely that your customers are Internet host sites.)

Person-to-person modeming is easier and cheaper than running your own online service. Unlike operating your own BBS (see Chapter 12), person-to-person modeming does not require dedicating a computer, modem, and phone line to your electronic correspondents, or the considerable amount of time and effort that can go into designing and maintaining a BBS. The techniques in this chapter are quickly and simply used whenever you need them; then they go back in the toolbox until you need them again.

Answering Calls from Other Modems

You must learn how to greet guests with your modem, and how to get your modem to greet guests when you are not around. This section deals with

+ Immediate manual answering: telling your modem to pick up the phone line right now and establish a connection with the modem that is calling.

+ Auto-answering mode: setting your modem to listen for incoming calls and automatically answer them, even when you are not at the keyboard.

The software discussed in the following sections generally makes it easy to switch quickly from *originate* (call out) mode to manual or auto-answering. But before delegating these functions to a program, you should know how they work and how to implement them at home or at the office.

11

Immediate Manual Answering

Most modems are preset at the factory to make outgoing calls. A simple AT command typed from your keyboard is all it takes to make your modem answer the next call that comes to your phone line. (See Chapter 6 to refresh your memory of AT commands.)

When you need to accept a modem's call, you normally will tell someone to use their modem to call you "right after we hang up" from a normal voice phone call. (Some BBSs use call-back verification doors, and *they* tell *you* to prepare for a modem call; see Chapter 7.) You expect the next incoming call to be from a modem, and you will want to have your modem answer without delay. This section tells you how to do it. (Practice this technique alone; you do not need an incoming call to learn how manual answering works.)

Load your terminal software and be sure it is in command mode (listening to you, not the phone line) by typing **AT** and pressing the (Enter) key; you should get an "OK" response indicating that the modem is responding to your commands.

To tell your modem to answer the next incoming call, type the following AT command line and press the (Enter) key:

```
AT M1 S0=0 A
```

✦ *AT* gets your modem's attention to accept commands.

✦ *M1* turns on the modem's speaker; you will want to hear what happens next.

✦ *S0=0* tells your modem not to wait for the phone to ring before answering.

The *A* command tells your modem to pick up the phone (take the line *off-hook*) and try to answer an incoming call (even though there is no incoming call). You should hear a click as the modem "lifts the receiver," followed by the steady dial tone you would expect if you personally picked up an idle phone's handset.

Then the modem will generate some awful noises; do not panic. The sounds you hear are the modem's way of saying, "Hello! Can we talk?" The answering modem in any connection starts this handshaking routine, in which it signals its presence online to the incoming caller, and attempts to negotiate a mutually compatible connect speed, communication parameters, and so on. (The calling modem is silent, listening for a handshaking greeting, just as you are silent when you make a phone call until someone answers and says, "Hello?")

To make your modem hang up and stop making those annoying sounds, press any key on your keyboard. Your modem may report "No carrier" after it hangs up. This result code indicates your modem did not detect another modem's *carrier wave* signal in response to its attempted handshaking; no connection was established.

Automatic Answering: Make Your Modem Listen and Wait

If you do not know exactly when an incoming modem call will arrive, you do not have to hover over the keyboard all day, poised to type **AT A**. You can set your modem to monitor the phone line constantly, and to automatically answer any incoming call.

Type the following (while in command mode) and press Enter:

```
AT S0=1 S7=30
```

Your modem acknowledges your commands with "OK," then just sits there, quietly waiting for an incoming call. The *S0=1* command tells the modem to answer any incoming call on the first ring. The value of S0 can range from 0 (do not answer) to 255 (answer on the 225th ring).

The *S7=30* command tells your modem to attempt handshaking for up to 30 seconds before giving up. After 30 seconds of no carrier in this example, your modem will disconnect and go back to waiting for another incoming call. The value of S7 can range from 1 second to 255 seconds (4 minutes, 15 seconds).

Giving Modems More Time to Shake Hands

The S7 *no-carrier timeout delay* also applies when your modem is making outgoing calls. The factory default usually is S7=30 (try for 30 seconds to detect carrier, then hang up) in answer *or* originate mode. Sometimes 30 seconds is not long enough, especially if you are calling long-distance or over a noisy phone line, when handshaking can take an unusually long time.

You can change this default value before any given call, by entering a new S7=<some value> in command mode before placing a call. You also can change the no-carrier timeout delay in your terminal software's initialization string or by programming the change in command mode and then saving it in your modem's NVRAM user profile. (See Chapter 6 for details on initialization strings and user profiles.)

11

If another modem had been on the line, the pair would have shaken hands, established the best connection both could maintain, and turned over control to the software on each end of the link. What happens then depends on the software you and your online partner are using, and how you use it. The following sections discuss different types of person-to-person software.

Personal-E Mail: Skipping the Stamp and the Mailbox

Our first example of person-to-person software is designed for easy, fast delivery of electronic mail. *Personal-E Mail* (PEM) from AmerCom is ideal for novice modem users who want to occasionally exchange mail with friends, relatives, or business associates, but do not want to pay for a permanent online mailbox with a third-party service or learn the much more complex features of e-mail software such as cc:Mail or Microsoft Mail.

PEM is also good for intensive correspondence in business, educational, or personal applications where ease of use is important to the majority of users. PEM can function as a 24-hour *mail hub* on one computer in a group of correspondents, accepting and delivering mail for many callers. PEM operates in the background in *hub mode*, allowing full use of the computer while PEM monitors for incoming calls and performs mail operations.

PEM is available in shareware and commercial versions. The commercial version, which can be tailored to specific business needs, includes predesigned questionnaire forms that callers can fill out and return to a hub, and a unique module that can translate electronic mail text into formatted fields readable by spreadsheet, database, or statistical software. These features make it easy to analyze thousands of e-mail messages to determine consumer attitudes, frequency of common questions, and so on. Some current PEM users include:

✦ A bank and its best business customers use PEM to exchange information about market rates and account transactions, query customer service and conduct customer surveys. PEM's simplicity makes it easier to get customers to use it, and lets users avoid the red tape of obtaining MIS departments' participation in installation and training.

✦ A radio station has distributed hundreds of copies of PEM to listeners, who e-mail questions and opinions to talk show hosts. PEM's data conversion facilities make it easy to tabulate listener votes and analyze essay-style responses.

Sending Messages with Personal-E Mail

Installing PEM is a simple matter of inserting the distribution diskette in a floppy drive, typing **INSTALL**, and answering three questions about your COM port, which ring of the phone you want PEM to answer, and whether you want wide-character or normal display mode. The setup utility creates its own subdirectory and copies all necessary files to it.

To load PEM, switch to the PEM subdirectory and enter one of these batch-filenames:

✦ **HOME** to run PEM while you are also available to take voice phone calls

✦ **AWAY** to run PEM when your computer and answering machine will take calls

✦ **BACK** to run PEM in background mode and use your PC to run other programs

✦ **QUICK** to run PEM in high-speed mode (see following note)

✦ **TDD** to run PEM with a Telephone Device for the Deaf

The following example session uses the QUICK startup mode, and assumes you are going to call another PEM user to deliver or pick up mail. Figure 11-1 shows the PEM startup screen in normal text mode (80 characters wide).

Whereas some e-mail programs assume that the user knows the jargon of computing and telecommunications, PEM keeps things simple, bite-sized, and in plain English. You do not even have to remember which key to push for help; explanations are already on each menu. Power users may get impatient with this baby-step approach, but PEM is ideal for the modem-innocent and infrequent users.

11

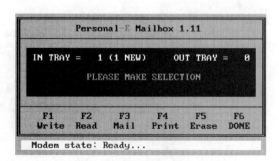

Personal-E
Mail main
menu
Figure 11-1.

Creating or Editing Mail with Personal-E Mail

To compose a new message or edit one in your electronic out-basket, press the F1 function key. Figure 11-2 shows the resulting submenu and your options.

Creating a new message involves filling in the addressee's name and modem phone number, adding your return address, and entering a subject for the message. The shareware version of PEM does not offer a dialing directory in which to permanently store frequently called correspondents; you have to fill in the addressee and return address information for every message. See Figure 11-3.

After a letter is addressed and written, it goes into your electronic out-basket, ready to be sent when you select Mail from PEM's main menu. You can edit any message in your out-basket before sending it.

Dialing and Exchanging Mail

When you are ready to send mail, press the F3 function key on PEM's main menu (Figure 11-1.) You will be shown the headers of all messages in your out-basket, so you can select which one(s) to send now. PEM takes over when you select Done (F6). It dials each message's phone number, logs on to the receiving PEM user's computer, delivers your mail, and logs off.

If you own a high-speed modem, you can save more than half of long-distance connect time costs by using PEM's QUICK.BAT startup mode. Most v.32/v.42bis modems go through a complicated handshaking routine that takes about 10 to 15 seconds before carrier is detected and real communication begins. This delay is due to the many different combinations of connect speed, error-correction protocols, and data compression protocols that must be tried in order to find a combination both modems can sustain. PEM's Quick mode skips this automatic

PEM Write
submenu
Figure 11-2.

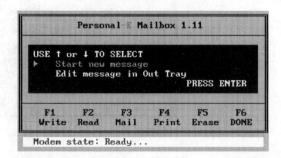

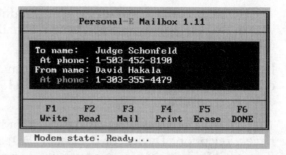

PEM message-addressing screen
Figure 11-3.

adjustment procedure, directing your modem to dial at 2400 bps without trying to get an error-free connection. The result is an immediate handshake, saving 10 to 15 seconds per call. Since most e-mail messages take only three to five seconds to deliver, you get on and offline faster.

Receiving Mail with PEM

PEM is ready to answer calls and receive mail whenever you start it. The key differences in how you receive mail lie in which batch file you use to start PEM and whether you exit PEM by unloading it or by leaving PEM running in background mode.

PEM is unique in how it answers calls and decides what to do with them. Instead of delivering a blast of handshaking squeals to every incoming caller, PEM keeps your modem mum and listens for either a fax tone or a special tone that indicates another PEM system is calling. If neither tone is heard, PEM assumes this is a voice call and routes it to your answering device. Fax calls are routed to your fax machine, and of course PEM callers are immediately handled by PEM. The HOME.BAT startup file lets you answer the phone first. If a modem is calling, the line will be silent when you say hello. Hang up, and if the caller is indeed a PEM user, the two systems will connect within 20 seconds.

You can leave PEM running in background mode while you work with other software in the foreground. Just run the BACK.BAT file to start PEM in background mode, or start PEM any other way and choose Exit with background ON. PEM takes up a scant 24K of memory, leaving plenty of room for other applications.

The AWAY.BAT startup mode assumes you are gone, leaving just PEM, an answering machine, and perhaps a fax machine or modem to handle all calls. PEM answers calls after the number of rings you specified during the setup procedure. If a PEM inbound call is simultaneously answered by an answering machine, PEM will wait until the machine's outgoing message ends and the machine shuts off before transferring e-mail.

11

The HOME.BAT mode assumes you are around to pick up the phone. When you answer the phone, you will hear silence if a modem is calling. Just hang up and PEM will take over.

Use the QUICK.BAT startup mode if you run a dedicated PEM system. Then other PEM callers who use QUICK.BAT will log on and off your machine as quickly as possible.

The TDD.BAT mode is specially designed for hearing-impaired users who have a Telephone Device for the Deaf (TDD) attached to their PEM systems. It uses PEM's Autochat feature to facilitate simultaneous mail transfers and interactive chat between users.

Remote Control Software: WizLink

Remote control software lets you run a remote computer as if you were sitting at its keyboard. The connection can be made via modem, through a Local Area Network, or over a hardwired RS232C serial link. You can run any of the remote computer's software, copy files between its disk drives and yours, and even chat with the operator of the remote computer if he or she is around. Two people can share the remote computer's keyboard as if they were sitting side by side in the same room. This makes remote control software ideal for training and troubleshooting users' problems.

In a remote control session, one computer runs *remote* software and dials out to the other computer, which runs *host* software to receive the call. Sometimes the remote and host programs are identical except for the way they are started up, but more often two different programs are provided.

Remote control software must meet two special criteria in order to perform satisfactorily:

✦ *Very small host memory requirements* You need all the free RAM you can get to run large application programs while the host program remains in memory to maintain the communications link. For an IBM-compatible computer with 640K of conventional memory, host software should not take up more than 100K to 120K. Most host software, like the WizLink program reviewed in the following sections, takes up less than 10K of memory.

✦ *Efficient screen-refresh* Running software in real time involves many little changes in what you see on the screen: cursors move one row/column at a time, characters are written and deleted in fields, and so on. Good remote control software transmits over the phone line only the portions of the screen that have changed, rather than repainting the entire screen every time you press a key. The most efficient remote control software includes its own data-compression techniques to further speed up screen-refreshes. This feature is handy when using non-data-compressing modems. It is less important on LAN or hardwired links, which run at much higher speeds than modems can achieve over dial-up phone lines.

Introducing WizLink

WizLink is a good shareware example of remote control software. Released in April 1992 and updated for 1993, WizLink includes the following features:

✦ Only 6K required for background operation in host or remote mode.

✦ Selective screen-refresh and optional data compression.

✦ File transfers with error correction at speeds up to 115K over hardwired links.

✦ Live chat feature during remote control or file-transfer operations.

✦ A 100-entry built-in dialing directory for managing multiple host sites.

✦ Extensive online help, including access to the full user manual.

✦ A screen-saver that blanks your screen to avoid burn-in while you are away from a host computer.

✦ Host mode can be set to disconnect and call back to a remote user. Consultants like this feature, since it makes their clients (who usually run the host program) pay for each call.

✦ User-definable password protection in the host program provides vital security against unauthorized callers. But password security can be disabled for quick in-house use.

WizLink can be installed in background remote mode and popped up at any time by pressing the (Alt)-(Shift)-(H) key combination. This option lets you remain available to dial out to a host, without having to exit your current foreground program and start WizLink. Hosts will generally load WizLink only when they need to accept a call, but the program also can be kept in background mode at host sites.

Once the remote and host software connect (and any required password is correctly entered from the remote), the remote user shares control of the host. Commands typed at either end of the link will be executed as if they were typed at the host's keyboard. Additionally, users can perform these special functions:

✦ Resynchronize and refresh remote screen. Line noise can knock the remote view of the host's screen out of kilter. This command retransmits the whole screen so both users see the same thing.

✦ Receive (download) files from host.

11

◆ Send (upload) files to host.

◆ Reboot the host computer from the remote without losing the modem connection. Sometimes pressing `Ctrl`-`Alt`-`Del` is the best way to get out of a lockup and start over.

◆ Shell to DOS on a remote computer. Often you will need to locate a file on your disk, edit a file you just downloaded from the host, and perform other local tasks. This feature lets you out of WizLink to run DOS commands and other programs. You can return to WizLink by typing **EXIT** at the DOS command line.

WizLink is shareware, with a registration fee of just $45. Commercial remote control programs such as Carbon Copy and PC Anywhere generally cost $100 to $300. Commercial packages include more robust features such as multiple passwords and access privileges, script languages for automated sessions, and unlimited support for hundreds of users.

Windows and Other Graphical Software

Windows 3.x and other software that relies on bit-mapped graphical displays present special challenges to remote control software. Whereas a text-based screen might be refreshed by transmitting less than 3K of data, a screenful of high-resolution graphics can easily exceed 250K. A full-screen refresh of that size would take over 100 seconds at 2400 bps! Mouse control is another challenge in remote control; the very fine movements and flickering speed of mouse-controlled cursors place high demands on modems and software.

Close-Up, from Norton-Lambert Corp. of Santa Barbara, California, is one of the best commercial packages for Windows users and anyone who must remotely control a graphical interface program such as AutoCAD, Ventura Publisher, and so on. Close-Up's proprietary data compression efficiently handles bit-mapped graphics, and the software refreshes only the portions of a screen that have changed. "PerfectPointer" patented technology provides fine mouse control.

File-Transfer and Self-Installing Software: LapLink V

Our final example of person-to-person modem software solves one problem—moving data from one computer to another. This seems simple enough until you consider the possible glitches:

◆ *Incompatible floppy disks* What if one computer has only 5.25-inch drives and the other has only 3.5-inch drives?

✦ *Incompatible operating systems* Macintosh computers cannot read disks formatted for MS-DOS.

✦ *File version control* If you frequently copy files from a laptop to a desktop computer and edit them on both machines, how do you keep track of which copy of a file is the most recent version?

✦ *Selective multiple-file transfers* It can be very tedious to type **COPY <filename.ext>** when you have to move a lot of files and all of them have different names. Using wildcards to match filename patterns in a single COPY operation is not always possible.

LapLink V is the latest version of Traveling Software Inc.'s sophisticated solution to these and other file-transfer problems. As you might guess from its name, LapLink was originally developed with laptop computer users in mind; laptop owners often copy files from desktop to laptop and back. In the early days of portable computing, desktops usually had 5.5-inch floppies while portables used space-saving 3.5-inch drives.

LapLink V performs file-transfer functions most people never think of but are very glad to learn are available:

✦ *Automatic operations* You can record backup routines and play them back later, and even schedule LapLink to perform recorded operations in your absence.

✦ *Direct network connections* On Novell networks, LapLink does not burden the file server, but connects two workstations directly to one another.

✦ *Background operation under Windows* LapLink can transfer files and even run scheduled recorded operations in the background while you work in other windows.

✦ *Automatic port sensing and speed maximization* A boon for communications novices and busy professionals, this feature automatically detects which serial and parallel ports are available for use. LapLink also can detect a modem or mouse attached to a serial port, and automatically adjust the port speed to the highest possible rate.

✦ *Intelligent file-transfer options* Files can be selected by date, name, attributes, and other criteria. With one command you can make an exact copy of any drive, directory, or set of subdirectories. Another command lets you synchronize files—perform a two-way exchange so that two different directories or disks have the same versions of the same files.

✦ *Remote installation over modem or wire* This feature seems like sorcery the first time you use it. Other software presents the chicken-egg problem of getting the host software to the remote computer before you can log on. LapLink has the ability to call another modem that does not already

11

have LapLink installed, copy itself over the line, install itself on the remote computer, and begin a two-way LapLink session. The remote user need only enter three ordinary DOS commands to prepare to receive a remote installation. Figure 11-4 shows LapLink running under Windows, and the remote installation setup screen.

LapLink Mac can be used to transfer files from Macintoshes to DOS computers and vice versa. The package even includes a cable with both Mac and IBM serial port connectors on each end.

Either version of LapLink can use parallel ports to achieve transfer speeds of over 800,000 bps, a significant improvement over the 115,000 bps maximum speed of regular serial ports. LapLink also uses data compression to achieve a fourfold increase in effective throughput.

The Host Mode in Your Terminal Program

Most retail terminal programs and many shareware products include built-in host functions or separate host software at no additional cost. *Host software* configures your modem to answer incoming calls, and lets you control whose calls are accepted and what authorized callers can do on your computer.

Host mode capabilities vary from one terminal program to another. The simplest host modes are intended to be used only when the operator of the host computer is at the keyboard. More sophisticated hosts are miniature BBSs, offering secure, unattended access to e-mail, chat, file lists, and so on.

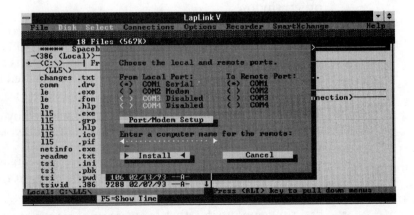

LapLink V remote installation
Figure 11-4.

Simple Hosts: "Come On In, Here's My DOS Prompt"

The simplest type of host mode just answers callers, verifies their passwords, and drops them into DOS (usually in a predefined directory). After logging on, callers are pretty much on their own. Within the limits you have set on which directories they can access, callers must find their own way to whatever they need.

Callers to such primitive hosts can browse directories, run software on your computer, copy files from your hard drive to their own (or vice versa), and generally act as if they were sitting at your keyboard instead of their own. But they cannot leave or read e-mail.

Complex Hosts: Miniature Bulletin Board Systems

More sophisticated and user-friendly host modes are miniature BBSs in their own right. HostPlus, the host-mode script included with the popular Telix terminal program, looks and feels like a BBS in every respect. Figure 11-5 shows the main menu callers see when they call a HostPlus system.

Complex hosts can serve as your online secretary, taking messages, passing out files, and offering callers a selection of bulletins you create. Such hosts can be left unattended for days; they will faithfully log every call and every action each caller takes (reading bulletins, transfering files, and so on) for you to review when you return.

Multitasking Host Mode

Many people run a copy of their terminal software in host mode under Desqview, Windows, or another multitasking operating environment. Multitasking lets you and your host software work simultaneously. The host works in the background, monitoring the phone line for calls, transferring files, and so on, while you work on other things in the foreground.

NOTE: If you want to run a host constantly, you will need another modem and phone line just for the host.

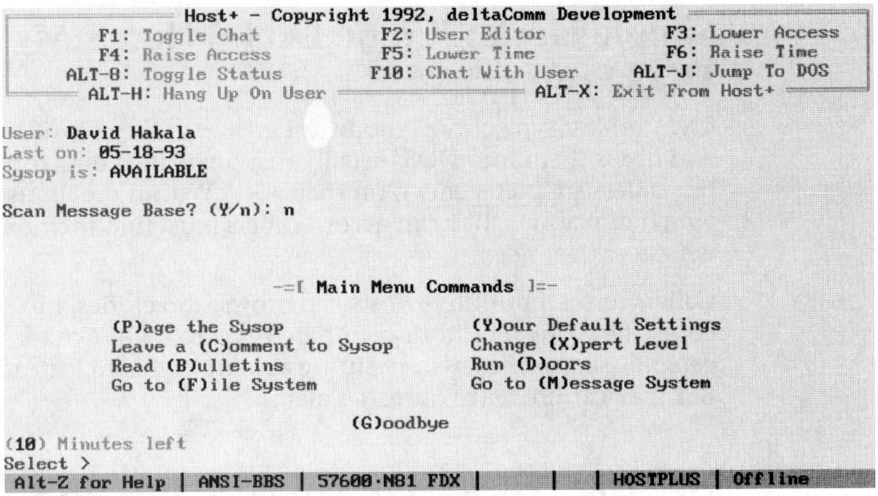

```
┌──────── Host+ - Copyright 1992, deltaComm Development ────────┐
│      F1: Toggle Chat         F2: User Editor       F3: Lower Access │
│      F4: Raise Access        F5: Lower Time        F6: Raise Time │
│   ALT-8: Toggle Status      F10: Chat With User  ALT-J: Jump To DOS │
└──── ALT-H: Hang Up On User ─────────────── ALT-X: Exit From Host+ ──┘
User: David Hakala
Last on: 05-18-93
Sysop is: AVAILABLE

Scan Message Base? (Y/n): n



                     -=[ Main Menu Commands ]=-

         (P)age the Sysop            (Y)our Default Settings
         Leave a (C)omment to Sysop  Change (X)pert Level
         Read (B)ulletins            Run (D)oors
         Go to (F)ile System         Go to (M)essage System

                         (G)oodbye
(10) Minutes left
Select >
 Alt-Z for Help │ ANSI-BBS │ 57600-N81 FDX │     │   │ HOSTPLUS │ Offline
```

HostPlus main
menu
Figure 11-5.

Limitations of Host Mode

If free host scripts such as HostPlus did everything that dedicated BBS
software does, no one would buy BBS software—yet thousands of people *are*
buying BBS software. Host software has limitations that make it unsuitable
for use in high-traffic online service applications:

✦ Host software can only provide access through a single phone line.
   Callers cannot chat with each other, and a single-line system that gets
   more than about 20 to 30 calls per day will be busy more often than not.

✦ Host software is relatively slow compared to BBS software written in
   fast-executing languages like C++ or assembler code. Menus do not
   display as quickly, searches of file directories and message headers take
   longer, and so on.

✦ The capacity of features such as the user database, file directories, and so
   on, is usually limited in host software. You may not be able to present
   more than 1,000 files to 500 authorized callers, a limitation many busy
   systems quickly outgrow.

Setting Up an Unattended Host

You will usually have to configure your host software the first time you start
it up. These are some of the options you can tailor to your needs:

✦ How many rings your modem should wait before answering

✦ Whether to accept unknown callers (new users) or simply hang up
   on them

✦ Whether an alarm should alert you to an incoming caller

✦ What hours of the day callers can page you to chat

✦ What access level a caller must have in order to download files from your computer

✦ How long a caller can stay online

✦ Whether call-back is used to provide security

✦ When, if ever, your host software will execute *external events:* separate programs that automatically perform various housekeeping chores at preset times

The preceding list is just a taste of the power and responsibility you assume when setting up your own online service. Chapter 12 goes into much more detail about the joys and trials of running your own BBS.

Summary: Getting Personal with Your Modem

Individuals and small businesses can stay in touch with their close circles of friends, relatives, and customers using person-to-person programs like the ones described in this chapter. Such intimacy may require a few voice phone calls, mailing software to your intended partner, and more coordination of modem calls. But you and your circle of modem friends will be able to do much more than a third-party service allows.

11

CHAPTER

12

STARTING YOUR OWN BBS THE "MADE EASY" WAY

This chapter discusses inexpensive, easily maintained Bulletin Board Systems (BBSs) that are recommended starting points for a hobbyist BBS or a small business system. Two popular BBS programs, WildCat! and Sapphire, are examined from the perspective of an aspiring sysop (SYStem OPerator). This chapter covers BBS design, maintenance, and performance issues. It also prepares fledgling sysops for the last thing they generally expect: success beyond their wildest dreams!

If the urge to run your own BBS strikes you, do not dismiss it. Thousands of people start their own BBSs each year. Reasons for crossing the line between information consumer and information provider vary, but career sysops and even reformed addicts who have taken The Pledge never to run a BBS again heartily agree on one thing: the experience is exhilarating and rewarding.

This chapter emphasizes the low-risk, short learning curve, and minimal maintenance approach to starting a BBS. If you already have a computer, modem, and phone line, you can start a BBS in about 20 minutes without spending another dime. Or you can make a full-time career of being a sysop, and invest your life savings in an information business. The more sophisticated and costly BBS packages are briefly discussed at the end of this chapter.

Planning a New BBS

Even if you were only building a birdhouse, you would normally sit down with paper and pencil to do some planning before reaching for a saw and hammer. You would have to consider such factors as the materials available, the types of birds you hope to attract, the aesthetic appearance of the birdhouse, how you will clean and maintain it, and so on. A BBS requires at least as much planning, and usually more.

Planning ahead will help you avoid the traps some sysops fall into when they dive into the first BBS software package that comes their way. Planning encourages the design of logical, intuitive menu structures and command names. It helps focus your attention on the things that really make a difference to your audience, saving time that might otherwise be wasted on tinkering with fascinating but obscure capabilities of your BBS.

Experimental Versus Mission-Oriented BBSs

First, decide whether you are creating a BBS for yourself or for other people. An *experimental* BBS is your personal workshop, a place where you can tinker and putter around for the sheer joy of seeing what happens. It does not have to be neat and tidy, or even particularly easy to understand. You may invite a few friends in to see your creation, but it will not be a public showcase.

Perhaps more importantly, an experimental BBS can be put away and forgotten for weeks on end. You do not assume responsibility for maintaining constant access to the system.

Most people create *mission-oriented* BBSs, which are born from the sysop's inner vision and desire to somehow be of service to other people. This definition sounds rather grandiose at first, until you consider the enormous personal power a BBS confers upon its creator.

If you run a BBS, whatever you choose to do with it can potentially affect the lives of many millions of people around the world. This potential appeals to the visionary in most people. Often a BBS is the most viable way to realize a long-held ambition to serve humanity in a specific way. In short, a mission-oriented BBS is a dream come true.

Missions need not be altruistic. Your mission may be to do the job your boss gave you: set up a BBS for the field sales force to use. Many corporate sysops report that the "incidental" duty of running the company BBS quickly grows to become their most satisfying and time-consuming occupation. Your mission also could be a profit-centered business plan, designed to provide whatever people will pay to receive. But whatever your mission is, it will strongly affect the planning and design of your BBS, and your own inner attitude toward your powerful creation.

By definition, mission-oriented BBSs must be constantly available and easily used by anyone. You will not be personally greeting and guiding each new caller 24 hours a day. The BBS must be thoughtfully designed to be intuitively obvious in its functions and purpose to the lowest-common-denominator caller.

The mission you envision will determine the ultimate shape of your BBS, and the amount of effort and money required to realize and nurture your dream. The following sections examine some of the most common missions for business and personal BBSs.

Internal Uses of Corporate BBSs

Most business BBSs are created for specific internal communication needs; the general public does not even know these BBSs exist. Such closed systems make the sysop's job much easier, since the audience is limited to employees and every member is known. This makes it possible to provide advance training, detailed user manuals, and other intensive aids for users.

These are just some of the benefits and reasons for creating corporate BBSs:

◆ *Avoiding third-party information services charges* A BBS can replace MCI Mail, CompuServe, and other value-added services for e-mail, file transfer, and even fax applications.

◆ *Maintaining security by keeping control of information* Any data too sensitive to be allowed out of the company computer system may be too sensitive to put on a third-party service's computer. A BBS keeps your vital data in-house.

◆ *Internal corporate communications* A BBS can dramatically increase the flow of employee suggestions, save tons of memo and fax paper, and

12

encourage formation of ad hoc workgroups to solve specific problems anywhere in a company.

✦ *Management information collection* A BBS can collect, collate, and distribute vital management information in a startlingly short amount of time. Wal-Mart's hundreds of stores all report the day's sales, closing inventory, and other critical data to headquarters within *15 minutes after closing time*. Small businesses can enjoy such timely information too; I have personally installed systems for firms with as few as three stores. Reporting software can be integrated into the BBS, making automatic generation and delivery of management reports possible.

Improving Customer Relations with BBSs

Some businesses invite existing customers to use their BBSs. Such limited-access BBSs may offer the following:

✦ *User group participation* Customers often solve each other's problems and brainstorm new applications for a company's products in the message areas of a BBS.

✦ *Technical and price information on demand* A 24-hour BBS is enthusiastically welcomed by anyone who needs help outside of regular business hours. The current boom in home-based and part-time small businesses means that millions of people need after-hours access to technical and pricing information.

✦ *Instant software upgrades* Compare the efficiency and ease of downloading the latest version of a program to the labor and time required to order it by mail, pack the upgrade in a box, and ship it by traditional methods. The benefits to both customer and supplier are obvious.

✦ *Customer feedback* Paper surveys packed with products are often thrown away. A BBS can encourage and sometimes even require a caller to complete a questionnaire. Less formal feedback from customer messages can provide suggestions that lead to profitable innovations. Some companies run monthly contests to encourage such customer feedback.

Marketing and Public Relations Uses of BBSs

A growing number of companies consider a BBS to be another store, branch office, or media relations center. Such BBSs are generally wide open to the public, allowing anyone who calls to shop for products, order online, or learn more about a company.

Few things cause a sales manager more agony than missing an order because the buyer called at 5:05 p.m., or because all the sales reps were in a meeting. Modem-based ordering systems can work 24 hours a day, 365 days per year. They never enter the wrong color code for a product, misspell a valued customer's name on the invoice, or forget to get a purchase order number.

Sophisticated order-processing systems can inform absent sales reps that they owe customers a thank-you note, update the billing department's records, transfer products from the inventory database to the shipping database, print invoices and shipping labels... in short, do everything except put the box on the delivery truck.

While over 100,000 companies operate BBSs, they are still newsworthy. Press releases announcing a corporate BBS have a very high probability of being printed in trade journals and major business publications. If the BBS is open to public access, its name and phone number will find its way into lists of specialty BBSs distributed worldwide, seemingly by magic. The BBS community thrives on such lists, and most callers submit one or more of their favorite systems' names and numbers to a list keeper who publishes and distributes it, at no cost to the BBS operator.

A growing number of corporate BBSs are started as self-contained profit centers, rather than as support systems for other products. Desktop publishing centers, for example, may run a BBS that sells access to typefaces, shareware utilities, vendor databases, and other related products or services. Mailing list vendors distribute limited editions of selected lists through BBSs. The sysops hope that callers will also buy the company's main products or services, and the strategy works quite well.

Stand-alone BBS Enterprises

By far the fastest growing segment of the BBS industry, *BBS enterprises* rely entirely on the content of a BBS to generate revenues. Customers may come from carefully controlled, understated marketing efforts, or from efficient electronic mass marketing.

12

Many sysops become entrepreneurs by default, sometimes even reluctantly. What would you do if a grateful user of your free public-service BBS sent you a donation; return it? Voluntary donations are customary among BBS users; most sysops use the money to improve their BBSs. It is a short step from there to mandatory donations, which can be a difficult option to resist as the benefits of a positive cash flow become apparent.

Many sysops have reluctantly "gone commercial" because the alternative was to close their BBSs (or sell their homes). The more callers you serve, and the more services you provide, the more it will cost you. Most sysops who start charging fees quickly discover that only the undesirable, eternally complaining, parasitic *users* abandon a BBS-gone-commercial. Activity in message bases and file areas rarely declines, because the most active and desirable members are willing to pay their fair share of "taxes" to maintain their online community.

A skyrocketing number of unabashedly profit-driven BBSs is rapidly transforming the BBS industry. Indeed, one could not have called BBSing an industry just two years ago. It was a grassroots phenomenon, composed of a high-turnover assortment of BBSs widely varying in their purposes, reliability, and quality. Today, professional sysops are the rule rather than the welcome exception.

The BBS industry has even spawned satellite industries such as system design consulting and BBS maintenance services, third-party software written specifically for BBS business management, $150 newsletters such as *Making Money With Modems,* even an international trade show (ONE BBSCON) that attracts thousands of sysops, would-be sysops, and vendors each August. (See Appendix A for contacts in these and other BBS satellite industries.)

Earning a substantial income entirely from a BBS is not impractical, as Kevin Behrens discovered shortly after starting his Aquila BBS in the Chicago area. An electrician laid up with an on-the-job injury, Behrens started a BBS to relieve his homebound boredom. Six months later, when he received doctors' permission to return to his union-scale job, Behrens found he could not afford to do so; the BBS was bringing in more money! Aquila has one of the nation's largest and most current collections of shareware, Internet newsgroups, and lively callers.

Checklist for Planning a BBS

Whatever your motives for starting a BBS, begin with a plan that covers at least the decision points covered in this section.

Is the BBS for You or Others?   Is the BBS primarily for you (experimental), or for others (mission oriented)? If you have a mission in mind, who are the people you plan to serve, and what do they need? Avoid the common ego-trap of offering only what you think your audience *should* have; do the necessary market research to learn what people really *want,* or your BBS will languish for lack of market interest.

What Will You Give and How Will You Get It?   What services will you provide, and how will you obtain them? Message areas are easily set up for special interest groups. Shareware and data files are readily purchased or downloaded from other systems. Door programs and custom software design services are widely available.

How Will You Present Information?   In what form(s) do you want to present information? Some BBSs emphasize just one of a BBS' capabilities (messaging, file transfers, information bulletins, or database searches) as the primary means of presenting what they have to offer. Others make the same information available in two or more forms. Consistency for users and easy maintenance for the sysop are the benefits of the one-medium approach. Accommodating a wider range of user preferences and thereby attracting more users are the benefits of the several-media approach.

What Laws Affect Your BBS?   What are the legal considerations for your BBS? *Syslaw*, written by veteran BBS attorney Lance Rose, is a good place to start learning about the legal environment of BBSing. (See Appendix A for contact information.) Give at least passing thought to local home-business zoning laws; you may need to seek a zoning variance or operate undercover, the way most sysops do. Telephone company policies on BBSs that accept voluntary donations may force you to pay business service rates even if you do not intend to earn a profit. Keeping copyrighted uploaded software out of your BBS file areas is critical; BBSs have been confiscated *in toto* as evidence in software piracy cases. Adult-oriented BBSs should consult an attorney experienced in telecommunications and pornography laws.

How Big Will the BBS Get?   Do you intend your BBS to grow or remain small? Many personal and business BBSs never grow beyond one phone line. But one line will comfortably support only about 24 daily callers, hardly enough to earn a living. Expanding to multiple lines is much more complicated and expensive than just ordering more lines and modems; see the discussion of multiline BBSs later in this chapter. Decide in advance whether to grow or stay small, and start budgeting accordingly from the very first day you go online.

12

How Often Will the BBS Change?   Must the BBS structure be stable, or will users tolerate and even welcome constant change? The answer determines when you will be ready to go online, and how much work you will have to do after opening day. Do you plan to serve busy people, long-distance callers, modem novices, or anyone who would benefit from long-term familiarity with a stable, unchanging BBS—one they can log on to and navigate without much thought? On the other hand, socially oriented BBSs generally attract modem-literate callers who, like nightclub patrons, thrive on new and entertaining variations.

How Much Will Access Be Controlled?   What will your access policies be? A BBS that is by design open to everyone and treats everyone the same does not need the many access-privilege categories that a highly controlled-access BBS does. Access privileges are a sysop's favorite method of encouraging the type of behavior desired from users. First-time callers can have free run of the BBS for a limited time, or be restricted to read-only demonstrations, bulletins, and other sales pitches. Frequent contributors of files may be given larger downloading limits, while the most active contributors to message areas are often given more access time per call or per day.

How Many Rules Will You Have?   What will your user policies be? Generally speaking, the fewer rules you impose, and the more discreetly you word them, the better. The only policy I have ever posted on my BBS proved adequate for all occasions: *"We do business only with people who are pleasant."* When deciding how to communicate the rules to callers, remember that you are in the hospitality business. Few nightclubs, for example, hold up a line of eager patrons by reading each of them a pageful of rules and regulations before allowing them to enter.

How Much Time Will You Have for the BBS?   How much time per day can you devote to BBS maintenance, answering user questions, and other administrative duties? If your time is limited, keep the BBS simple to use and take advantage of every built-in or third-party utility that can automate mundane tasks such as providing instructions, verifying the location and identity of new callers, sorting and listing uploaded files, purging deleted messages, and so on.

Will the BBS Be Full- or Part-Time?   Must the BBS be online all the time? Most BBS software requires some offline maintenance time in which to process incoming mail from other networks, perform file cleanup, and do other housekeeping chores. While it is possible to keep a BBS online around the clock (usually by using a LAN to move such chores to a second, offline computer), maintaining 24-hour availability can be expensive. But constant availability may be important to your callers and your cash flow.

How Important Is Reliability?   How much *random* downtime is acceptable? Every BBS freezes up, burns out a hard drive, or otherwise misbehaves at some time or another. More costly commercial BBS software tends to be more reliable than "version 0.5" experimental shareware. Let me hasten to add that many shareware BBS packages, such as Sapphire, which is described later in this chapter, have been tried, tested, and debugged by thousands of satisfied sysops. You can get references readily by calling the support BBS for a given program and downloading its list of BBSs that use the software; then call a few systems and ask the sysops how they like the program. Hardware reliability is the other half of the mean-time-between-failures equation. Better hardware also costs more. Ask a few sysops which computers, disk drives, and modems they use.

How Will You Pay for Ongoing Costs?   How much, if anything, will you charge for full access? You will hear BBS industry pundits assert that most fee-based BBSs charge between $10 and $120 per year, per user. But do not let the market average determine the value of your services. We know of at least one attorney who gladly pays $1,200 per year for access to his favorite home-based BBS. Fledgling sysops, like new artists uncertain of their talents, often hesitate to charge what they are worth, and what they need in order to survive and grow. It is much easier to lower prices later than to raise them.

How Will You Collect User Fees?   If you decide to charge callers, how will you collect fees? Credit cards are the ideal payment medium, but card issuers are increasingly reluctant to give merchant accounts to any business they consider to be mail-order, and most card issuers have difficulty distinguishing a BBS from a mail-order operation. If your prospects prepay by check, they run the risk of logging off then losing your mailing address and BBS phone number. 1-900 phone lines usually give more of each minute's charges to the 1-900 service provider than the sysop gets to keep. If you deal with a known circle of reputable customers (corporations, professionals), monthly billing is an option.

How Will You End Your BBS Business?   This is a question few people consider when starting any type of business, but it may be important to you. It is certainly important to your customers, some of whom you might meet again. Ending a BBS is as simple as cancelling its phone service. But if you abandon the BBS on which callers came to depend, you may suffer sleepless nights and loss of reputation in the business community. Arranging transfers of privileges to a similar BBS or selling out to another entrepreneur are more palatable ways to get out of the BBS business. I have not yet heard of anyone *inheriting* a thriving BBS business, but the industry is still young, and the average sysop's age is just 36.

12

Personal Reasons to Start a BBS

People generally start nonprofit, home-based BBSs to form a community that shares a common interest. Often the intended audience is very, very small. Recall from Chapter 7 that the first BBS was started by two guys in a local Chicago computer club, who did not want to brave the snow for meetings. Dartmouth College runs the Dante BBS, where scholars around the world (maybe 87 of them, as a tongue-in-cheek estimate) can find 600 years' worth of commentaries and annotations on Dante's *Inferno*, in a dozen or so languages.

A BBS can be a rallying point for special interest groups whose members are widely scattered as well as few in number. The National Association of Cave Divers runs a thriving BBS, where members buy, sell, and trade specialized equipment, swap esoteric technical data, and exchange tips on the best dive trips available.

Some BBSs are born of sheer love for a subject, and a desire to share years of experience with the world. The Bird Info Network BBS, in Denver, Colorado, is a delightful showcase of information on the care and habits of exotic birds. Sysop Terry Rune offers a wealth of articles, graphic images, specialty shareware, and even books and magazines for bird-lovers everywhere.

Many sysops start a BBS to save money. Hard-core modem maniacs regularly run up thousands of dollars per year in long-distance service charges and BBS subscription fees. Almost in self-defense, they reverse the charges by starting their own BBSs. 'Tis better to receive a call than to make one.

Often a BBS is started out of sheer frustration. Many online cosmopolitans, disenchanted with what they consider the poor design of other BBSs, start their own just to prove that they can do it better.

Some sysops, like Kevin Behrens mentioned in the preceding section, get into BBSing as a hobby and quickly find it a rewarding, exciting career. Most examples of large, fee-based BBSs cited today had success thrust upon them as Behrens's Aquila BBS did.

With the myth of corporate job security in cinders, and legions of MBAs fighting over a shrinking pool of middle management and executive jobs, many highly competent businesspeople are seeking financial and personal liberation in self-employment. A growing number of these talented, ambitious, visionary people are turning to BBSing.

Whatever your original reason for starting a hobby BBS, be prepared to see it snowball into a thriving community. You too may have success forced upon you.

Choosing the Right BBS for Your Purposes

All of the decisions you make while planning your BBS determine the types of hardware and software, telephone service, and personal skills you will need to realize your vision. There are more than 50 different BBS software programs available at this writing, and new packages with different design philosophies seem to pop up every other month. Planning your goals and needs in detail quickly narrows this confusing list to a few prime candidates. Choose the right software for your needs, and the hardware required will be self-evident.

Here are some very broad guidelines for minimum hardware and software needed to satisfactorily operate two types of low-traffic BBSs.

Minimum Requirements for a Low-Volume Hobby BBS

Just about any computer will do; some BBSs still run on Commodore 64 machines. One 2400-bps modem should cost no more than $50. Any shareware or public domain (no registration fee) BBS program such as Sapphire (shareware; $51) or RBBS (public domain) can handle low-volume, low-speed traffic.

If you have an IBM-compatible computer and a multitasking operating environment such as DesqView or Windows 3.1, you may be able to run a single-line 2400-bps BBS in the background while using the computer for other things in the foreground. Then you do not need to buy a dedicated computer.

You may not even need a second phone line. A *voice/data switch*, which costs around $75, will answer your phone, detect whether the caller is a human or modem, and route the call to the phone or BBS.

This low-budget approach should comfortably accommodate up to 20 callers per day. If you offer an attractive BBS, word will quickly spread around the online community. Be prepared to step into bigger shoes, or at least dedicate a second phone line and computer to your hobby, to avoid conflicts over computer and phone line availability with others in your household.

12

Minimum Requirements for a Low-Volume Business BBS

A dedicated computer and phone line are essential to provide adequate customer service. If you expect 50 or fewer calls per day, a $200 IBM PC-XT or clone will handle up to two 2400-bps lines without strain. If you use more than one high-speed modem, plan on buying an 80386SX or faster computer.

The BBS will represent your business, so its reliability is important. Consider these factors before purchasing your BBS software:

◆ *Installed base* How many BBSs use the software, and are they similar in business and volume to your planned BBS?

◆ *Technical support* Support should be available through a BBS as well as voice and fax lines. A full-time support staff is another indication of a company's stability and resources.

◆ *Third-party software vendors* Independent programmers know a good bet when they see one. If plenty of third-party utilities from a number of different vendors are available, that is a good indication that those who know BBSing have confidence in this software and its vendor.

◆ *Multiline upgrade path* How difficult and expensive is it to expand your call capacity? The cost of multiline software licenses is only part of the story. You may need an additional computer for each extra line, plus LAN hardware and software, and someone who knows how to install and configure a LAN for use with a BBS.

◆ *Ease of use for novices* Most of your customers probably do not call many BBSs. It is important that they be able to easily and intuitively grasp and be able to navigate your BBS' menu structure, messaging and file-transfer commands, and other options. People rarely return to a place where they got lost. Call the vendor's support BBS and test ease-of-use yourself. Better yet, have a modem novice call.

◆ *Ease of customization* Can you fine-tune menu options to exactly suit your needs and the terminology used in your industry? Is the overall look and feel of the BBS hard-coded into the program, or can you control the colors, menu layouts, command options, and other factors? For callers, a BBS program that looks and acts pretty much the same no matter whose BBS you call means that the screens and the user interface are familiar and easy to navigate. The downside of a fixed-presentation BBS is that your system tends to look like every other one out there.

With these general considerations in mind, let's examine two specific BBS software programs, one shareware and the other a commercial retail product. Both are leaders in their respective categories, with thousands of satisfied sysops.

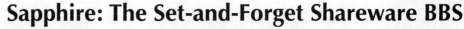

Sapphire: The Set-and-Forget Shareware BBS

Sapphire 4.00A, from Pinnacle Software, is widely hailed as the easiest BBS to set up. Letters from sysops confirm that Sapphire can be completely installed in 20 minutes or less. Many people take more time to plug in an external modem.

Ease of setup and maintenance requires some tradeoffs in capacity and your ability to customize. Sapphire strikes an excellent balance for any personal or small-business application for which installing and maintaining a BBS is a relatively low priority.

Sapphire's User Features

Sapphire's menu structure is fixed, meaning that the look and feel of a Sapphire BBS Main Menu options is the same no matter whose BBS you call (see Figure 12-1). But within this familiar presentation there is plenty of room to customize colors, the name of the BBS, the behavior of commands, and so on.

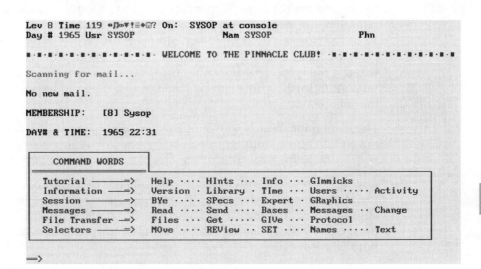

Sapphire's
Command
Words menu
Figure 12-1.

12

The Command Words are organized in rows, each of which corresponds to a major activity:

- ✦ *Tutorial* is the first item in the Command Words menu, which is appropriate since this provides online assistance. Tutorial is especially useful for novice and infrequent callers, who tend to spend a lot of time looking for help and recalling functions they can perform on a BBS.

- ✦ *Information* includes a Library of text files created by the sysop, the caller's remaining time on the system, the number of calls the system has received, a lookup database of users, and the version of Sapphire they are using.

- ✦ *Session* utilities customize the callers' environment with graphics and short or long menus, and allow them to log off quickly.

- ✦ *Messages* provide functions such as reading, sending (writing), selecting new message areas, editing messages, and checking for personal messages.

- ✦ *File transfer* functions include listing files, getting (downloading) files, giving (uploading), and choosing a protocol.

- ✦ *Selectors* are various ways to select which files and messages will show up in searches, or to move a message from one area to another.

Sapphire help screens, like the one shown in Figure 12-2, are actually useful to novices, unlike some help screens that use too many technical terms and ramble on for pages. Notice the Notepad feature at the bottom of Figure 12-2; the Notepad is available on almost every screen in Sapphire. The sysop or a user can write notes to themselves about what they are reading, where a file is located, and other things that occur to them during a session. A finished note can be saved in a message addressed to the writer for later review.

The Command Words shown at the bottom of Figure 12-1 need not be typed out in full. Some commands can be invoked by typing a single key (F for File, H for Help) while others may require two or three keystrokes.

The Sapphire file-transfer system supports the two most common Xmodem variations, Ymodem for faster file transfers, and Zmodem for fast, auto-downloading transfers. These four file-transfer protocols are enough for most callers; BBSs that list a dozen or more protocols tend to confuse nontechnical callers.

Installing and Configuring Sapphire

Yes, I *did* install a working Sapphire BBS in less than 20 minutes—17 minutes, 34 seconds, to be exact. The Sapphire software can be ordered on

```
Lev 8 Time 114 *♫∞♥!≡♦☺? On:  SYSOP at console
Day # 1965 Usr SYSOP             Nam SYSOP              Phn

ACTIVITY    Display system activity for past 7 days
BANISH      Devalidate user (remove from user list)
BASES       Display list of available message bases
BYE         Disconnect from  system  (i.e. logoff)
CHANGE      Modify a message you've sent previously
CHAT        Page system operator for a conversation
CLOSE       Shut down system; prevent further calls
DOORS       Update  your  list  of  "Door"  programs
DOS         Shell  out  to  DOS;  type  EXIT  to return
DUMBTERM    Start dumb terminal  for outgoing calls
ERASE       Remove  a message  from  a message base
EVENTS      Schedule your BBS's  close-down  events
EXPERT      Switch  between  casual and expert mode
FILES       List software available for downloading
GET         Get some software  from our  collection
This is the "Notepad" editor, which you can use this to write down ideas.
Later on, you can use the SEND command to send everything as one message.
If you started the Notepad by mistake, enter Q on an empty line, to quit.

For help:  enter  ?  on an empty line.
```

An example of
a Sapphire
BBS help
screen
Figure 12-2.

disk from Pinnacle Software, or downloaded from their BBS; see Appendix A
for contact information. After inserting the Sapphire distribution disk in
your floppy drive, type **SYSOP** to start the automatic installation process.
Sapphire prompts you for the name of the main directory where you want
the BBS programs installed. Then it creates all the subdirectories and support
files it needs.

After installing itself, Sapphire displays the System Operations menu shown
in Figure 12-3. There are few choices, and all of them are in plain English.
Selecting the DEMO option starts the BBS in local mode, meaning you, the
sysop, get to see exactly what a remote caller would.

Sapphire's Automatic Maintenance Features

Sapphire automatically handles the mundane maintenance chores of
running a BBS. The user database, for example, has room for 350 entries.
When the 351st unique caller logs on, Sapphire deletes the user with the
lowest access-privilege level who has been inactive for the longest time. This
logic lets you keep special users active indefinitely; just assign them
relatively high access levels, and all users with lower levels will have to be
deleted before one of your VIP's turn comes up.

There are 15 message areas that hold a total of 225 messages. The oldest
message is automatically deleted to make room for a new message,
eliminating the need to run daily purges and compressions of the message
files. You can name any of the 15 message areas whatever you wish.

12

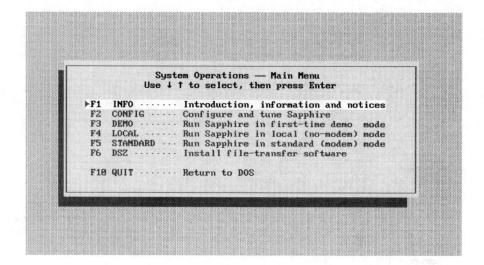

```
          System Operations — Main Menu
        Use ↓ ↑ to select, then press Enter

 ▶F1  INFO ········ Introduction, information and notices
  F2  CONFIG ····· Configure and tune Sapphire
  F3  DEMO ········ Run Sapphire in first-time demo  mode
  F4  LOCAL ······ Run Sapphire in local (no-modem) mode
  F5  STANDARD ··· Run Sapphire in standard (modem) mode
  F6  DSZ ········ Install file-transfer software

 F10  QUIT ······· Return to DOS
```

Sapphire
System
Operations
Main Menu
Figure 12-3.

Bulletins, text files offered to callers in one-line picklist format, are also easy to maintain and update. The description of each bulletin is taken from the first 39 characters of the bulletin itself, so you can write the bulletin and add its description to the picklist in one operation. Sapphire recognizes any file in its Library subdirectory with the extension *.TXT as a bulletin. All you need to do is copy text files into the Library subdirectory, or delete such files using the DOS DEL command.

Up to 500 files can be available for listing and downloading. When Sapphire needs space for a new uploaded file, it deletes the least popular file according to a formula that takes into account a file's age, the number of times it has been downloaded, and how many days have passed since it was last downloaded. No file that has been downloaded within the past 14 days is ever deleted.

Doors and External Events

Sapphire supports both doors and external events. Doors, as you recall from Chapter 7, are separate programs that use the communications functions of a BBS program to extend their reach to the person calling the BBS. The BBS removes most of itself from memory to make room for loading the door program, keeping just enough of the BBS in memory to maintain the modem link. Doors may include third-party software such as database programs, games, callback verification systems, registration questionnaires, and so on.

External events are housekeeping chores for which the BBS must shut itself down. The BBS restarts itself automatically when the external event is over. Making backup copies of messages, user databases, and other vital data is one common external event. Other external events you might commonly perform include dialing out to other BBSs to retrieve e-mail and new files, or deleting old messages and files and reorganizing indexes.

Limitations of Sapphire BBSs

Sapphire is a single-line BBS. Do not try to run multiple copies of Sapphire on multiple phone lines under a multitasker such as DesqView; Sapphire is not designed for safe file-sharing. You might get away with it for a while, but inevitably you will corrupt all of your message and file system data.

Because it's a single-line BBS, Sapphire is vulnerable to the failure of its phone line or modem. In fact, there is no redundancy protection in the event of a failure of any system component. WildCat!, the multiline BBS described in the next section, can keep going even if one of its hard drives crashes.

Sapphire has a relatively limited set of commands, for the sake of simplicity. Additional commands can be programmed, but that requires a knowledge of Turbo Pascal and a source-code license from Pinnacle Software.

The limits on messages, files, and users are acceptable in most single-line low-volume BBSs, but a message-oriented social BBS may find it needs more storage space.

The next section examines an industrial-strength BBS program that can handle multiple lines and tens of thousands of files or messages, yet is still relatively easy to set up and use.

WildCat!: Multiline Commercial BBS

WildCat! (the exclamation point is part of the name) is sold by Mustang Software Inc. (MSI). It is the only BBS program (at this writing) available in retail stores such as Software Etc., Waldensoft, and CompUSA. Retailers hate to see products returned, and cannot train their staff to support every package they sell. WildCat!'s acceptance by the retail community is powerful testimony to its ease of installation and overall reliability.

Wildcat! installs almost as easily as Sapphire. Figure 12-4 shows the main installation menu. Note the helpful explanation of the highlighted menu item at the bottom of the screen.

12

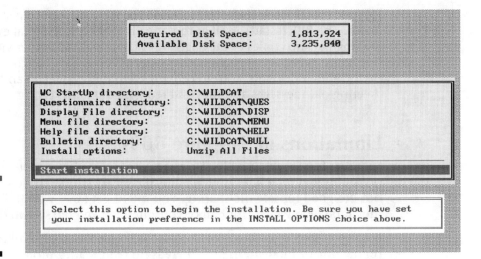

Required Disk Space: 1,813,924
Available Disk Space: 3,235,840

WC StartUp directory: C:\WILDCAT
Questionnaire directory: C:\WILDCAT\QUES
Display File directory: C:\WILDCAT\DISP
Menu file directory: C:\WILDCAT\MENU
Help file directory: C:\WILDCAT\HELP
Bulletin directory: C:\WILDCAT\BULL
Install options: Unzip All Files

Start installation

Select this option to begin the installation. Be sure you have set
your installation preference in the INSTALL OPTIONS choice above.

WildCat!'s
installation
menu
Figure 12-4.

You need to run a configuration program called MAKEWILD.EXE in order to change any of the default settings in the WildCat! demonstration BBS. Figure 12-5 shows the main items that can be configured using MAKEWILD.EXE.

WildCat! User Features

File searching and downloading are two of WildCat!'s strongest points. See the WildCat! file listing screen in Figure 12-6. You can search for files by filename, using DOS wildcard patterns such as *.TXT, PHOTO????.ZIP, and so on. You can search the full description of a file, which can run many lines and take quite some time. You also can search just six key words entered by the uploader. When files are listed, you can page up or down, read long or short descriptions, and best of all, select a file to download by entering just one or two numbers, instead of an often cryptic and easily misspelled full filename.

Messages can be written using a full-screen editor that gives you cursor control similar to that of word processors. Files can be attached to messages, a handy and natural way to send a package and its cover letter.

WildCat! supports more file-transfer protocols than Sapphire. The list includes Zmodem and Kermit for mainframe and other non-PC callers. Additionally, external protocols can be added to WildCat!'s built-in selection. Some sysops prefer to drop the antiquated Xmodem protocol and add newer, more efficient protocols distributed as standalone programs.

Bulletins and doors are fully supported. Online questionnaires can be designed to collect user feedback, registration and credit card data, and other data collection functions.

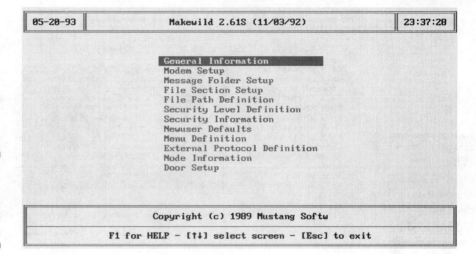

WildCat!'s
configuration
utility,
MAKEWILD.EXE
Figure 12-5.

Multiline WildCat! systems also support chat functions, including the ability
to page a user on another line and ask them to join you in the chat area.

Customizing WildCat! Menus and Commands

Figure 12-7 shows a sysop's view of the MAKEWILD.EXE Main Menu
Definitions screen. This is where you customize the look and feel of your
WildCat! BBS. The Description line can be changed from the defaults

```
Scanning file area - Free Public Files
[ 1] 3D-BLDR.GIF    214,746   04/03/92 | 3D terrain view - Boulder to Flagstaff
     Dwnlds: 88      DL Time   00:03:46 F - neat!

[ 2] 3D-WORLD.GIF   184,868   03/24/92 | 3D color shaded map of World Topography
     Dwnlds: 69      DL Time   00:03:14 F 640x480x256                    *Info*

[ 3] 4CORNER.GIF    232,703   04/02/92 | Color-shaded relief map of Four Corners
     Dwnlds: 34      DL Time   00:04:04 F area      799x657x256          *Info*

[ 4] ALLFILES.TXT    57,795   05/21/93 | List of all files on GISnet BBS
     Dwnlds: 97      DL Time   00:01:00 F

[ 5] ALLFILES.ZIP    19,080   05/21/93 | List of files on GISNET BBS (compressed
     Dwnlds: 268     DL Time   00:00:20 F version)

[ 6] BRRANET7.ZIP    12,239   04/14/93 | About BRRAnet (AutoCAD network), how to
     Dwnlds: 3       DL Time   00:00:12 F join, etc.                     *Info*

[ 7] CSHOW843.ARJ   130,538   03/22/92 | CompuShow v 8.43  our favorite GIF
     Dwnlds: 34      DL Time   00:02:17 F viewer

-Pause- [C]ont, [H]elp, [N]onstop, [M]ark, [D]wnld, [I]nfo, [V]iew, [S]top? [C]
 Unregistered  | ANSI-BBS | 38400·N81 FDX |      |    |     | Online 00:01
```

A WildCat!
file listing
screen
Figure 12-6.

12

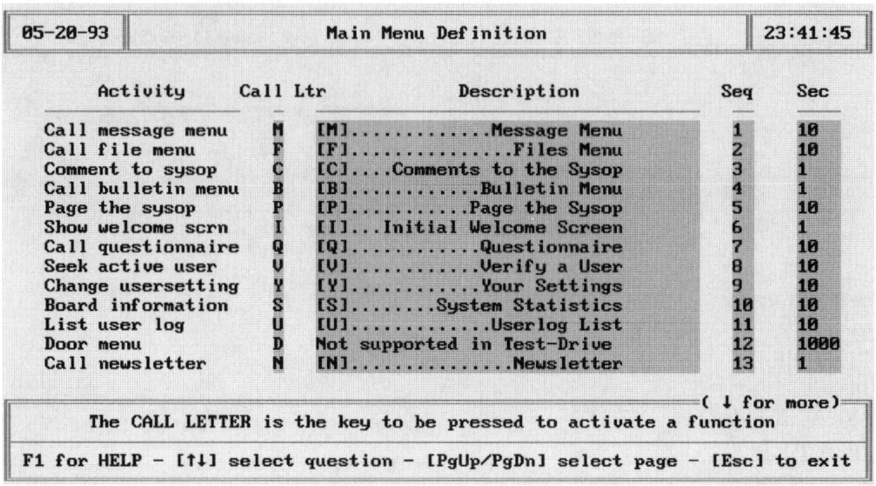

```
┌───────────┬──────────────────────────────────────┬───────────┐
│ 05-20-93  │         Main Menu Definition         │ 23:41:45  │
└───────────┴──────────────────────────────────────┴───────────┘

      Activity        Call Ltr        Description        Seq    Sec
    ─────────────────────────────────────────────────────────────────
    Call message menu    M    [M]..............Message Menu    1     10
    Call file menu       F    [F]................Files Menu    2     10
    Comment to sysop     C    [C]....Comments to the Sysop     3     1
    Call bulletin menu   B    [B]............Bulletin Menu     4     1
    Page the sysop       P    [P]...........Page the Sysop     5     10
    Show welcome scrn    I    [I]...Initial Welcome Screen     6     1
    Call questionnaire   Q    [Q].............Questionnaire    7     10
    Seek active user     V    [V]...........Verify a User      8     10
    Change usersetting   Y    [Y]...........Your Settings      9     10
    Board information    S    [S].......System Statistics      10    10
    List user log        U    [U].............Userlog List     11    10
    Door menu            D    Not supported in Test-Drive      12    1000
    Call newsletter      N    [N]...............Newsletter     13    1
                                                       ─( ↓ for more)─
    ┌─────────────────────────────────────────────────────────────┐
    │  The CALL LETTER is the key to be pressed to activate a function │
    └─────────────────────────────────────────────────────────────┘
    F1 for HELP - [↑↓] select question - [PgUp/PgDn] select page - [Esc] to exit
```

A sysop's view of the MAKEWILD.EXE Main Menu definitions
Figure 12-7.

(shown in Figure 12-7) to anything you like. Each menu option is selected by pressing its CALL letter, which you would also change so that readers can match it intuitively to the description. For example, if you prefer to name the Messages function "Post Office," you might change the CALL letter from M to P.

There are only 13 main menu commands to worry about—another step toward simplicity that many sysops appreciate in WildCat!'s programming. (TBBS, a fully programmable BBS, builds menus from scratch with over 1,000 possible commands and options.) Each main menu command leads to a submenu of specific commands (read, write, scan messages, for example) or immediately executes a function, such as showing users their current configuration settings.

To the right of the Description field in Figure 12-7 are two columns, Seq (for sequence) and Sec (for security). Seq controls the order in which Call letters and Descriptions are displayed, so you can position the Message Menu option in the upper left, followed by Comments to the Sysop, if you wish. Sec determines whether a menu option appears at all on a given caller's screen; the caller must have a security level of 10 or higher to access either the Message or Files menus in this example.

Figure 12-8 shows the custom welcoming menu from a WildCat! BBS. Designed using ANSI color and IBM graphics characters, such screens can add a great deal of distinction to a BBS. ANSI screen design is such a popular task among sysops that many shareware ANSI-drawing programs are available; THEDRAW and ANSIPAINT are two popular examples. WildCat! and other BBS software lets you define specific files that will be displayed when callers log on, proceed to the main menu, select a file area, and so on.

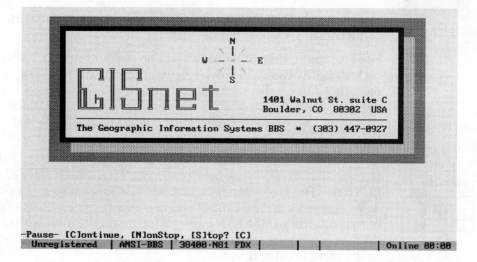

A custom
welcoming
menu from a
WildCat! BBS
Figure 12-8.

Multiline WildCat!

WildCat! is available in a single-line and three multiline versions. The
single-line version supports only one incoming line. The computer may be
attached to a LAN, but no other LAN workstation can access the BBS
computer while WildCat! is running, because the single-line version does
not support file-sharing and record-locking.

WildCat! Professional: Up to 250 Incoming Lines

The Professional version of WildCat! supports a mixture of phone lines and
hardwired LAN connections. A LAN connection lets the sysop access the
WildCat! computer's hard drive while the BBS is running, a very useful
feature when you want to move or add files without bumping paying
customers offline or waiting until 3:00 a.m. when no one is online.

NOTE: A LAN link also lets LAN users log on to the WildCat! BBS
workstation and use it just as if they were dialing in over the phone
lines; this is often called an in-house BBS, and can be a very useful
workgroup tool.

12

When running on a LAN, the Professional version supports two lines for
each workstation that is running WildCat!, using the standard COM1 and
COM2 serial ports. An 80386 PC can easily accommodate two 38,400-bps
connections in this way. Adding connections involves adding another

workstation, LAN adapter and software, and cabling. A maximum of 250 connections (LAN plus phone lines) are allowed.

The Professional version also can run up to four lines on a single 80386 PC if no LAN is involved. This trick requires the help of DesqView, a multitasking operating environment similar to Windows 3.x. DesqView creates up to four *virtual computers* in an 80386's memory, each a software imitation of a complete 8088 IBM PC. Each virtual computer independently runs its own copy of WildCat!, controlling its own phone line while sharing file access with the other copies.

NOTE: The Professional version will not support four lines on a LAN because DesqView cannot simultaneously handle the I/O requirements of four BBS lines and a LAN connection. If you want to expand beyond four lines, you must use the two-line-per-computer, LAN-link method described in the preceding paragraphs.

WildCat! Multi-Line: Up to Ten Incoming Lines

The only difference between this version and the Professional is that WildCat! Multi-Line will support only ten lines in a LAN configuration. Four lines are still the maximum under DesqView. The affordable Multi-Line version is designed for small networks and BBS applications.

WildCat! IM: Up to Eight Lines Per Computer

The Intelligent Multiport (IM) version of WildCat! is specially designed for use with the DigiBoard intelligent multiport card. This card replaces the standard serial ports of an IBM-compatible PC with its own unique hardware and memory addressing methods. Effectively, it allows up to eight modems to be connected to a single port via a special connector/cable apparatus appropriately called an *octopus* cable.

The IM version can use DesqView to support up to eight high-speed modems and incoming phone lines on a single computer. A fast 80486 computer is essential to handle all of this traffic. Multiple IM workstations can be linked by a LAN to provide capacities of 16, 24, 32 and more lines, up to a maximum of 250 connections.

Clearly, operating a multiline WildCat! system is considerably more complicated than running a single-line WildCat! or Sapphire BBS. The cost of adding lines skyrockets quickly once you move beyond the 8-line limit of the IM version; add up the prices of another 80486 computer, LAN adapter, LAN software license, cabling, DesqView, and a DigiBoard card. These items must be purchased whether you need one more line or a full complement of eight more lines. Most multiline sysops will postpone this huge expenditure until their traffic load is so great they can be sure of immediately getting full use of another eight lines.

Where to Learn More about Running a BBS

There are many, many more aspects to running a BBS than this introductory chapter can explore. There are another 50 or so BBS software programs, for example. The business management side of a for-profit BBS could easily fill a book, and third-party utilities for sysops would fill a large hard drive.

BBS software vendors' support BBSs are good places to learn more about BBSs before starting one. Many support boards offer shareware or demo versions of BBS software, so you can download and test-drive a product before buying it. The user message forums are full of testimonials, tips, and tricks from sysops using each vendor's BBS; these forums are usually open only to customers. Bulletins on support BBSs may include feature lists, case studies of business and personal applications, and lists of BBSs that use the software.

Most sysops will be glad to answer your questions about the BBS software they run, how they got started, and what it is like to run a BBS. Nationwide echomail conferences devoted to specific BBS software packages carry hundreds of messages a day from sysops; generally you will find a related echo on a BBS running a specific package.

John Hedtke's definitive book, *Using Computer Bulletin Boards* (2nd Ed., MIS Press, 1992), contains two exhaustive chapters on the mechanics of choosing and designing a BBS, and examples of business and personal BBS applications. Hedtke includes throughout the book detailed tours of how major BBS software looks and operates from a user's perspective.

BBS Press Service, Inc., publishes *Making Money with Modems*, a monthly newsletter for serious infopreneurs. Experienced and novice sysops report that MMWM has invariably opened their eyes to additional income opportunities, improved their cash flows, helped cut expenses, and increased the efficiency of their online businesses. Call 913-478-3157 voice, or log on to their BBS at 913-478-9239.

Boardwatch magazine, published monthly since March, 1987, is widely considered the bible of the BBS industry. It covers everything from the latest modems, multiport serial cards, and other hardware, to telephone company policies and legal issues affecting sysops, communications-related software, the Internet, MacIntosh BBSs, and it also spotlights new and intriguing BBSs and their sysops. *Boardwatch* is widely available in computer stores, bookstores, even grocery stores. Call 303-973-6038 (voice) or log on to their BBS at 303-973-4222 to order a sample copy or browse the index of back issue articles.

12

The ultimate learning experience for would-be and experienced sysops is surely the *Online Networking Exposition and BBS Convention* (ONE BBSCON), sponsored by ONE, Inc. Literally everyone who is anyone in BBSland attends: leading sysops such as Ward Christiansen (who started the first BBS); publishers of BBS-related magazines; every commercial BBS software vendor and many shareware BBS vendors; modem, computer, and other hardware vendors; third-party BBS utility developers; and over 2,000 sysops and aspiring sysops from around the world. Call 303-693-5253 (voice) for an information kit. Be sure to ask about audio tapes of the hundred or so workshops held each year.

Is There a Sysop Inside You?

The itch to try your hand at running a BBS is a strong one, and should be scratched at least lightly. Thousands of ordinary people discover extraordinary talents, knowledge, and pleasure in themselves and their callers after starting a BBS. Whether you just read about it, experiment with a part-time BBS, or go for the personal and financial freedom of running a BBS business, you owe yourself the chance to see what it's like to be a sysop.

CHAPTER

13

MONEY-SAVING IDEAS FOR MODEM MANIACS

Exploring the online universe is inexpensive compared to many other forms of recreation or education (golf, pottery, an MBA degree), but as with anything worth having, online adventure is seldom entirely free. This chapter suggests numerous ways to avoid getting a telecomputing bill that exceeds your mortgage payment.

Buy a Better Modem Than You Think You Need

The speed and reliability of your modem affect the cost of connecting to and using online services more than any other factor. First-time modem buyers generally make the mistake of trying to save a few dollars by making do with a 2400-bps modem. Most second-time buyers know that even if you have to finance the purchase at credit card interest rates, you will save money in the long run by buying the best modem you possibly can afford.

While modems overall are the best bargain in computer equipment, the difference in price between a low-end and a high-end modem can be hundreds of dollars. Spending that extra money without plenty of hard evidence to support your decision may be difficult; that is why this section on the cost/performance ratio of various types of modems intentionally goes into great detail to prove the case for buying a better-than-adequate modem.

Data Compression Saves More Money Than It Costs

A plain-vanilla 2400-bps modem may cost $30 to $40 less than the same modem equipped with v.42bis data compression, but the cost of *using* these two modems differs even more. Data compression, by squeezing more information into each second of connect time, reduces the time you spend on long-distance telephone service and pay-per-minute online carrier services.

You can easily recover the extra $30 spent for a data-compressing 2400-bps modem in just three months, and save more than $10 per month for as long as you use that modem. Assume you download 10M of archived files per month; that's only three 250K files every other day or so. Data compression will cut the connect time needed to download that much data by about 10 percent. If your long-distance or online carrier service charges $0.15 per minute, you will save more than $10 per month by using a 2400-bps v.42bis modem instead of a plain 2400-bps model with no data compression features.

Your actual savings will vary depending on what you do online. Most people spend the majority of their online time transferring files or waiting for a remote computer's menus to finish scrolling down their local screens. Data compression saves money on both activities. However, if you spend a lot of time typing or reading while connected to a remote computer, data compression will not save much time. Your own typing and reading speeds limit how quickly you can log on, do what you came to do, and log off.

Connect Speed Costs Versus Savings

The ongoing savings are even greater when you buy a high-speed modem. The 10M of downloads in the preceding example will take about 700 minutes at 2400 bps, but only 175 minutes or less at 9600 bps. At a cost of $0.15 per minute, the 9600-bps modem saves $78.75 per month! A top-of-the-line 14,400-bps modem would save $89 per month versus a 2400-bps modem, and over $10 per month versus its 9600-bps rival.

The street price of a generic 9600-bps modem today is around $200, versus $40 for a plain-vanilla 2400-bps modem or $80 for a data-compressing 2400-bps modem. A 14,400-bps modem costs about $250 to $300. Most modem users will quickly recover the added cost of higher speed.

Fast Modems Need Buffered Serial Ports

The standard serial ports built into an IBM-compatible computer or sold as $15 to $20 add-on cards cannot keep up with modern data-compressing modems at port speeds higher than 19,200 bps. Standard serial ports are based on a chip (called a UART, or Universal Asynchronous Receiver/Transmitter) that has no buffer, a small memory block in which to temporarily store bits of data that arrive faster than the chip can process them. Such overflow data is lost if your computer sends data to the serial port faster than the chip can process it and pass it on to the modem. Lost data can corrupt or abort uploads, and effectively limits you to 19,200 bps throughput instead of 38,400 or 57,600.

For $15 to $20, you can replace the UART chip in your serial port with one that is buffered; ask your computer dealer for a buffered UART, often called a *16550-compatible UART*. (National Semiconductor's NS16550 chip was the first buffered UART produced for the mass modem market, and the 16550-compatible designation has become generic for buffered UART chips.)

Replacing board-level UART chips may require a soldering iron, desoldering tool, and great confidence. Since the last item cannot be bought, you may prefer to buy a complete serial port card, with buffered UARTs built into it, for about $40 to $120.

13

Invest In Quality

All modems are not created equal, even if they include the same connect-speed and data-compression features. While virtually all of the 300-plus modem manufacturers out there make *good* products, a few make *better* products. These are just some of the factors that affect the quality of a modem and the cost of using it:

✦ *Ability to establish carrier under adverse conditions* Your long-distance charges start when the remote modem answers, but your modem session does not start until the two modems shake hands and the CD (Carrier Detected) light on your external modem goes on. (Internal modems lack panel lights.) Line static and minor malfunctions on either your computer or the remote computer can prevent carrier detection, leaving you with a bill for a call that was not usefully completed. Better modems use advanced circuitry and quality control that reduce such wasted phone calls.

✦ *Ability to recover from mid-session changes in line quality* A thunderstorm hundreds of miles from you or the BBS you are calling can inject static into an established connection. Some modems cannot tolerate such interference at all. You will lose your connection, probably in the ninth minute of a ten-minute download. Better modems can ride out such storms.

✦ *Ability to connect with a wide variety of other modems* In theory, any Hayes-compatible modem should cooperate with any other. In practice, some modems are finicky about who they will talk to. The best modems make an extra effort to compensate for the idiosyncrasies of less forgiving modems, reducing the number of answer-but-no-carrier calls on your phone bill.

✦ *Ability to maintain connect speed* Most modems adapt to noisy line conditions by falling back to a lower connect speed; your 9600-bps modem may drop back to 4800, 2400, 1200, or even 300 bps and stay there throughout the call. If this happens during a file transfer, you will see the transfer rate plummet from its usual 960 to 2500 characters-per-second (depending on the type of file and its compressability) to a sickening 500 to 800 cps (5000 to 8000 bps) or less. (Each character transferred requires 10 bits, so cps equals bps divided by 10.) Unless you abort the transfer and call back, your cost for that download will at least double. Calling back often means repeating lengthy log-on procedures, finding the right file again, and starting the transfer over from scratch. More often than not, the lesser of two evils is to finish the transfer at subnormal speed (or hang up and forget it).

Manufacturers noted for high-quality, ultra-reliable modems include but are not limited to: US Robotics, Hayes, UDS Motorola, AT&T Paradyne, ZyXel, Telebit, GVC Technologies, Intel, Multi-Tech, and Supra Corporation. US Robotics has long held the lead in quality, especially among BBS sysops. But a number of challengers to USR's supremacy have emerged in the past year. This competition on quality has had a welcome impact on USR's notoriously high prices: USR recently cut 30 to 50 percent from the manufacturer's suggested retail prices for the outstanding USR Sportster line of 2400- to 14,400-bps fax/data modems.

Quality rarely comes cheap. The difference in price between a generic middle-of-the-pack modem and a name-brand quality leader of seemingly identical features can stop your heart for a moment. But the long-term cost savings of buying a high-quality modem should not be underestimated, as the following section explains.

Analyzing the Long-Distance Cost of "Adequate" Quality

My own 1993 phone bills clearly illustrate the difference modem quality makes. I prefer to live and work in an apartment building, an environment where phone line conditions are often less than ideal. Residential lines are often installed with less care than office lines. The phone wires for many units are jammed into the same conduits, increasing the possibility of electromagnetic interference with each other's signals. Then there are the children in the neighborhood who like to kick, climb, and otherwise abuse the phone company's junction box outside.

During the first four months of 1993, I used a $300 9600-bps v.42bis modem whose manufacturer I will not name. (When I bought this modem two years ago, $300 was a phenomenal bargain.) My long-distance modem bills averaged $150 per month, from January through April. *Close to 40 percent of all calls lasted one minute or less*, which generally meant I got an answer, but could not establish carrier and had to disconnect. Those little $0.12 to $0.23 calls added up to 9 percent of my total bill, or about $54 in wasted long-distance charges over four months.

File transfer speeds on long-distance connections were generally 20 to 40 percent slower than they should have been. I wasted about $70 on inefficient connections during the same four months.

The average total cost of my bargain modem's performance was over $30 per month! During the two years since I bought it, I could have saved enough money to buy any of the most expensive modems on the market.

I switched to an *AT&T Paradyne Dataport* 9600-bps v.42bis modem in mid-May; since switching, I have *never* failed to connect and establish carrier. Long-distance file transfers now proceed at the same speed as local calls. As an added and welcome bonus, the Dataport includes send/receive fax capabilities.

13

The Dataport carries a suggested list price of $445 versus $300 for the nameless modem, but I fully expect to recoup the difference by Labor Day, and the entire cost of the Dataport by Valentine's Day, 1994. Street prices are generally lower, and BBS sysops can get a Dataport for just $209.

NOTE: AT&T Paradyne has been making top-quality data communications equipment for decades. The Dataport line is a relatively new and uniquely effective entry in the modem market. See the following box to learn why the Dataport is so reliable and adaptable.

AT&T Paradyne's Dataport Modem: The Best Today?

The Dataport line of modems from AT&T Paradyne has a unique feature that may well make the Dataport the most adaptable and reliable modem available for personal or most business uses. The Dataport's *Optical Line Interface* (OLI) greatly reduces mismatches between the electrical characteristics of your modem and the one to which you connect. (For a detailed technical explanation of OLI, contact AT&T at one of the phone numbers listed at the end of this box.)

Using OLI results in far less line noise and an exceptional ability to adapt to the idiosyncrasies of almost any other modem. Even if the online service you call (or the person calling you) uses a low-end modem, the Dataport will probably compensate for the other party's shortcomings.

The Dataport line includes v.42bis/MNP-5 data compression in all models. Choices include v.32 (9600 bps) or v.32bis (14,400 bps) speeds in both internal and external models. Group 3 (9600 bps) send/receive fax capabilities can be ordered. QuickLink II terminal/fax software is included in both DOS and Windows versions for IBM-PC compatibles; a Macintosh version is available.

Dataport modems are backed by a very unusual *lifetime* warranty on parts and labor, and toll-free technical support. The warranties for most modems cover five years or less, and tech support is often a toll call for the customer.

AT&T Paradyne
8545 126th Avenue North
Largo, FL 34649
Information: 1-800-554-4996
Public BBS: 1-813-532-5254

In addition to buying the best hardware you can afford, there are other ways to get better performance out of almost any modem. The following sections discuss a few of these simple methods.

Getting Top Performance from Your Current Modem

Like an automobile, a modem needs fine-tuning once in a while to maintain peak performance. Unlike a car, a modem is generally a very stable device; solid-state circuits rarely burn out, and NVRAM seldom loses its settings. But the environment in which a modem must operate often changes. Line noise is the most common change you will experience, but environmental changes can include new hardware or software in your computer, moving the modem from home to office, and other things that can make your existing configuration obsolete and inappropriate.

Fine-Tune Modem and Terminal Program Options

Like two dance partners who know the steps but have not danced with each other often, your modem and terminal software may be getting by without perfectly meshing with one another. Double-check both the modem's settings (DIP switches and user profile settings) and the terminal program's settings. Read and thoroughly understand the documentation for modem and software before performing such tinkering. These are some items to check:

✦ *Flow control* For any modem that includes hardware-based error-correction (v.32, v.32bis, MNP 1-4 or v.42bis) software flow control (XON/XOFF) must be turned off. The DSR/DTR signal should *always* be turned off when modems are in use.

✦ *File transfer disk buffer size* Your terminal software may get too busy when it writes a block of data to disk while simultaneously handling more incoming data. Most terminal software can create a buffer in your computer's RAM, a temporary holding area where data is diverted until the terminal software finishes a disk-write and can pay full attention to new arrivals. If you have a high-speed modem and a slow hard drive (28 milliseconds access time or greater), or if you use a hard-disk compression utility such as Stacker, you may experience CRC errors (indicating lost data) when your terminal software writes to disk. Increasing the size of the buffer often eliminates this problem.

✦ *File transfer window size* Protocols such as Zmodem generally use an error-checking routine called *sliding windows*, which simply means the amount of data transmitted without a pause (the *window* of uninterrupted data flow) to listen for an acknowledgment from the

13

receiving modem can vary (slide) during any file transfer. The default window for such protocols is zero, meaning data is sent continuously unless an error is detected. This is much more efficient than pausing every 1,000 bytes or so to listen for an acknowledgment. Set a non-zero value for the window size only if you regularly experience errors in file transfer that cause pauses while the modem retransmits blocks of data.

✦ *Use slow handshaking on error-prone lines* If you get errors at regular intervals during downloads, set your terminal software to lower the RTS (Ready To Send) signal while it is writing data to disk; this technique is called *slow handshaking*. Momentarily lowering RTS tells the remote modem to stop sending data for a while. It is more efficient to receive data only when your software is ready for it than to detect a partially lost data block, send a retransmit request, and download the entire block all over again. Consult your terminal software's manual to see how RTS can be lowered during disk writes.

Different terminal programs offer different fine-tuning mechanisms. Unfortunately, you must often dig through mounds of documentation to learn all of your software's options.

Double-Check and Minimize Cable Connections

Line noise often starts right in your own home, not in a distant part of the telephone network. Check all of the connections between your telephone line, modem, and computer.

✦ Make sure that modular phone jacks fit snugly into their sockets on the modem and at the wallplate; replace loose-fitting cords. Wallplate sockets may become obstructed when a room is repainted; be sure the gold contacts inside the socket are clean. Replace wallplate sockets if a new cord still fits loosely.

✦ Avoid splicing two short modular cords into one long cord in order to reach your wallplate from your modem. Every extra juncture in a wire is a potential source of trouble. Buy a cord as long as you need.

✦ If you have an external modem, tighten down the screws that hold the cable connectors in place on modem and serial ports. Some cheap cables may be loosely or incorrectly wired; a replacement cable costs about $10, and may solve static problems.

✦ If you have a desktop phone, answering machine, or other device plugged into the PHONE auxiliary jack on your modem, unplug it. Other devices can inject noise into modem connections.

Does Your Modem Need Its Own Phone Line?

If your household includes a number of extension phones, answering machines, or other devices that share a single phone line, you probably will have trouble with line noise when using your modem. A second phone line used only by your modem may be the only way to enjoy efficient modeming while preserving domestic tranquility.

TIP: Some regional telephone companies offer discounted second residential lines called "Teen Lines." These lines are the same as regular phone lines, but are offered at lower prices as an incentive for parents frustrated by the constant busy signals generated by adolescents. Be sure to specify that you want your "teenager's" phone number to be *unpublished*; otherwise, your modem's phone number will be listed in the White Pages and Directory Assistance. You do not want a bunch of telemarketers calling this new listing.

Minimize Online Reading and Typing

Chapter 7 describes in detail ways to quickly capture messages from a BBS, log off, read and answer your mail offline, then upload your replies at modem speed instead of your relatively slow typing speed. A quick review follows here:

✦ Turn on session-logging before logging on.

✦ Turn off page-pause to log bulletins and messages nonstop.

✦ Write messages offline and upload them into message forms on the BBS, using the ASCII protocol if no option is provided to upload a prepared message just as you would any other file.

✦ Log file listings nonstop, or look for a downloadable file listing. Pick the files you want offline, then call back with a list of downloads prepared.

✦ Create keyboard macros to automate error-free entry of your name, address, home phone number, and other small bits of frequently needed data.

✦ Use your terminal program's Record feature, if it has one, to create scripts that quickly blaze through routine menu navigation. Take the time to study script language programming to create complex scripts with branching logic.

13

All of these money-saving tips can be implemented on your end of the telephone line, or on any BBS you may encounter. The following section discusses money-savers that require the right capabilities on the remote computer; some are more commonly available than others.

Using Money-Saving Features of Online Services

Most online services offer ways to save you connect time charges. Even services that charge by the minute have finally realized that customers want to squeeze as much value from each minute online as possible, and offer custom tools that save time and connect charges, although usually for a hefty price.

One-line BBSs have the most incentive to help callers get on and off as fast as possible. Even the largest multiline BBSs operate as close to capacity as members will tolerate. Because most BBSs charge a flat fee per year (if they charge anything), it is in the sysop's best interest to reduce the length of an average call as much as possible; then more paying subscribers can use the same number of lines.

✦ Use a QWK-compatible mail packer if a BBS offers one. You will need a shareware QWK-compatible offline reader on your computer. SpeedRead and Blue Wave are two popular examples.

✦ Use the most appropriate file-transfer protocol a specific online service offers, that matches one in your terminal software. Zmodem works well just about anywhere. Avoid using Xmodem with high-speed modems; Xmodem pauses every 128 characters to listen for an error-checking acknowledgement, a waste of time on already error-correcting v.32 and v.32bis links.

✦ Avoid ANSI color if you want maximum throughput of menu screens. Each ANSI code consists of at least three characters, which translates into a slight hesitation each time a color changes on your lovely screen. This effect is most noticeable on 2400-bps connections that lack data compression, but ANSI characters add invisible overhead to communication at any speed.

NOTE: Many online door programs, and all full-screen editors used in writing messages online, require that ANSI color/cursor control be turned on. Some door programs will not even attempt to load themselves when you select them unless you have ANSI enabled.

✦ Use *offline front-end software*, similar to QWK offline message managers, whenever an online service you regularly use offers it. Front-end software often imitates the same screens you would see online and use for data entry, message composition, database search specification, and other time-consuming chores. Then at the press of a key, the front-end can log on to the remote computer, flash all of your instructions to it, upload messages and download replies, retrieve the results of database searches, and log you off. Do not let the sometimes high price of specialized front-end software deter you. If you frequently run searches in a $120-per-hour database, a $250 front-end will soon pay for itself in connect time savings.

CompuServe has its own front-end software, the CompuServe Information Manager (CIM), in DOS and Windows versions. Many people prefer OZCIS, a shareware front-end written by a CompuServe customer. GEnie also has a shareware front-end, Aladdin.

These tips as well as those in preceding sections will help you minimize the amount of time you spend online, which will reduce your monthly phone bill and information carrier surcharges. The following section explores ways to reduce the per-minute cost of long-distance telephone calling.

Buy the Right Long-Distance Service

Long-distance modem calling can run up your phone bill faster than you can say, "Pull the plug!" Even though I use most of the time-saving techniques described in the preceding sections, my monthly long-distance bill averages over $150. The problem is that work (or play) expands to fill the time available for it (Parkinson's Law). Many people do not reduce the number of minutes they spend online each month, they just make more calls more efficiently. This section explores some ways to reduce the per-minute cost of telecomputing.

Night and Evening Discount Rates

Every long-distance service offers automatic discounts on calls made after 7:00 p.m. local time (your time zone) on weekdays, and from 7:00 p.m. Friday until 7:00 a.m. Monday morning all weekend. This discount is generally known as the *evening/weekend rate*. An additional discount, the *night rate*, kicks in after 11:00 p.m. every night. The difference between regular day rates and night rates for the same long-distance call can be 40 percent or more.

You do not have to stay up past 11:00 p.m. or wake up an hour earlier than normal to take advantage of night rates. If you learn your terminal program's script language, you can write a *timed-execution script* that will wait until after 11:00 p.m. to dial any number of online services, perform specific tasks on each one, log off, and have your mail ready for you to read with breakfast. Scripts can keep track of which phone numbers were busy, and call those numbers as many times as you specify before giving up on them.

13

Long-Distance Discount Programs

Competition among the many long-distance carriers is a mixed blessing for consumers, bringing them lower overall prices at the cost of great confusion. The major long-distance carriers—AT&T, MCI, and US Sprint—have numerous calling plans designed to save customers money (and steal market share from other long-distance carriers).

Choosing the best calling plan is a tedious business of collecting marketing literature from all the carriers, analyzing your long-distance calling patterns, and seeking the best match between calling plans and your calling habits.

Calling plans can be pretty complicated, but in general they offer discounts based on two types of calling behavior: volume (minutes per month) and frequency (how often you call a given phone number). Volume discounts fall into two categories:

✦ *Overall volume* The more minutes you use, the less each one costs you. This is the easiest discount to understand, but it can still get confusing. Some price schedules charge a higher rate for the first minute of a call than they do for additional minutes. If the majority of your calls last ten minutes or more, the extra cost of the first minute may be negligible.

✦ *Guaranteed minimum purchase* AT&T popularized this discount plan with its Reach Out America program. If your monthly long-distance use is fairly constant and relatively high ($20 or more), you can save money by paying a fixed minimum monthly fee that includes a specific number of "free" minutes. The cost of minutes that exceed the basic allowance is usually lower than a non-plan price, and lower than the overall volume discount plan described in the preceding paragraph. But the cost of each excess minute can be significantly higher than the average cost-per-minute of your basic allowance.

All three major long-distance carriers offer such plans in various sizes, so it pays to shop around. Beware of startup fees; they can dramatically inflate the cost of your first month's usage. It pays to ask if any special promotions are currently in effect that waive the startup fee or refund it after a few months.

Volume-based calling plans are best suited for online gadabouts who make a lot of long-distance calls to many different places. If you find you spend a lot of money calling just a few different phone numbers, the following types of calling plan may save you more money:

✦ *Frequently called numbers* An automatic discount may be applied on calls made to the phone number(s) you call most often. US Sprint calls this plan "The Most." If you find most of your long-distance time is spent on one or two BBSs, this type of plan may be the right choice.

♦ *Designated discount numbers* MCI has made a killing on this idea, under its Friends & Neighbors calling plan. You specify up to six phone numbers on which you receive a 20 to 25 percent discount, day or night. The catch is that each number you add to your Friends & Neighbors list must also be an MCI customer. Some BBS sysops will gladly let you add their BBSs to your Friends & Neighbors list, if they already use MCI. Leave a message to the sysop asking if you can add the BBS to your Friends & Neighbors list.

Shopping for the best long-distance service can shave 10 to 30 percent off your monthly phone bill. Consistently taking advantage of automatic evening and night discount rates is even more effective. The following section explains how to make long-distance modem calls for much less than the lowest public network rates.

Packet-Switching Networks

Packet-switching is a data communications technique that takes advantage of idle moments in a communications channel to simultaneously squeeze more than one user onto a single line. When a BBS sends you its opening menu, data passes through the phone line. But while you are reading that menu and deciding what to do, no data is moving through the phone line. There are hundreds of such idle moments in every online session, as tiny as the time span between one keystroke and the next when you are typing a message, or as lengthy as the time it takes to find and display one file in a list of 50,000.

Packet-switching divides your stream of stop-and-go data into evenly sized bundles called *data packets*. Each packet is routed to a packet-switching computer that finds a space of idle time on a channel leading partway or all the way to your destination, and inserts your data packet into someone else's idle time. The first computer to receive your packet may have to forward it to another packet-switching computer to deliver your packet at its destination. All of your packets are reassembled before entering the final destination. Data from a remote computer reaches you by an identical process.

The overall effects of packet-switching are to let many users share one phone line, and maximize the amount of traffic the line handles. These efficiencies make substantial cost savings possible. But packet-switching has its drawbacks for certain online activities.

13

When Packet-Switching Makes Sense

Packet-switching is most compatible and cost-effective with highly interactive online activities, such as live chat, one-by-one message reading, and online message writing, each of which involve many brief exchanges between caller and remote computer. Such activities naturally include a great deal of idle time, so the stop-and-go delivery method used by packet-switching is hardly noticeable.

Packet-switching is not recommended for lengthy file transfers (more than 50K per file) or nonstop scrolling of bulletins and messages. A 9600-bps v.42bis modem that should normally achieve over 1,050-characters-per-second throughput will be lucky to hit 800 cps over a packet-switched connection. A 2400-bps modem may stumble along at 180 cps or less in file transfers. Nonstop scrolling becomes a joke; you will see significant pauses between packets, but at least you will not have to press the (Enter) key after every page.

My own analysis of packet-switching performance and prices versus using the public telephone network showed that the latter cost very little more per online session than the former, when transferring large files. If most of your online activity is stop-and-go, try a packet-switching service. But if continuous high-speed data transfer is important, stick with traditional long-distance carriers.

Packet-switching services do not reach every telephone in the U. S., let alone the world. When shopping for a packet-switching service, carefully check its geographic coverage to be sure you can reach the places that you want to go.

Following are some brief descriptions of the major packet-switching networks in the U.S.

PC Pursuit and SprintNet

US Sprint operates a packet-switching network known as SprintNet (formerly Telenet). SprintNet reaches hundreds of cities and thousands of local telephone exchanges in the U.S., and is one of the largest domestic packet-switching services.

PC Pursuit is a calling plan, a subset of SprintNet that is available only in about 40 major metropolitan areas, and only during evening and weekend calling hours. Back in 1988, Telenet started the PC Pursuit calling plan in an effort to capture the growing BBS market. For a flat monthly fee, BBSers received unlimited connect time to any PC Pursuitable destination, during weeknight and weekend hours.

US Sprint inherited the PC Pursuit customer base when it bought Telenet, and all indications are that US Sprint wishes the entire BBS crowd would just go away. Minimum monthly fees have been raised several times; the least you can buy now is 30 hours a month for $30. "Excess usage fees" have been added. PC Pursuit is not advertised or promoted in any way. Access is limited to 2400 bps, and there are no plans to upgrade to modern speeds. Only about 4,500 customers still use PC Pursuit.

But using PC Pursuit costs less than $0.02 per minute as long as you stay within your monthly limit, compared to $0.12 to $0.25 per minute over public long-distance carriers. If customer appreciation is less important to you than cash savings, you can sign up for PC Pursuit by calling (voice) 1-800-877-1130.

Tymnet and BT North America

British Telecom, the national telephone service company of the United Kingdom, operates a packet-switching network that links over 1,000 cities in 100 countries. Its subsidiary, BT North America, runs the Tymnet network.

Tymnet has no calling plan comparable to PC Pursuit, or anything remotely cost-effective for personal modem users. The minimum monthly charge for a Tymnet outdialing account is $229, and connect time costs $12 per hour in low volumes, day or night. Tymnet prefers to bill information providers, and let them concentrate all the small monthly checks from end users.

If you are the sysop of a BBS that logs thousands of minutes of inbound long-distance calls per month, you may be able to save your callers some money by offering Tymnet access. Call 1-800-872-7654 to speak with a sales representative.

Beware of Packet-Switching Resellers

Several enterprising firms have tried to buy low and sell high in the packet-switching market, invariably with disastrous results for the entrepreneurs and, at the least, inconvenient for their customers. Tymnet, SprintNet, and other packet-switching networks will gladly sell blocks of time at substantial discounts. Resellers then sell time to customers at rates far less than low-volume end users could usually afford.

The buy-wholesale, sell-retail theory should work, but so far it has not. No packet-switching reseller has been able to build up a big enough end-user base fast enough to keep up its monthly payments to the packet-switching service provider. Negative cash flow usually drives resellers out of business in a year or less, leaving end-users without service.

Dozens of BBS operators have invested $10,000 to $20,000 in packet-switching equipment to give their callers savings touted by resellers. These sysops were stuck with unusable, highly specialized equipment when their resellers went bankrupt.

13

My advice is to buy direct from a packet-switching service, or do not buy at all.

Saving Time Saves Money

Even if your modem use is strictly recreational, your time is valuable and should be counted when figuring overall dollar savings. Try to strike a good balance between saving hard dollars and spending the time necessary to write scripts, tune software, and use a packet-switching service such as PC Pursuit, as well the extra effort required by all the other tips in this chapter. Remember, the ultimate goal is to enjoy using your modem!

CHAPTER

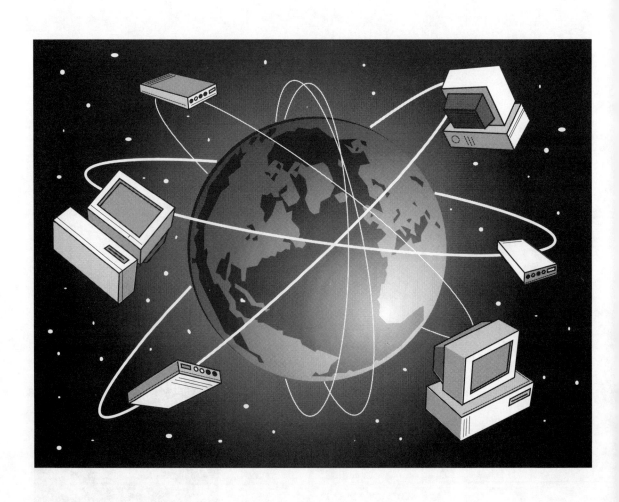

14

MODEM SHAREWARE YOU DON'T WANT TO MISS

This chapter describes useful modem-related shareware and public domain software. Beginners and advanced modem users will find these programs make setting up and using modems easier and more fun. All of the programs described here are widely available on BBSs, information carriers, and the Internet, but it can take years to discover them if you do not know they exist.

Shareware, as described in Chapter 4, is copyrighted software you get to try before you buy. Public domain software is not copyrighted, and does not require a registration fee. Both kinds of software are intended to be copied and freely distributed, and modems make an ideal distribution medium.

Understanding Archiving (Compression) Utilities

Newcomers to the world of shareware are often confused and frustrated when the software they downloaded will not run. Generally, such recalcitrant programs end with an unfamiliar filename extension such as *.ZIP, *.ARC, *.LZH, or *.ARJ. If you try to run such a file in the ordinary way, by typing its name, you will get a "Bad command or file name" error message.

The problem is that the program is still in its "shipping container." Files that can be run under MS-DOS always end with the extension *.EXE, *.COM, or *.BAT. These files and others are *inside* of the file you downloaded, and must be unpacked before you can put them to work. How did they get there, and how do you get them out?

Archiving utilities (archivers for short) squeeze one or more files into a single file, which occupies fewer bytes than the original file(s) did. (Archiving utilities are also called *compression utilities* for this reason.) Fewer bytes mean less transmission time when transmitting an archived program over a modem connection, often one-half to one-quarter of the time required to transfer the uncompressed file(s).

Convenience is a less obvious benefit of archiving. Even relatively simple programs generally consist of more than one file; at the least, the executable file is accompanied by a documentation file. Archiving all of a program's component files in a single file lets you download just one file instead of many, and keeps the essential components from getting separated as the program is passed around online.

Many commercial programs distributed on disks now take advantage of archivers. Microsoft's Excel for Windows, for example, occupies over 15Mb in its uncompressed state, or about thirteen high-density 5.25-inch floppy disks. Using archived files, Microsoft distributes Excel on just five such disks.

Recognizing Common Archive Formats: ZIP, ARC, ARJ, and LZH

To unpack an archived file, you must use the same archiving utility that was used to pack it in the first place (or an archiver than can handle one or more of its competitors' formats). The bad news is, there are over 30 different archivers available; one BBS we know makes a specialty of maintaining lists and tables of all these archivers' relative performance characteristics. You could easily fill up a substantial portion of your hard disk with archivers, and take forever to find the right key to a given archive.

The good news is, only four archivers "own" 99 percent of the market, and you can generally tell which utility created an archived file by glancing at the file's extension (the three characters to the right of the period in a file's name, such as MYFILE.EXT). The following table is a guide to archive filename extensions and the utilities that create them.

Archive Extension	Archive/Decompression Utility	Comments
myfile.ZIP	PKZIP.EXE/PKUNZIP.EXE	The most common and powerful by far
myfile.ARC	ARC.EXE/XARC.EXE	Often used in commercial software
myfile.ARJ	ARJ.EXE	Only one utility needed
myfile.LZH	LHA.EXE	Also one utility

The archivers listed in the preceding table can be found anywhere online that their compression formats are used, or on the disks that carry compressed commercial software. Key words to look for are "archiving" and "compression." Often a file library will have an entire section devoted to archivers and the many third-party utilities that have cropped up around each leading format (a following section describes some third-party utilities).

Get PKZIP/PKUNZIP if you get no other archiver; it is by far the most widely used, and, in your author's opinion, the most versatile. ARC/XARC is the oldest archiver, and PKZIP's arch rival. ARJ and LHA are relative newcomers with substantial followings, but are not nearly as common as their older cousins.

NOTE: The latest version of PKZIP/PKUNZIP (v2.04G as of this writing), is not entirely backward-compatible with the earlier v1.11. Archives created with v2.04G cannot be decompressed using v1.11 of PKUNZIP, but v1.11 archives can be unpacked using PKUNZIP v2.04G. You can download the latest version of PKZIP/PKUNZIP from the PK Ware BBS: 414-354-8670.

14

Whichever archiver(s) you collect, put them in a directory on your hard disk that is part of your MS-DOS path; that way, you can invoke an archiver utility from any other directory on the drive.

How to Unpack an Archived Program

When you receive a package in the mail, the first thing you probably do is peek inside to see what's in it. Depending on the contents, you may then clear some work space to hold all of the parts before unpacking things. If there are instructions in the box, you will want to read them before assembling the parts.

Archivers include features that make viewing the contents of an archived file and extracting selected files easy. To view the contents of a *.ZIP file, for example, you would type

```
PKUNZIP -V path\filename
```

where *filename* is the portion of the file's name to the left of the period; PKUNZIP assumes the extension .ZIP unless you specify another extension. If you invoke PKUNZIP while in the same directory that contains your archived file, you need not specify the *path*.

PKUNZIP's View option produces a listing similar to Figure 14-1. Take special note of the number in the lower left corner of the screen. It tells you how many bytes of disk space are required to hold all of the archive's contents in uncompressed form. You must have at least this many bytes of disk space available or you will not be able to unpack the entire archive. To find out how many bytes you have available, enter a DIR command and check the "bytes free" shown at the end of the resulting directory listing.

```
PKUNZIP (R)    FAST!    Extract Utility    Version 2.04g  02-01-93
Copr. 1989-1993 PKWARE Inc. All Rights Reserved. Shareware Version
PKUNZIP Reg. U.S. Pat. and Tm. Off.
■ 80386 CPU detected.
■ EMS version 4.00 detected.
■ XMS version 3.00 detected.

Searching ZIP: WINZIP4B.ZIP -
 Length  Method   Size  Ratio   Date     Time    CRC-32   Attr  Name
 ------  ------   ----  -----   ----     ----    ------   ----  ----
   1063  DeflatX   613   43%  04-02-93  00:00  d2c90fc2  --w-  README.1ST
   1427  DeflatX   702   51%  04-02-93  00:00  c04a6862  --w-  WHATS.NEW
  19930  DeflatX  6890   66%  04-02-93  00:00  c431e86f  --w-  WINZIP.DOC
 148480  DeflatX 67238   55%  04-02-93  00:00  0bec1ea2  --w-  WINZIP.EXE
  85397  DeflatX 43263   50%  04-02-93  00:00  a1a2e45c  --w-  WINZIP.HLP
  32256  DeflatX 15843   51%  04-02-93  00:00  49d3a8e5  --w-  WZ.DLL
   2367  DeflatX  1355   43%  04-02-93  00:00  fa5ed94b  --w-  WZ.COM
    545  DeflatX   158   72%  04-02-93  00:00  60fa7410  --w-  WZ.PIF
   3353  DeflatX  1549   54%  04-02-93  00:00  b6c09fc6  --w-  LICENSE.DOC
    429  DeflatX   289   33%  04-02-93  00:00  b8db0428  --w-  FILE_ID.DIZ
   3548  DeflatX  1504   58%  04-02-93  00:00  1da41990  --w-  VENDOR.DOC
   2948  DeflatX  1294   57%  04-02-93  00:00  e92bb468  --w-  ORDER.DOC
 ------          ------  ----                                        --
 301743          140698   54%                                        12
```

PKUNZIP -V *filename* tells what's inside a ZIP archive

Figure 14-1.

Before unpacking the whole archive, unpack just the instructions that usually are included, and read them thoroughly. Instruction files often include important information on how to properly extract and install the program files in an archive. Instruction files often have obvious names like MANUAL.DOC, README.1ST, and so on. But look for any file that ends in a telltale extension such as TXT (text), DOC (document), MAN (instruction Manual) or WRI (Windows' Write format).

Archivers make it easy to locate or unpack only selected files. Entering the following command at the DOS prompt:

```
PKUNZIP filename *.DOC READ*.* *.TXT *.MAN *.WRI
```

will extract from the archive *filename*.ZIP only the files whose names match the wildcard patterns specified.

Following the instructions, create any necessary directory to hold your program files before extracting them. You can switch to this program directory before extracting the archived files, or tell the archiver to put the files it extracts in a specific directory. For example, the command

```
PKUNZIP filename C:\PROGRAM
```

tells PKUNZIP to put everything extracted from the archive *filename*.ZIP into the directory C:\PROGRAM. After extracting all of the files from an archive, you can save hard disk space by deleting the archive or moving it to a floppy disk in case you need it again.

Self-Extracing Archives

Sometimes you will encounter archive files that end with the extension .EXE. These are *self-extracting archives* which unpack themselves when you type their filenames. Self-extraction does for archives what pop-top cans do for soda pop: you don't need a can opener. Part of the unpacking utility's code is built into the archive itself, and goes wherever the archive goes.

Archive utilities themselves are generally distributed as self-extracting archives, for instance PKZ204G.EXE. This makes sense; if you get this file, you get it because you do not already have it or its unpacking capabilities.

Self-extracting archives are often preprogrammed by their creators to perform complex installation procedures for the software they contain. For example, a self-extracting archive may create subdirectories as it goes, or extract instructions and display them on your screen before proceeding to install the entire archive. You could do these things yourself, but self-extraction gives the author of a program more control over its installation and puts less of a burden on the user during installation.

14

Other Uses for Archiving Utilities

Archivers are good for more than just transporting software. A modern archiving utility is a versatile tool you can use every day on your local computer and floppy disk collection. Common archiver features include

Comments attached to archive and component files. If you ever forget what a particular program is (and who doesn't?), you can refresh your memory by invoking a short comment attached to the archived file, such as "Checkbook/personal finance manager." Comments can be attached to individual files within the overall archived file, so you can figure out exactly what each component is and whether it belongs to the original program or is one of your own data files.

Encryption with password protection prevents an archived file from being unpacked by unauthorized persons. You create a password for the encrypted file at the time you archive it. Any time someone invokes the decompression command, they must enter the correct password before the archive will disgorge its contents. Even peeking into an archive using a file-viewing utility will not reveal its secrets; encrypted archives are scrambled into a hopelessly random mess until they are properly unpacked.

Backups of hard disks can become a breeze with the help of an archiver. By invoking the right options in a batch file, you can tell the archiver utility to scan your entire hard disk (or selected directories) and pack up only those files that have been created or modified since the last time you performed a backup sweep. Some archivers, such as PKZIP, can create archives that span multiple floppy diskettes. A 72Mb hard disk compresses into just eighteen 1.2Mb floppies using PKZIP, and any file or subdirectory can quickly be located and decompressed.

Archivers are essential to enjoying the world of shareware. A sophisticated archive utility also saves time and disk space around the home or office when you are not using your modem.

SHEZ: A Front-End Processor for Archivers

Modern archivers are extremely versatile, but their sophistication has a price: complexity, in the form of many options and command-line switches. Figure 14-2 shows just one of three highly abbreviated help screens (bare-reminder screens, really) that PKZIP displays when you type **PKZIP** all by itself. The complete reference manual for PKZIP/PKUNZIP is over 100 pages long.

Multiply this complexity by four, because you may well need to learn the ZIP, ARC, LZH, and ARJ archivers to deal with the leading archive formats you are likely to encounter. Pretty discouraging, isn't it?

```
PKUNZIP (R)    FAST!   Extract Utility    Version 2.04g  02-01-93
Copr. 1989-1993 PKWARE Inc. All Rights Reserved. Shareware Version
PKUNZIP Reg. U.S. Pat. and Tm. Off.

Usage:   PKUNZIP [options] zipfile [@list] [files...]

-c[m]                    extract files to Console [with More]
-d                       restore/create Directory structure stored in .ZIP file
-e[c|d|e|n|p|r|s] Extract files.  Sort by [CRC | Date | Extension | Name
                         | Percentage | Reverse | Size]
-f                       Freshen files in destination directory
-j|J<h,r,s>              mask|don't mask <Hidden/System/Readonly> files (def.=jhrs)
-n                       extract only Newer files
-o                       Overwrite previously existing files
-p[a/b][c][#]           extract to Printer [Asc mode,Bin mode,Com port] [port #]
-q                       Enable ANSI comments
-s[pwd]                  Decrypt with password [If no pwd is given, prompt for pwd]
-t                       Test .ZIP file integrity
-v[b][r][m][t]           View .ZIP [Brief][Reverse][More][Technical] sort by [CRC|
    [c,d,e,n,o,p,s] Date|Extension|Name|natural Order(default)|Percentage|Size]
-x<filespec>            eXclude file(s) from extraction
-$                       Restore volume label on destination drive
-@listfile              Generate list file
```

PKZIP has
many
versatile, but
confusing,
options
Figure 14-2.

Take heart; where there is a need, there is a shareware solution. A number of shareware utilities have been written to shield the user from the complexities of archivers, and to make converting archives from one format to another easier.

SHEZ v8.8 is one such archiver front end. Figure 14-3 shows one of the many user-friendly screens in this combination DOS-shell/file-editor/archive manager. This screen illustrates the seven different ways you can extract a given file from a ZIP archive. SHEZ makes it easy and obvious to choose the option you want to use. Some of these options would require three or four command-line switches or multiple operations if executed by using the basic PKZIP/PKUNZIP utilities. SHEZ also includes online context-sensitive help to further explain your options.

SHEZ and similar shareware programs can convert a batch of archives in different formats (ZIP, ARC, LHA, and ARJ) to one standard format in a single operation. Mouse support and directory trees make it easy to navigate your hard disk. You can view or even edit a text file without extracting it from its archive. SHEZ relies on external hooks to the original archiver utilities, so updating SHEZ's capabilities to keep pace with new versions of archivers is a simple matter of installing the new archiver and telling SHEZ where to find it. You can also tell SHEZ to use your favorite editor and file-viewing programs. SHEZ even includes a macro record/playback feature, making it easy to automate multistep archiving functions.

GIFLite: Compression for GIF Images

14

One of the most popular types of file available for downloading is full-color graphic images stored in the Graphics Interface Format (GIF), developed by

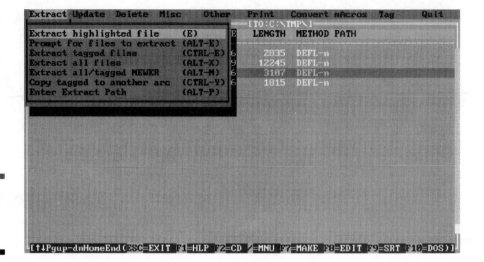

SHEZ makes
working with
archives easy
Figure 14-3.

CompuServe and now an industry standard. GIF images can be gloriously detailed; see Figure 14-4 for an example. A collection of GIF files can be your own private poster gallery, full of fast cars, nature scenes, or movie stars.

GIF images can take up a lot of bytes. A 256-color VGA-quality (640 × 480 pixels) GIF averages about 150K in size; it takes ten minutes at 2400 bps to download such a file, almost three minutes even at 9600 bps. A high-resolution SVGA GIF (1024 × 768) can easily swell to 500K; that takes over half an hour to download at 2400 bps, and nearly nine minutes at 9600 bps.

Then there is the question of where to store so much data once you download it. You could archive GIF images like other files, but that has its downside, in that you would have to decompress an image before you could view it (see the following section on graphics image viewers).

A unique shareware program called *GIFLite* compresses GIF images while keeping them in a format you can view, print, and even edit just like a normal GIF file. The size of the compressed GIF varies between 50 and 70 per cent of the original uncompressed file, depending on the number of colors and amount of detail contained in an image. Developed by Winfred Hu of Canada, GIFLite is distributed as a standalone program and is also bundled with Hu's popular Telemate terminal program.

Picture

Photographic-quality GIF images are popular downloads
Figure 14-4.

PKLITE: Double Your Disk Space Without Decompression

You have probably seen commercial software such as Stacker (by STAC Electronics), which promises to "double your disk space" by compressing *all* of your files. MS-DOS 6.0 includes a DoubleDisk utility that does much the same thing as Stacker. Such disk-doubling software is different from archiving utilities in that you need not unpack files before using them. After running a disk-doubling program on your hard drive, you can continue to work with all executable and data files just as you did before. It just appears that your hard disk's capacity has suddenly doubled.

PKLITE is a shareware disk-doubling utility developed by the same folks who created the PKZIP/PKUNZIP archiver. The latest version is v1.15, and it has some limitations. The most notable flaw in PKLITE is that it cannot transparently handle certain executable files that include overlays (data that paints a screen, for example) and expect to find each overlay at a specific point inside the executable file. Nothing fatal will happen if you run such a program after compressing it with PKLITE; it will simply abort with an error message. PKLITE provides command-line options that let you omit files containing overlays from the compression process, or restore compressed files to their original uncompressed form.

14

Another consequence of compressing files with PKLITE only crops up if you update or patch a program. Because PKLITE rearranges all of a file's internal code in order to achieve compression, patch utilities provided by software developers might not be able to find the portions of code they are supposed to upgrade or correct. The only solution is to decompress a file, patch it, and then recompress it with PKLITE.

PKLITE probably will not evolve beyond version 1.15. Competition from Stacker, DiskDoubler, and other heavyweight commercial utilities have pretty well overwhelmed this shareware utility. But nonbusiness users need not pay a registration fee, and business licenses start at a modest $35 for two to nine computers. If a more robust commercial disk-doubler is beyond your budget, PKLITE can give you more disk space for little or no cost.

Anti-Virus Protection

Computer viruses are the dark side of telecomputing. A computer virus (just "virus" for short) is a program deliberately designed to vandalize your other software and data, or to disrupt the normal operation of your computer system.

The truly diabolical aspect of viruses is that they literally *reproduce* before doing their destructive work. A virus can duplicate its own program code and insert the replica in another program many times before the virus finally starts deleting or scrambling files, causing your computer's monitor to start displaying letters backward, or whatever mischief the virus is programmed to cause. The infected program can then be copied to a floppy disk or downloaded via modem. When the infected program is run on another computer, the virus code embedded in it begins duplicating and infecting other software on the new machine.

The people who write virus programs generally have very specific targets in mind. A disgruntled employee might leave a virus on his employer's computer network before leaving. Bright but twisted students have infected nationwide networks of university computers "just to see what would happen."

Contrary to sensational press reports, it is unusual to find a virus on a public bulletin board system. Your author has visited thousands of BBSs and downloaded gigabytes of unknown shareware since 1986, none of which has carried a virus. The vigilance of BBS operators is one reason viruses seldom appear, but the main reason is that most BBSs are just too small to attract a virus programmer—not enough people can be hurt to justify the programming effort.

Still, "virus mania" has created a booming industry in anti-virus software. *SCAN,* an anti-virus program distributed by McAffee & Associates, is a good example. Updated every four to six weeks as new viruses are discovered, SCAN lists over 2,000 known virus "species" against which it is effective. SCAN is offered in DOS versions, OS/2 versions, network versions, and foreign-language versions. As a further indication of SCAN's success, the parent company was the first shareware developer to go public with a well-received initial stock offering.

SCAN is easy to operate: just run the program by typing its name and the letter of the drive you want to check for viruses. In its default mode, SCAN first sweeps your computer's RAM to see if any active viruses have been loaded and are hiding in memory. Then it scans every file on the designated drive that ends with the extension .EXE, .COM, or .PIF (Microsoft Windows' Program Information File format). If it finds a known virus, SCAN neutralizes it and excises the virulent code from the program file in which it was found.

It is important to note that SCAN checks only executable files, files which can "run" when their names are typed. *A virus cannot do anything at all until you run it or the program it has infected!* You cannot catch a virus from a text file, because text files cannot be run. Similarly, an unopened archive file might contain a virus-infected executable file, but unless the executable file is unpacked and run, the virus remains dormant.

SHEZ and other archiver front ends can cooperate with virus-killing software like SCAN, to inspect and disinfect executable files while they are still inside their archives. SCAN by itself will not find viruses inside of archives.

McAffee & Associates maintains a BBS from which you can download the latest shareware version of SCAN: log onto 408-988-4004. There is no monetary registration fee for using SCAN on home computers, but the license agreement requires home users to complete and mail in a registration form. Corporate users must pay a registration fee, which varies according to the number of computers on which SCAN will be used.

Modem Setup and Diagnostic Shareware

Beginners often have trouble identifying which COM ports are available for use with their new modems, or identifying IRQ conflicts (see Chapter 5 for discussion of COM ports and IRQs). Intermediate and advanced modem users sometimes need a diagnostic tool to read the many status registers in modems and UARTs to track down a particularly subtle problem.

Modem Doctor (MDR) v5.1 is my favorite all-round diagnostic utility. MDR is a powerful tool, but its user interface and report functions are so logically and neatly organized that beginners can readily learn to use it too. The first

14

thing Modem Doctor does is locate all of the active COM ports for you. Any modem owner will appreciate this feature; it saves lots of guesswork trying to find an available COM port when configuring internal modems and terminal software.

MDR also identifies and tests the type of UART built into each serial port, as shown in Figure 14-5. Some problems with data loss and disconnections that occur when using high-speed modems on older, unbuffered serial ports can be solved with a 16550 UART; Modem Doctor tells you if you already have one or not, and if your existing serial port hardware is working properly.

MDR will tell you if it finds a modem attached to a serial port, and its speed, also shown in Figure 14-5. Internal modem owners will really appreciate this feature; it is all too easy to forget what is out of sight. External modem owners can easily forget which COM port their modem uses; a quick MDR check reminds them.

The modem hardware tests MDR runs are exhaustive, but easy on the user. The values stored in every status register (S register) are displayed, as you can see in Figure 14-6. Compared to the manual method of typing **AT S#?** to peek at each status register's value one at a time, using Modem Doctor is a convenient luxury.

If Modem Doctor detects a problem, it provides helpful suggestions as to what may be wrong and what to investigate to verify MDR's diagnosis. Figure 14-7 shows Modem Doctor's recommendation when it discovered a faulty UART on a serial port.

Modem Doctor identifies modem and UART types on COM ports
Figure 14-5.

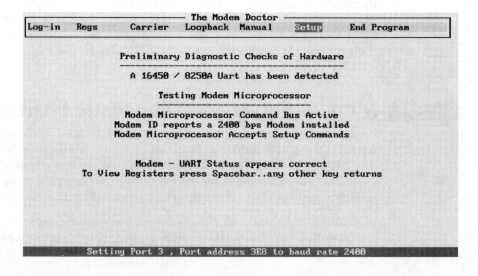

```
───────────────── The Modem Doctor ─────────────────
│ Log-in   Regs      Carrier   Loopback  Manual   Setup        End Program │

            Preliminary Diagnostic Checks of Hardware
         ----------------------------------------------
              A 16450 / 8250A Uart has been detected

                    Testing Modem Microprocessor
         ----------------------------------------------
              Modem Microprocessor Command Bus Active
              Modem ID reports a 2400 bps Modem installed
              Modem Microprocessor Accepts Setup Commands


                 Modem - UART Status appears correct
        To View Registers press Spacebar..any other key returns



      Setting Port 3 , Port address 3E8 to baud rate 2400
```

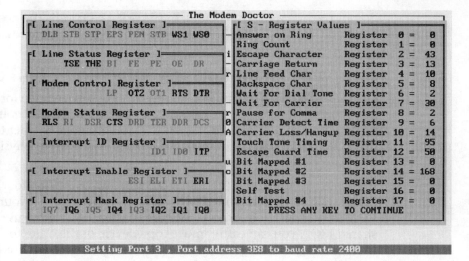

Your modem's status registers are revealed at a glance
Figure 14-6.

Status Lights for Internal Modems

LITES11.COM is a tiny memory-resident utility that discreetly displays on screen the status of a modem's RS232 control wires. External modems have front panel lights or LCDs that show you whether your modem has connected and detected a carrier wave (the CD signal), whether it is receiving data (RD) or transmitting data (TD), whether it has taken the phone line off-hook (OH) as it is supposed to, and so on. Internal modems

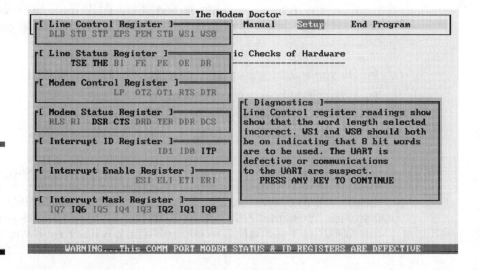

Complete diagnosis and prescription for a faulty UART
Figure 14-7.

14

do not provide such visual clues, but LITES11.COM fills the need to know what your modem is really doing when you give it commands.

Swapping COM Ports to Solve IRQ Conflicts

Chapter 5 discussed the rule of sharing an IRQ between two (or more) COM ports: only one serial device can use a given IRQ at a time, though several COM ports can take turns using an IRQ. Sometimes it is easier to switch the COM port memory address your modem uses than to physically change the COM port that the modem uses.

COMSET v10A provides the ability to swap any of the first four COM port addresses (COM1 through COM4) with any other. Thus, if your mouse on COM1 and your modem on COM3 are conflicting over the use of their shared IRQ2, you can easily "move" one device or the other to COM2 or COM4 without having to unplug cables or reconfigure an internal card. COMSET provides other useful communications capabilities, such as setting the speed of serial port data transfer from 300 to 57,600 bps, detecting and resetting internal modems.

Telix Terminal Program and Utilities

General-purpose terminal programs are thoroughly examined in Chapter 4. My personal favorite is Telix, originally developed by Colin Sampaleneau, now distributed and supported by deltaComm Inc., of Cary, North Carolina (1-800-TLX-8000). Telix is an MS-DOS, character-based application, though it can run in Microsoft Windows in either full-screen or windowed mode.

Telix is easy for beginners to set up and learn. When you start Telix for the first time, it looks for a file named TELIX.CNF. If the file is not found, Telix asks four simple questions to help you configure the program for the first time:

✦ Do you want color or monochrome display?
✦ What COM port is your modem attached to?
✦ What is the highest baud rate your modem supports?
✦ Do you want a status bar displayed on the bottom line?

This simplified setup routine makes a lot of assumptions about the IRQ used by your COM port; specific modem make and model's required settings; and miscellaneous options such as bells, scrollback buffer size, and other details discussed in Chapter 7. The simplified setup routine assumes you want to use XON/XOFF software flow control, which is incorrect if you have an error-correcting modem.

But Telix also comes with an external modem configuration utility that offers a pick list of 66 modem vendors, with submenus of specific modem models beneath each vendor, as shown in Figure 14-8. Just pick your modem's vendor and pick the model you own. The configuration utility automatically sets TELIX.CNF to the ideal settings for that specific modem.

Telix is well supplied with internal file-transfer protocols, listed in Figure 14-9. You can also add external protocols: standalone programs that implement file transfer protocols not included with Telix. Add-on protocols appear on the same pick list shown in Figure 14-9.

The latest shareware version of Telix is v3.21, and it is the last major shareware release of this now-commercial terminal program. Version 3.21 includes a handy pick-list method of selecting a single file or tagging several files for uploading, as you can see in Figure 14-10. This technique eliminates a lot of mistyped filenames and "file not found" error messages.

Telix includes not one but two script languages: a simplified, easy-to-learn language for beginners and a more complex powerful version for modem maniacs and programmers. The registered version of Telix includes a recording feature that stores your online keystrokes and converts them to a script file.

Telix Add-on Utilities

Many external programs have been written to make Telix even easier to use. Telix's script language is so powerful and flexible that many add-on utilities

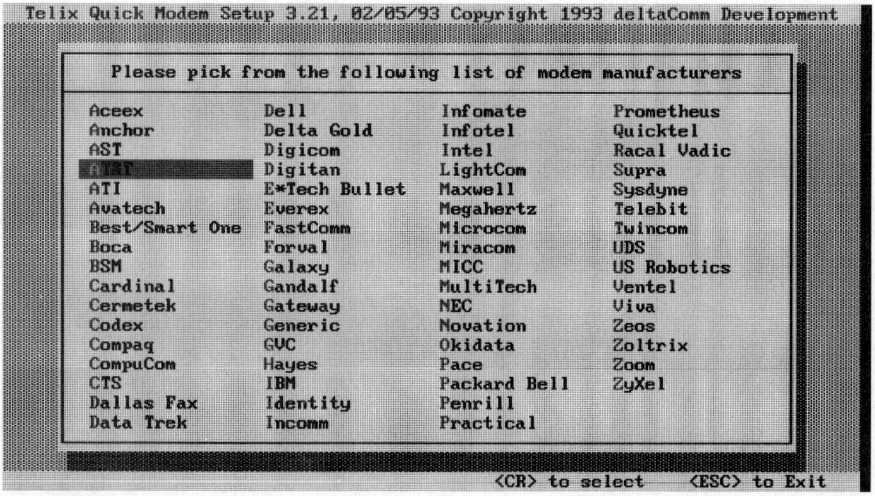

Telix's modem
configuration
utility
Figure 14-8.

```
Telix Quick Modem Setup 3.21, 02/05/93 Copyright 1993 deltaComm Development

        Please pick from the following list of modem manufacturers

   Aceex          Dell           Infomate       Prometheus
   Anchor         Delta Gold     Infotel        Quicktel
   AST            Digicom        Intel          Racal Vadic
   AT&T           Digitan        LightCom       Supra
   ATI            E*Tech Bullet  Maxwell        Sysdyne
   Avatech        Everex         Megahertz      Telebit
   Best/Smart One FastComm       Microcom       Twincom
   Boca           Forval         Miracom        UDS
   BSM            Galaxy         MICC           US Robotics
   Cardinal       Gandalf        MultiTech      Ventel
   Cermetek       Gateway        NEC            Viva
   Codex          Generic        Novation       Zeos
   Compaq         GVC            Okidata        Zoltrix
   CompuCom       Hayes          Pace           Zoom
   CTS            IBM            Packard Bell   ZyXel
   Dallas Fax     Identity       Penrill
   Data Trek      Incomm         Practical

                                    <CR> to select    <ESC> to Exit
```

14

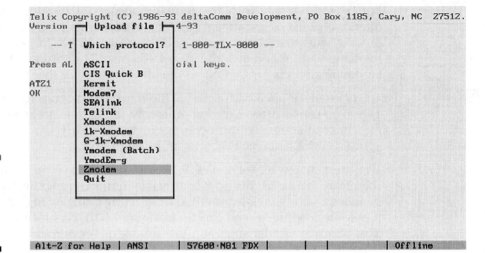

Telix offers all
the popular
file-transfer
protocols
Figure 14-9.

have been written entirely in the script language. HostPlus, the sophisticated
mini-BBS host program described and illustrated in Chapter 11, is written

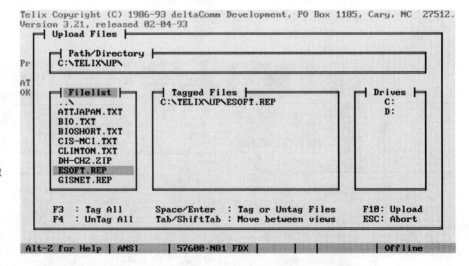

Point-and-shoot
file selection
makes
uploading easy
Figure 14-10.

entirely in the Telix script language. Two of my favorite Telix utilities and scripts include

✦ PICK-UP v1.3, by Mark Harrison, adds a number of sophisticated, time-saving features to Telix's already user-friendly interface. In "Message" mode PICK-UP lets you write messages offline or online with your favorite editor. Then just select your message from a pick list at the proper time, and PICK-UP sends the message for you. PICK-UP makes regular uploading easy too. Just select the file you want to upload from a pick list, select a protocol and PICK-UP sends the file for you. In "Script" mode PICK-UP makes writing, compiling, and testing scripts convenient. PICK-UP also makes general file maintenance chores easy, providing instant access to DOS directory-navigation commands and file-manipulation functions. Selecting a new dialing directory (if you use more than one) can also be done from a pick list; Telix, by contrast, makes you remember and type in the name of a new dialing directory.

✦ TFE (Telix FON Editor), v2.21, by Paul Roub, makes creating, editing, and managing Telix dialing directories a breeze. TFE can translate other terminal programs' dialing directories into Telix's format; sort a dialing directory by entry name, phone number, and other fields; provide full-screen editing of a dialing directory entry (Telix makes you cursor through every field in a top-down fashion); merge two FON files into one; change the value in a given field for a whole group of entries (very useful if you buy a faster modem and want to update every entry's baud rate in a large dialing directory); and a good deal more.

Graphics-File Viewing and Editing Programs

As mentioned in the preceding section on GIFLite, graphics files are among the most popular downloads on almost every BBS, information carrier, and Internet node. The GIF format is a *de facto* industry standard, and a host of file-viewing and editing utilities have cropped up to support it.

You need a special utility to view, edit, or print a graphic image, because all graphics images are composed of data that is much different from standard ASCII characters your word processor or text-viewing utility can read. Image files contain data that specifies which individual pixels (dots on your screen) to turn on or off, the intensity of illuminated pixels, and the color(s) each pixel should display. Hundreds of thousands of bits of data are required to specify one screenful of 640 × 480 VGA graphics. When printing a graphics image, all of this information must be translated into black-and-white dots

14

that a dot-matrix or laser printer can print. Clearly, specialized software is needed.

VPIC v6.0 is an excellent graphic file *viewing* utility for beginners and experienced users who only want to display graphics files and convert one graphics format to another; VPIC does not allow editing of images. It is easily configured for a variety of video adapters, allowing you to take full advantage of your monitor's highest resolution, memory, and other features. VPIC can convert graphics files from one format to another; conversion and viewing capabilities include GIF, CUT (Dr. Halo), LBM or IFF (Deluxe Paint), MAC (Macintosh, display only), PIC (Pictor/PC Paint), PCX (Zsoft), Targa, and Microsoft Windows BMP formats.

Graphics Workshop v6.1 allows editing, as well as viewing image files, and supports even more graphics formats than VPIC. Figure 14-11 shows a list of supported formats. GWS, as Graphics Workshop is called, is much more powerful than VPIC, but more challenging to learn. GWS lets you crop (trim), reduce, enlarge, rotate, and reverse images. You can also *dither* color images to translate them into grayscale black-and-white images for printing on monocolor printers. GWS supports a variety of printers and plotters, including color PostScript laser and inkjet printers. If you have an external scanner, GWS will accept its input and let you edit your own collection of image files.

Huge graphics files can take a long time to download, even at 9600 or 14,400 bps. It is very frustrating to spend five, ten, fifteen or more minutes downloading a large GIF image, only to discover that it is not what you thought it was, or that the file is corrupted and unusable.

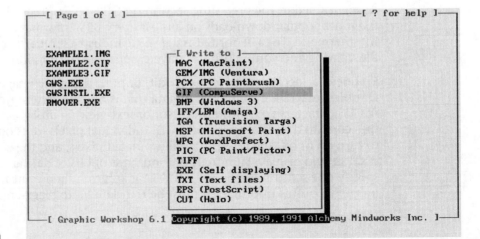

Graphics Workshop can edit or convert many image formats

Figure 14-11.

SHOWGIF v5.5 is an *online* viewing utility that lets you see a GIF image as it is downloaded and abort the download if you do not like what you see. SHOWGIF is a memory-resident (TSR) program that coexists with your terminal program in RAM. It monitors incoming data from your modem, and detects the unique file header that identifies a GIF file. While your terminal program stores the file on disk, SHOWGIF displays the image to your screen. The program automatically detects the type of video adapter you have and displays files in the highest possible resolution. If you do not like what you see, just press the (Esc) key to abort both the download and the display.

HINT: Aborting your terminal program's download function often will *not* force the remote modem to stop sending a file; your screen will rapidly fill up with garbage characters. Generally, you can stop this runaway display by pressing the (Ctrl)-(X) key combination three or four times; this tells the remote computer to abort its file transfer and return you to the regular menus.

SHOWGIF can also be used as an offline GIF-viewing utility like VPIC, and in many cases displays files faster than VPIC. SHOWGIF is for display only; you cannot edit files with it, as you can with Graphics Workshop. But you can copy, move, and delete files. You can also tag a number of files, and SHOWGIF will display them one after another in slide-show fashion. Figure 14-12 shows the options available in SHOWGIF's interactive (offline) mode.

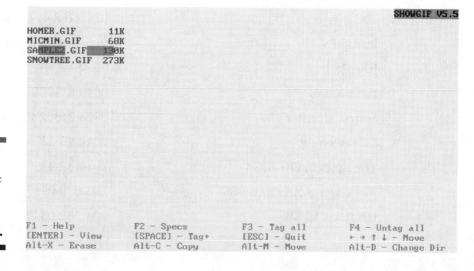

SHOWGIF offline interactive GIF viewing options
Figure 14-12.

14

Where to Find the Best in Shareware

Your author is indebted to the following BBS operators for many of the helpful shareware programs described in this chapter:

✦ The File Bank: 303-534-4646, Denver, Colorado

✦ Aquila BBS: 708-820-8365, Chicago, Illinois

✦ Nautilus Commercial Data Systems: 316-365-7631, Iola, Kansas

In addition to these outstanding megaBBSs, the ASP's (Association of Shareware Professionals) list of authorized distribution BBSs will help you find the latest versions of the highest quality shareware. As of May 30, 1993, 387 BBSs in the U. S. and overseas carried ASP members' shareware; see the following table to find one near you. The latest updated list of ASP distribution BBSs can always be found on the following online services:

✦ CompuServe SHAREWARE forum, Library 2 (filename ASPBBS.ZIP)

✦ RoadHouse BBS: 317-784-2147

✦ East Bay X-Change: 803-556-7485

✦ Collector's Edition 214-351-9859

✦ Boardwatch BBS 303-973-4222

Here is a list of some names and phone numbers of ASP bulletin boards, ordered by area code:

ASP BBS Name	BBS Phone
Media Concept BBS	011 32 411300
IDC BBS	011-3258-421-963
Icaro BBS	011-34-1-519-4645
JIX BBS	06 351-6074
Paramount	0843 851722
Softels Monster BBS	0923 213373
Evergreen BBS	201-398-2373
The Bytes 'n Bits BBS	201-437-4355
The Cygnus X-I Opus BBS	203-620-0757
Hh Info-Net BBS	203-738-0342

ASP BBS Name	BBS Phone
The B.I.B.S. System	205-271-5385
Take-A-Byte	205-553-9952
Bluestarr BBS	205-637-9448
Maxnet BBS	205-943-7530
F1 Computing BBS	206-338-2078
PCpulse	206-377-8508
Sales Automation Success!	206-392-8943
Ten Forward	206-452-7681
The Hotline PCboard	206-644-1882
501 Wildcat Plaza	206-720-4187
The Sceptic Tank	206-754-4878
Bits N'bytes BBS	207-873-1937
Stingray, Stingray II	209-434-4215
Ameriserve	212-876-5885
The Red Phone Information Sys	212-924-1138
Thundervolts BBS	213-225-5474
Lapalma Communictions	213-865-7374
The Westside	213-933-4050
The Modems Delight BBS	213-944-1221
JR's Graphics	214-235-1004
Collector's Edition	214-351-9859
Byte Back!	214-361-6756
DFW Programmers' Exchange	214-398-3112
Private Eye's BBS	214-475-8708
Two Ravens BBS	214-618-9578
Puss N Boots	214-641-1822
BBS America	214-680-3406

14

ASP BBS Name	BBS Phone
U.T. Dallas Undergraduate	214-690-2168
Embedded	214-727-2610
The Seeker's Place	215-237-1281
Del Ches Systems BBS	215-363-6625
The Glass Menagerie Ii	215-376-1819
DSC BBS	215-443-9434
Logon: Philadelphia, Inc.	215-572-8240
The Round Table BBS	215-678-0818
Dreamline II BBS	215-721-7039
The Storm Front BBS	215-788-4662
The Newtown Express Inc.	215-860-9724
PC-Ohio	216-381-3320
The Odyssey BBS	216-527-2186
Lecar BBS	216-532-2122
The G-Net BBS	216-782-6135
Merrifield PC BBS	218-829-6340
The Bertha BBS	218-924-2060
Surreal BBS	219-262-9371
Lighthouse BBS	219-464-2455
Geofract BBS	219-484-9740
Hollywood News/Info System	301-373-3530
RRR	301-464-1372
Capitol Area Network	301-499-4671
Hug & Lincoln Software	301-733-6456
CBUG BBS	301-750-1253
Technical Information & Freeware	301-926-4367
Alternatives Plus, Inc.	302-328-0381

ASP BBS Name	BBS Phone
DTEL	302-739-2818
George's Computer Room BBS	303-344-9547
Valuecomm BBS	303-388-0336
The File Bank, Inc.	303-534-4646
The Circuit Board	303-666-0302
The Global-Link Network BBS	303-680-4563
The Graphics Edge	303-795-9583
Boardwatch Magazine BBS	303-973-4222
The Cat Eye	304-592-3390
Pav's Place	304-725-8709
Mindless Ones BBS	304-748-0491
Who Knows BBS	305-383-7717
The Wild Thing	305-587-3496
The Miami PC Users Group	305-680-9481
Corsair Online	309-925-5916
Tess	31-30-522171
Specta Graphix BBS	310-532-0278
Sleepy Hollow	310-859-9334
Online Resource	312-631-7191
The Crossroads BBS	312-743-5439
Gateway Online	313-297-5571
The Firebox Express	313-588-0815
Logic Board Amiga BBS	313-659-9861
HAL 9000 BBS	313-663-4173
Techno-Babble	313-737-2912
Toledo's TBBS	313-854-6001
WSMR-Simtel20.Army.Mil	313-885-3956

14

ASP BBS Name	BBS Phone
Starview BBS	314-243-0227
Express Shareware Rpt.	314-256-0507
Charlie's BBS	314-442-6023
Nite-Air BBS System	315-339-8831
Excalibur Systems Network	315-736-3792
A.C.S. BBS	316-251-2761
Hanger 18	316-251-7460
The Mother Board BBS	316-284-2421
The Linker BBS	316-321-5933
ClassiComputerFieds	317-359-5199
JB's BBS	317-395-8203
The Roadhouse BBS	317-784-2147
Portal To Infinity	317-887-6043
The Dataexchange BBS	318-239-2122
PUMA Wildcat!	318-443-1065
Ultra BBS HQ & Support	318-487-0800
The Board Room BBS	319-927-3233
Hermes Center BBS	331 69007672
Hawk's Castle	344 411621
Skylab BBS	351 1 7269042
Cats-BBS	351 1-352 64 22
B-Link BBS	351-1-4919755
The Mail House BBS	351-19889047
Infonet Services	353-21-892582
ABM-BBS	38 61 218-663
Prime Cut BBS	401-334-3096
Hawg Wild! BBS, Inc.	402-493-2737

ASP BBS Name	BBS Phone
The Mages Inn	402-734-4748
T-8000 Information System	403-246-4487
Gorre & Daphetid BBS	403-280-9900
Action Net	403-346-7179
Malum Information Network	403-473-8875
Express Net	404-410-9139
The King's Palace	404-781-8435
COM1 Atlanta-Atlanta PCUG	404-808-4699
Thompson Towers BBS	404-941-0746
Positive I.D.	405-226-2223
OKC-PCUG	405-348-9810
The Red Baron's BBS	405-454-6551
PC-Montana BBS	406-284-3120
$Ensible $Oftware BBS	407-298-5830
Jupiter BBS	407-575-3853
The Black Cauldron	407-699-6613
The Fabulous BBS	407-834-6466
Windchimes BBS	407-881-9025
The Key Info System	407-951-1900
Globalnet	408-439-9367
The Motherboard III	409-539-2939
Housenet BBS	410-745-2037
Rosedale Data Line	410-866-1755
Magnus Computing BBS	410-893-4786
Quad-Tech Systems BBS	412-262-4794
JBJ Systems PC Board BBS	412-341-9323
MetroPitt BBS	412-487-9223

14

ASP BBS Name	BBS Phone
The Dew Drop Inn	412-854-0619
Springfield Public Access BBS	413-536-4365
Sharpenit! RBBS	413-786-4706
The File-Cache BBS	414-545-8545
Back Alley BBS	414-722-4774
Exec-PC	414-789-4210
Space BBS	415-323-4193
Random Walk Investment BBS	416-274-2381
Techline	416-332-4831
Alpha City BBS	416-579-6302
Otb Communication System	416-844-2483
The Computer Matrix	417-862-8910
The Menagerie BBS	419-935-0245
Globe	43 524265265
The BIXbox	44 0 634-200931
The Board! BBS	44 222 541688
The Shareware Support BBS	44 442 890303
Bath BBS	44-225-840060/70
Buller BBS	46-431-70909
The MakerBBS	4611 125248
Maus Mk	49 237114490
The Silverado	49 6221 767992
Kurpfalz BBS	49-6233-55087
Conway PC Users Group BBS	501-329-7227
Cindy And Eddie's BBS	501-942-4047
Arkansas River Valley	501-968-1931
National Data Exchange	502-942-2848

ASP BBS Name	BBS Phone
Electronic Publishing Service	503-624-4966
Random Access Information Netw	503-695-3250
ECCO Com...	503-775-6099
Southern On-Line Services, Inc	504-356-7090
Southern Star BBS	504-885-5928
The Garbage Dump	505-294-5675
The Albuquerque ROS	505-299-5974
Indigo	505-326-2436
Construction Net #6	505-662-0659
The Eagle's Talon	507-285-9639
PC-Profile	507-288-6347
PC-Monitor	507-373-1100
Crystal Mountain BBS	508-249-2156
Nordic Enterprises EDMS	508-356-1767
Software Creations	508-365-2359
Computer Confident	508-528-2295
Xevious BBS	508-875-3618
The Openwindow BBS	508-927-7224
Xanadu BBS	508-995-9876
Legal Ease BBS	509-326-3238
One Stop PCboard	509-943-0211
Turning Point Information Svc	512-219-7828
CCAT	512-242-2206
Computer Data Services BBS	512-887-0787
Multisystem TBBS	513-231-7013
Totoche BBS	514-326-8363
Computer Support Hot-Line	515-246-1353

14

ASP BBS Name	BBS Phone
L.I.N.E.	516-261-9701
America's Suggestion Box	516-471-8625
SOM Premium Info Network	516-536-8723
Time Slice BBS	516-981-1264
Law & Order BBS	517-263-0273
PJ Systems	517-451-2072
Wolverine	517-631-3471
JAPCUG	517-789-7556
Delight The Customer BBS	517-797-3740
The Times	518-452-4757
Knightec BBS	519-940-0007
Psychobabble	601-332-9453
BTB Fun Ware BBS	602-494-7080
The Nor'easter Premimum BBS	603-432-6711
Compuspec	604-479-0418
AIS Multiline	604-489-4206
Cyberstore Online	604-526-3376
Deep Cove BBS	604-536-5885
Bored Games BBS	605-692-2379
The Prof-BBS	606-269-1565
The Play House BBS	607-796-9078
Jade	608-757-3000
It's All Rock 'n Roll	609-252-0260
The Casino Bulletin Board	609-561-3377
The Radio Wave BBS	609-764-0812
NJ Computer Connection	609-895-0398
War On Virus BBS	612-255-5981

ASP BBS Name	BBS Phone
Shareware Solutions Inc	612-557-9764
Azcad BBS	613-481-6873
X-Connections BBS	613-748-9702
KanataCAD BBS	613-831-1449
The Wizard's Gate BBS	614-224-1635
Vicom Information Service	614-775-7083
The Lebanon Link	615-399-0707
Skyboard BBS	615-623-8203
The Bobcat BBS System	615-738-2509
The Dartboard BBS	615-885-3529
The 8-Bit Corner	616-722-0050
The Custom Computer Shop	616-722-2356
The Evans BBS	616-754-6180
Channel 1 Communications	617-354-3230
Abdex	617-665-0048
Argus Computerized Exchange	617-862-9373
The White Zone BBS	617-969-3138
The Omega Line	618-392-4607
[Parameters]Informationservice	618-549-8448
Pacific Rim Information	619-278-7361
Lakeside Wildcat! BBS	619-390-7328
Mushin BBS	619-452-8137
Diskoveries Online!	619-482-0972
Classified Connection	619-566-7347
The File Bank	619-728-4318
Tech Pro BBS	619-755-7357
Dragnet BBS	619-940-1985

14

ASP BBS Name	BBS Phone
The Cutting Edge BBS	619-947-5951
City Lites	701-772-5399
Charleston Communications Inc.	702-383-9939
Quicksilver	702-384-8503
Vegas Lights BBS	702-433-7940
Infospan BBS	702-474-7370
The Elusive Diamond	703-323-6423
GLIB	703-578-4542
The Break RBBS <East>	703-680-9269
The Looking Glass	703-823-1162
S7S Support BBS	703-949-4464
The Big Byte	704-279-2295
The Mind's Eye	704-322-1681
The Grapevine	707-257-2338
Uncle Bob's BBS	708-265-0698
Vampire's Lair	708-268-1245
The Cess Pool BBS	708-352-9231
Maranatha!	708-628-0330
Com-One	708-717-9370
Turbosof BBS	708-778-8620
Chicago Syslink	708-795-4442
Uncle Wally's Place	713-334-1136
Back To BASIC	713-470-8844
The Atomic Cafe BBS	713-530-8875
Software Expressions BBS	713-541-3910
Micro Archives	713-590-6267
Airboat Online	713-855-6724

ASP BBS Name	BBS Phone
The CAD BBS	714-364-1633
The Cutting Board	714-493-1006
The Kandy Shack	714-636-2667
U R Here	715-344-8786
The Point BBS	715-345-1327
Rapid River BBS	715-435-3855
The Twilight Zone	715-652-2758
The Byzantine Empire BBS	715-848-2833
PC-Cubed	716-723-8489
Pier 1 Exchange	716-875-0283
Pennsylvania Online!	717-657-8699
Apartment 2	718-347-1075
Jims' PC Paradise	718-458-0502
Mega-Source	718-545-3990
Systematic BBS	718-716-6198
The Consultant BBS	718-837-3236
DClipboard BBS	718-962-2403
Attard Communications	800-638-8369
Genie IBM R/T	800-638-9636
Novalink	800-937-7644
Rocky Mountain Software	801-963-8721
The Privy Ledged BBS	801-966-6270
East Bay X-Change	803-853-6687
Compu-Educare	803-873-1030
Crossroads, BBS	803-957-7077
Intercity BBS	804-353-4160
Club PC BBS	804-357-0357

14

ASP BBS Name	BBS Phone
Servant Of The Lord	804-590-2161
The Richmond Connection BBS	804-740-1364
The Blue Ridge Express	804-790-1675
Virginia Data Exchange	804-877-3562
The V.I.N.E. BBS	804-978-4134
The Grinder	805-583-5833
The Rosedale BBS	805-589-3715
The Seaside	805-964-4766
The Computer Station BBS	808-247-7328
The Wall Street Connection	808-521-4356
P & A BBS	81 425-46-9144
Ya! WeBeCAD!	812-428-3870
Digicom BBS	812-479-1310
EVSC BBS	812-985-7823
Mercury Opus	813-321-0734
Files America	813-349-0355
Software Plus	813-653-4892
Action-Link Systems	813-747-9295
The Linkup BBS	813-748-3983
R.B. Enterprises	813-748-5380
Studio PC BBS	813-862-8850
Gallifrey BBS	813-885-6043
The Southeast Data Link	813-954-DATA
At The Giffer's	813-969-2956
The Bad Attitude BBS!	814-456-6209
The Resting Place BBS	815-786-6240
Squirrel's Nest	815-795-6371

ASP BBS Name	BBS Phone
The Goose's Nest	816-221-6378
The Infomall	817-540-5419
The Board	818-366-8874
Inter-BBS	818-792-0419
The Ledge PCboard	818-896-4015
KBTC BBS	818-967-0701
Chatterbox! BBS	818-995-6959
Synapse BBS	819-561-4321
Phone Magazine	852 475-2772
Ilink Information Service	852-770-7611
SSC BBS	886-2 366-0101
Daemonworld BBS	886-2 703-5133
ATAB BBS	902-435-0751
Leroy's Domain BBS	902-679-6443
The Pooltable 2	904-260-2394
Dr. Sned's RBBS-In-A-Box	904-325-6558
Time Slice	904-334-4798
Wingit	904-386-8693
The Toy Shop-PC BBS	904-688-9124
The Hobbit Hole BBS	904-763-5165
The Northern Exchange BBS	907-479-3262
Computer Junction	908-354-6979
Eagle Command	908-446-0612
Data-Base BBS	908-735-2180
The After Hours BBS	909-597-3004
Attention To Details BBS	909-681-6221
The Library! BBS	909-780-6365

14

ASP BBS Name	BBS Phone
The Flash Point BBS	909-949-6238
Hubert Middle School	912-651-7232
Computer Users Exchange (CUE)	913-267-1903
<<Prism BBS	914-344-0350
Hudson Valley BBS	914-876-1450
24th Street Exchange	916-451-7179
The Cheshire Cat	916-542-3088
The Black Gold BBS	918-272-7779
Access America	918-747-2542
The Cannon Cocker	919-326-7839
The Pet Shop	919-497-2963
The Oracle BBS	919-675-3371
Seascape! BBS	919-726-9364
The Backdoor TBBS	919-799-0923
The Treasure Chest	919-922-1047

CHAPTER

15

MICROSOFT WINDOWS AND MODEMS

While Chapter 4 briefly touched on Microsoft Windows terminal programs, this chapter goes into much greater detail about the hardware, software, and performance considerations of using modems with Windows. Some of the information in this chapter can be found deep in the Windows user manuals, but much of it is hard-won experience passed on by word of mouth (or word of modem) among Windows users.

255

Windows promises the ultimate in telecomputing convenience. In theory, you should be able to

✦ Run multiple online sessions in separate windows, collecting and answering your e-mail, uploading and downloading files simultaneously, and receiving a fax in yet another window

✦ Transfer large files in the background while working on a spreadsheet, word processor document, or other application in the foreground

✦ Operate a multiline BBS with high-speed modems, using the same computer on which you perform your personal work

Reality falls a little short of these ideals for all but the most well-equipped and sophisticated power users. You would need an 80486 PC, equipped with about 16M of RAM, a high-performance disk cache, and buffered serial ports for all modems in order to achieve the multitasking productivity described in the preceding list. Most users do not have that kind of money.

If you own a PC of middling power (80386-33Mhz, 4 to 8Mb of RAM), the best you can expect is to run one or two MS-DOS applications in the background, while working on another program in the foreground. This chapter will help you achieve that realistic level of performance. This chapter will also help you make the best compromise between performance and cost that you can, using inexpensive shareware Windows programs and optimizing the way DOS applications run.

Understanding Windows Multitasking

Windows needs at least an 80386-based PC in order to work its *multitasking* magic, which allows more than one program to be actively processing data at any given time. The "magic" is actually a very good illusion; it only seems like multiple programs are running at the same time. Multiple programs actually take turns at using the PC's processor, but they take turns so fast that each program appears to be active constantly.

Windows allocates tiny bits of processor time—called *timeslices*—to each program in turn. A given program does as much work as it can in the tiny bit of time Windows gives it access to the PC's resources; then the program freezes in place until its turn comes around again. Timeslicing works fine as long as there are not too many programs taking turns, and each of them can finish a complete task (such as assembling an 8-bit data packet) in the amount of time allocated to it by Windows before pausing to await the next turn.

Windows need not be exactly even-handed in allocating timeslices to several applications. The *PIF Editor* in Windows' Main Program Group lets you control precisely how much priority (how many consecutive timeslices) is

15

given to an application when it is operating in background or foreground mode. These options can be set from the PIF Editor's Advanced screen, shown here in Figure 15-1.

Properly allocating timeslices and system resources is the key to getting modem-based programs to run well in background mode under Windows. If you are not thoroughly familiar with the PIF Editor and priority allocation considerations, read the chapter on PIF Editor in your *Microsoft Windows User's Guide* before continuing with this chapter.

Optimizing Windows for Use with Modems

Windows' time-slicing method of allocating system resources demands special attention when setting up modem-based applications. Unlike a spreadsheet recalculation or a database search, a telecommunications session is extremely time sensitive. If too little system resources are allocated for background use by a telecomm program, the program can lose characters, abort downloads, or drop carrier and disconnect.

Telecomm programs should be assigned relatively high background priorities when you set up their PIFs. Remember that background priority values are relative: a priority of 200 may be low compared to the 500 you have assigned to your spreadsheet. Review all existing background priority values in other PIFs and set the telecomm program's to a substantially higher value.

There will be noticeable slowdown in foreground tasks as a result of giving a high priority to telecomm programs running in the background. Don't compensate by setting the foreground priority to 100 percent, or you will rob the telecomm program of the power it needs to run in the background.

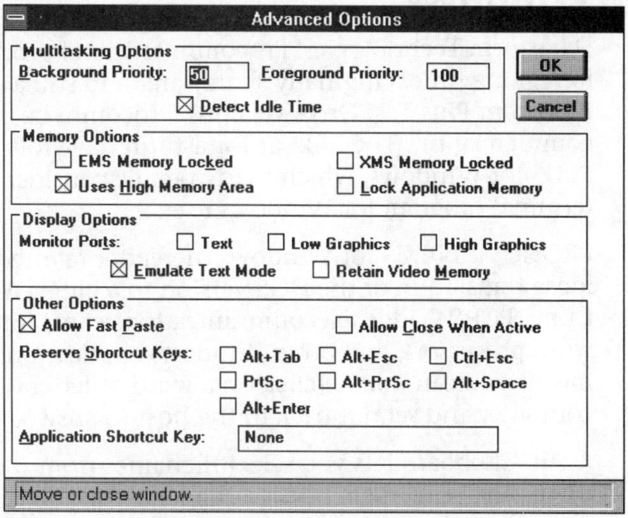

Windows' PIF
Editor
Advanced
options screen
Figure 15-1.

TIP: Telecomm programs don't need as much background priority to keep up with 2400 bps modems as they need for 9600 or 14,400 bps modems. Buffered serial ports are essential for effective background use of high-speed modems to avoid losing data while the telecomm program awaits its next timeslice.

Running telecomm programs in Windows' Enhanced mode can result in loss of some characters, even in foreground sessions. Add this line to the [386Enh] section of Windows' SYSTEM.INI file:

```
COM#BUFFER=2048
```

where # is the COM port number you are using (COM1, COM2, and so on). This increases the buffer size on your communications port from the usual 128 characters to a more forgiving 2,048 characters.

Fax modems that use *CAS (Communications Application Specification)* software drivers will cut down on serial port activity, improve overall system performance, and open up the widest range of Windows software and options to fax users. CAS driver software facilitates communications among the computer, the operating environment, and the fax hardware. The fax circuitry of a CAS board won't even need to use a COM port address, so the modem's COM port address can be used by other devices even while receive-fax software is loaded. The data functions of the modem will still need a COM port access.

Terminal Software: PROCOMM PLUS for Windows

Datastorm Technologies' Procomm terminal program has been around for a long, long time. Originally shareware (and still available as shareware in its Procomm Plus Test Drive version), Procomm became a shrink-wrapped commercial hit. The folks at Datastorm have followed up with PROCOMM PLUS for Windows, which many people consider the best all-around terminal program for Windows users.

PROCOMM PLUS for Windows (hereafter referred to as PCP/W) is not just a loose translation of the DOS version to a glitzy Windows interface. For one thing, PCP/W adds telecommunications capability to Windows spreadsheets, word processors, and other Windows applications. Extended mouse support means you can double-click on a word or letter displayed by a remote computer and send it back to the host to answer a screen prompt.

A File Clipboard lets you select filenames from the terminal screen, store them, and send them back to the host one at a time or in a batch. This means you do not have to type in filenames to download files.

15

PCP/W can be shrunk to an icon, reducing the amount of system resources it uses while performing automatic routines, such as scripts and file transfers. When transferring a file, the icon displays the amount of time remaining until the end of the transfer.

An online GIF file viewer is built into PCP/W; like the standalone program SHOWGIF described in Chapter 14, this viewer displays a GIF image as it is downloaded, so you can abort an unwanted download before it ends. The viewer can also be used offline, to examine your collection of GIFs.

The script language that accompanies PCP/W is called ASPECT, and it too is custom tailored for Windows. Scripts can include dialog boxes, bitmaps, metafiles, icons, list boxes, pushbuttons, and other tools familiar to Windows users and programmers. The included host program that turns PCP/W into a mini-BBS is written in ASPECT, and can be modified to suit your needs.

Installing PROCOMM PLUS for Windows

PCP/W comes on three disks; installation is a simple matter of running the INSTALL.EXE utility from Windows' File/Run option in Program Manager. INSTALL suggests directory names for the various parts of PCP/W, and allows you to edit them before continuing, as shown in Figure 15-2.

After creating directories and copying files to them, INSTALL presents you with an elegantly simplified terminal options selection menu, as shown in Figure 15-3. There are 34 terminal types and ten file-transfer protocols from which to choose.

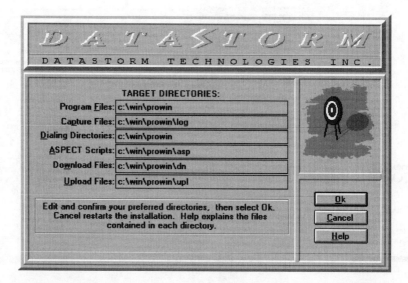

PROCOMM PLUS for Windows' installation dialog box
Figure 15-2.

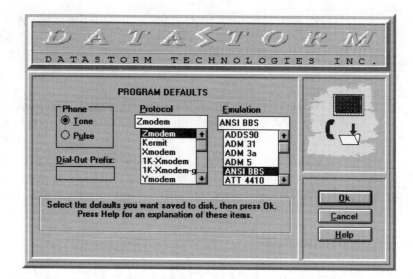

PROCOMM
PLUS for
Windows'
terminal
options
Figure 15-3.

If it is possible to go overboard in user-friendliness, PCP/W does so by offering over 200 different predefined modem configuration profiles. Fortunately, they are logically organized into two tiers; first you choose a manufacturer; then a second screen displays a list of models from which to choose, as shown in Figure 15-4.

After this simple installation procedure, PCP/W creates its own program group in Windows. The terminal program is activated by double-clicking the PCPLUS/Win icon shown in Figure 15-5.

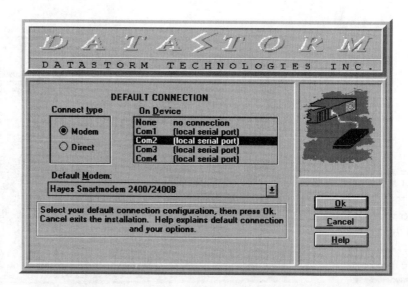

PROCOMM
PLUS for
Windows' 200
modem picklist
Figure 15-4.

15

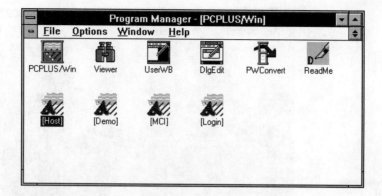

PROCOMM
PLUS for
Windows'
program group
Figure 15-5.

The several icons showing a large letter A are ASPECT script files, which can be launched directly from the program group screen. The script icons shown in Figure 15-5 perform the following tasks:

✦ *Host* Starts up PCP/W and configures it in host mode

✦ *Demo* Takes you through an offline demonstration of PCP/W

✦ *MCI* Logs on to MCI Mail and retrieves and delivers mail automatically

✦ *Login* Records your login procedures for a particular online service in an ASPECT script

Customizing PROCOMM PLUS for Windows

When you first start PCP/W in terminal mode, it displays a terminal window that uses a small, hard-to-read font and does not take full advantage of the space available on most monitors. The terminal window and the font can be enlarged by following these steps:

1. Double-click on the Windows menu bar option (shown in Figure 15-6)
2. Select Setup
3. Highlight the terminal type you use, such as ANSI/BBS
4. Select "Advanced" from the Setup menu bar
5. Select Font from the following menu
6. Set the default font to PCPlus SS, 15-point type
7. Select File from the Setup menu and save these settings

If it seems like a lot of trouble to set what should have been default settings, you might want to call Datastorm and tell them about it. You might as well use PCP/W to do it and see how easy it is to use this program.

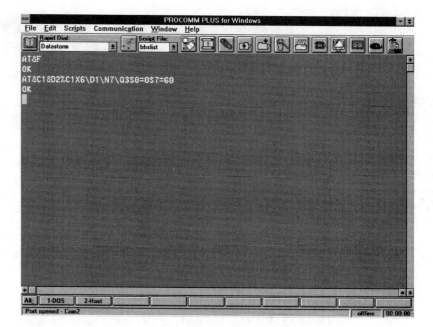

Terminal
mode display
of
PROCOMM
PLUS for
Windows
Figure 15-6.

Using PROCOMM PLUS for Windows

Figure 15-6 shows PCP/W's terminal-mode screen. In the upper-left corner of the screen, on the menu bar, is an open Yellow Pages book icon, which provides access to your dialing directory. Creating entries in the dialing directory is a rather ordinary process (described back in Chapter 5), but what you can do with the Rapid Dial option right next to the icon is not. Selecting Rapid Dial drops a pick list of your favorite online haunts. Double-click on a name, and PCP/W logs you on.

The running-man icon runs the script shown in the next drop-down window. Scripts are selected just like Rapid Dial entries. The script shown in Figure 15-6, BBSLIST, is a good example of what PCP/W's script language can do. It reads a text file containing the USBBS list, a national directory of Bulletin Board Systems updated each month. The script prompts you to enter an area code or state, and searches the USBBS list for BBSs in a particular region. You can highlight any or all of the search results and automatically add these BBSs to your dialing directory.

The folks at Datastorm do not tell you where to call to get a copy of the USBBS list, but your author is a kinder soul. Log on to any of the following primary distribution systems:

15

Log on to any
of these BBSs
where you can
download the
USBBS list.

BBS	Phone	State	City
Computer Connections	202-547-2008	DC	Washington
SPACE	415-323-4193	CA	Menlo Park
Darwin	301-251-9206	MD	Gaithersburg
Red Wheelbarrow	512-443-5441	TX	Austin
Toad Hall	415-595-2427	CA	San Carlos
VOR	707-778-8944	CA	Petaluma
YCS	813-842-8099	FL	Hudson (9600+ ONLY)
Blue Lake	503-656-9790	OR	West Linn
Virginia Connection	703-648-1841	VA	Reston
CompuServe	IBMBBS (Lib 7)		

Continuing from the Script drop-down menu to the right, the other icons on
the menu bar in Figure 15-6 activate the following functions:

✦ Setup allows you to change the current terminal emulation, file-transfer
  protocol, port settings, and other operating variables.

✦ Scrollback/Pause halts the display of characters in the terminal window,
  and lets you back up (scroll back) as many as 31 pages to review what
  has crossed your screen.

✦ File Clipboard is used to simplify selection of files to download from a
  remote computer. Just point and click on a filename (or several
  filenames) in the terminal window. Later, the File Clipboard feeds these
  names one at a time or in a batch to the remote computer's "download
  which file(s)?" prompt.

✦ Uploading and downloading are triggered by the next two icons (file
  folders with up and down arrows). Files to be uploaded are selected from
  a pick list that appears when you click on the upload icon. You can also
  change the file-transfer protocol from the upload-pick-list screen. Most
  people will use the autodownloading Zmodem protocol, and might
  never see the downloading protocol-selection screen. But it is there if
  you need to select another protocol.

✦ The butterfly net is not for those moments when you think you are
  going modem-mad; it represents Capture mode, which copies to a disk
  file everything that scrolls through the terminal window.

♦ The Printer icon routes output from the terminal window to your printer. Usually, this is not a good idea, since most printers are much slower than terminal displays. Windows' Print Spooler can be enabled to hold data until the printer can catch up, but most people capture to disk, edit the resulting text file, and then print what they need.

♦ The red telephone icon disconnects your modem phone call, equivalent to the AT H0 command.

♦ The next icon, a rather ambiguous computer monitor, clears the terminal window screen.

♦ The next two icons are used together. The cassette-tape icon starts recording your keystrokes in a script file. When you finish recording, you must save and compile the script by clicking on this icon and following the prompts. The following icon, a phonograph-record, displays a list of named scripts from which you choose one to play back.

♦ The last icon is a toolkit for creating, editing, saving, and deleting scripts.

Host Mode in PROCOMM PLUS for Windows

PCP/W includes a host mode (mini-BBS) program written in the ASPECT script language. Selecting the Host icon from the program group starts up PCP/W in host mode, or you can switch from terminal to host mode by clicking on the Host button found along the bottom edge of the terminal window (shown in Figure 15-6).

Host mode includes standard features such as up-/downloading, e-mail, chat with the sysop, and online help. Three classes of callers are supported: limited, normal, and privileged. Limited callers cannot download files, but can list available files. Privileged callers have access to remote control features in addition to the four basic functions. A privileged caller can abort host mode and return to the terminal window. From there, the caller can transfer files to and from any directory on your hard disk. Normal callers can only access the Upload and Download directories specified in the host mode's configuration.

Using PROCOMM PLUS for Windows as a DDE Server

One of the unique and intriguing capabilities of PCP/W is that it automatically functions as a *Dynamic Data Exchange* (DDE) server for other Windows applications. DDE lets two programs update each other's information. An Excel spreadsheet, for example, can contain a cell whose value changes, depending on the value of a cell in another spreadsheet; a profit/loss statement's quarterly-revenues cell will change as revenues and expenses are entered in other, subordinate spreadsheets. Pasting a DDE Link into the P&L spreadsheet cell for "sales revenue" would automatically update that cell each time the Sales Revenue spreadsheet is changed.

PCP/W automatically processes DDE requests from other programs. These requests can be inquiries for the value(s) of any of the 40 predefined global variables in the ASPECT script language, or more complex directives to run a script and return the results of calculations.

An interesting application of DDE is an ASPECT script that calls an online financial data service (such as Dow Jones News Retrieval), downloads a file containing stock quotes, and assigns each stock's current price to a global variable. You could enter a formula in an Excel spreadsheet cell, {=PW|dow.wax!f0}, that updates that cell with the current price stored in the PCP/W variable f0. Now your Excel stock portfolio is updated every time the script DOW.WAX is run; such a script could be programmed to dial and update its data every day, hour, or even more often.

Modem Shareware for Windows

Many of the MS-DOS shareware utilities discussed in Chapter 14 have their counterparts in the world of Windows. Generally speaking, true Windows applications are preferable to running DOS applications under Windows. Well-written Windows software will cooperate better with other applications when it comes to sharing system resources and timeslices, causing fewer system lockups and running better in background mode. True Windows programs also take advantage of Windows features such as drag-and-drop, DDE, Clipboard cut-and-paste, and so on.

Graphics Workshop for Windows

Graphics Workshop, the image file editor described in Chapter 14, comes in both DOS and Windows versions. The Windows version relies on icons and pushbuttons, instead of filename pick lists and function keys, as shown in Figure 15-7. GWS/Win is a more natural environment for editing graphic images. Cropping an image, for example, is more intuitive and precise than in the MS-DOS version. GWS/Win also supports more image formats when reading or converting image files.

WinZIP: Archive Management

If you download archived files, or use archiving to maintain backup files, you will love working with *WinZIP v4.0*. This archive manager, file viewer, and DOS shell combines the versatility and power of SHEZ (Chapter 14) with the easy, mouse-driven interface of Windows. When you select an archived

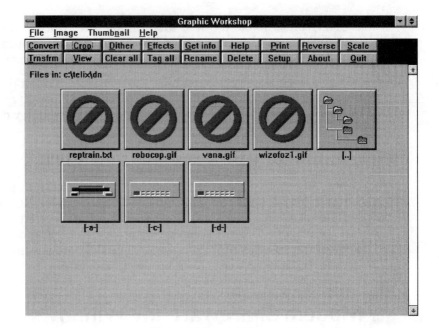

Compare
Graphics
Workshop for
Windows to
its DOS
version (Fig.
14-11)
Figure 15-7.

file (ZIP, ARC, LZH, and ARJ formats are supported), WinZIP displays its
contents in a listing much like Windows File Manager, as shown in Figure 15-8.

WinZIP treats
archived files
as File
Manager treats
normal files
Figure 15-8.

15

As with File Manager, you can click on any text file shown by WinZIP view it, using Windows Notepad, Write, or PKZIP's "extract to screen" feature, shown in Figure 15-9. This feature is extremely handy for examining program descriptions and documentation before you decompress an entire archive. Displayed text can be printed or copied to the Windows Clipboard.

WinZIP has a truly amazing feature called CheckOut. Click on CheckOut to create a temporary program group containing program item icons for all or some of the files in the archive. CheckOut extracts all of the files, assigns icons to them, and displays the Program Group shown in Figure 15-10. Now you can simply click on an icon to see how a program works, or to read a text file. No more shelling to DOS from Windows in order to test-drive shareware!

These are just a few of the extraction and viewing features built into WinZIP. This beautifully written Windows program can also create, update, and convert archives to self-extracting versions; check for viruses with the help of an external virus detector like SCAN (see Chapter 14); and even change the size and typeface of the font used to display files.

If you work with archivers and Windows, WinZIP is a must-have utility.

Microlink: Windows Terminal Shareware

Microlink v1.40A, as shown in Figure 15-11, is a good terminal program for beginners: simple, fully featured, and easy on the eye-cons (pun intended). Notice the row of modem status lights on the menu bar, a thoughtful touch for internal modem owners who wonder what's going on inside their PC's case. A built-in database of modem configuration profiles makes setting up Microlink a breeze. A good selection of file-transfer protocols is available: ASCII, several variations of Xmodem, Ymodem, Ymodem-batch, and Ymodem-G (for error-free high-speed connections), and the favorite, Zmodem.

WinZIP lets you read archived documents without extracting them

Figure 15-9.

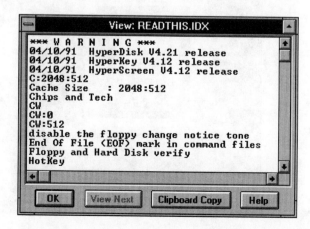

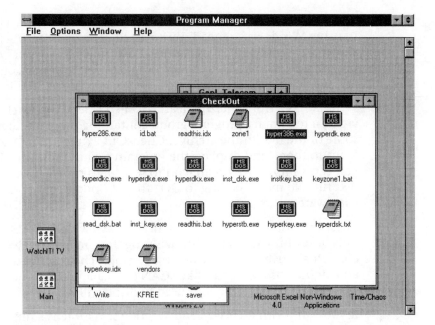

The CheckOut Program Group is automatically created from archives
Figure 15-10.

Microlink is a bit short on terminal-emulation types, supporting only ANSI, VT100, and TTY. But those three terminals probably accommodate 95

Microlink is a straightforward terminal program for beginners
Figure 15-11.

percent of the online services you are likely to encounter. Font typefaces and size can be selected from a somewhat limited list; only Windows' built-in Terminal font will properly display IBM graphics characters. There is a huge difference in size between 16 points (shown in Figure 15-11) and 18-point type, which is too large to permit 80-column display.

The latest version of Microlink can be downloaded from the author's support BBS: log on to 404-640-9225 (Roswell, GA). This is one shareware program you will want to check out.

WinModem: Modem Status Lights on Demand

Internal modem owners will appreciate this brightly colored Windows cousin of the LITES11.COM utility described in Chapter 14. WinModem v3.0 displays a small BMP image representing an external modem's front panel, complete with white (off) and red (on) status lights, as shown here:

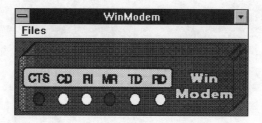

The documentation includes a good tutorial on what these lights mean.

WinModem supports COM ports 1-4. The postage-stamp sized image can be rotated from a horizontal to a vertical layout and conveniently moved to an inactive part of your terminal program's window.

Where to Find Windows Modem Shareware

Your author is indebted to Norm Henke, sysop *extraordinaire* of the enormous PC-OHIO BBS (35 lines, over 50,000 shareware files), for providing the latest versions of Microlink, WinZIP, and Graphics Workshop for Windows. Anyone looking for the latest shareware should make PC-OHIO their first stop; log on at 216-381-3320.

Two time zones west of Ohio, Frank Mahaney operates the Windows On-Line BBS, at 510-736-8355. As the name indicates, WOL specializes in Windows software; the downloadable directory of all files on the system is over 1Mb long! Frank and a team of freelance writers put out an excellent semi-monthly electronic newsletter just for Windows addicts; be sure to download the latest edition when you visit Windows On-Line.

A P P E N D I X

THE RESOURCE GUIDE

This appendix includes lists of hardware and software vendors, online services, bulletin board systems, electronic mail service providers, Internet access providers, books, magazines, and newsletters for novice and experienced modem users.

To pack more contacts into limited space, only vendor names and phone numbers are included in each category. Toll-free numbers are listed when available, followed by toll phone numbers for international and local callers.

Modem Vendors

There are over 250 modem manufacturers, ranging from Fortune 500 Intel Corp. to kitchen-table startup companies. The following table includes some of the better-known modem vendors with good reputations for quality and customer support. All BBS numbers assume communication parameters of 8-N-1 unless otherwise stated. If a vendor maintains a support BBS, its phone number is listed last.

Modem Manufacturers

Company Name	Toll-Free	Local/Int'l	Support BBS
AT&T Paradyne	800-554-4996	813-530-8276	813-532-5254
ATI Technologies		416-756-0718	416-756-4591
Cardinal Technologies		717-293-3000	717-293-3074
Computer Peripherals		805-499-5751	805-499-9646
Digicom Systems		408-262-1277	508-262-1412
GVC Technologies		201-579-3630	201-579-2380
Hayes Microcomputer		404-840-9200	404-446-6336
Image Communications	800-666-2496	919-395-6100	No BBS
Intel Corporation		503-629-7000	503-645-6275
Matron		407-695-4447	No BBS
Multi-Tech Systems		612-785-3500	612-785-9875
Practical Peripherals		805-497-4774	805-496-4445
Quadralink Technologies		416-538-0101	416-538-9999
QuickComm		408-956-8236	408-956-1358
Supra Corporation		503-967-2400	503-967-2444
Telebit Corporation		408-734-4333	408-745-3229
U.S. Robotics		708-982-5010	708-982-5092
Ven-Tel		408-436-7400	408-922-0988
ZyXel		714-693-0804	714-693-0762

Software for General Use, E-Mail, and Bulletin Board Systems

The following tables list software programs, vendors, and contact phone numbers. Each program's name is followed by one or more letters in parentheses, indicating the computer platforms supported (M=Mac, D=DOS, W=Windows). Note that some vendors support multiple platforms.

If a letter S appears in the parentheses, the software is available only as shareware. The letter T indicates a commercial product with a free test-drive or shareware version available.

General Terminal Software

The following table lists general-purpose terminal emulation programs. Terminal software is discussed in depth in Chapter 4.

Program Name	Vendor	Toll-Free	Local/Int'l	BBS
Boyan (DS)	Boyan Communications		301-805-7168	
COM-AND (DS)	Caber Software		213-439-6104	
COMMO (DS)	Fred Brucker		707-573-1065	
Crosstalk (DW)	Digital Comms. Assocs.	800-348-3221	404-442-4000	
Microphone II (MW)	Software Ventures	800-336-6477	510-644-3232	
Procomm Plus (DWT)	Datastorm Technologies		314-443-3282	314-875-0503
Qmodem Pro (DT)	Mustang Software	800-999-9619	805-395-0223	805-395-0650
Smartcom (DW)	Hayes Microcomputer		404-441-1617	404-446-6336
Telemate (DS)	White River Software			416-733-9052
Telix v3.21 (DT)	deltaComm	800-835-8000	919-460-4556	919-481-9399
Terminal Plus (W)	FutureSoft Engineering		713-496-9400	
Unicom (WS)	Data Graphics		206-932-8871	
White Knight (MS)	Freesoft Co.		412-846-2700	

Electronic Mail Software

The following table lists dedicated electronic mail programs and their vendors. These programs can be used in an inhouse network environment, on third-party e-mail service providers as discussed in Chapter 9, or for person-to-person e-mail delivery.

Program Name	Vendor	Toll-Free	Local/Int'l	BBS
cc:Mail (DW)	Lotus Development		617-577-8500	
Microsoft Mail (DW)	Microsoft Corp.		206-882-8080	206-936-6735
Da Vinci Mail (DW)	Da Vinci Systems		919-781-5924	
Personal-E Mail (DS)	AmerCom Inc.		503-246-6199	

Bulletin Board System Host Software

The following programs let you design and operate an electronic Bulletin Board System (BBS). An asterisk indicates that only a single-line version is available. The letter(s) in parentheses indicates the type of computer platform required: D=DOS, M=Macintosh, W=Windows, U=Unix.

Program Name	Vendor	Toll-Free	Local/Int'l	BBS
Falken (DT)	INFO*SHARE		703-491-5823	703-803-8000
Major, The (D)	Galacticomm	800-328-1128	305-583-5990	305-583-7808
PCBoard (DT)	Clark Development	800-356-1686	801-261-1686	801-261-8976
PowerBBS (WS)	PowerBBS	800-966-4832	607-777-5377	516-822-7396
Searchlight (DS)	Searchlight Software	800-780-5483		516-689-2566
Sapphire (DS)			514-345-9578	514-345-8654
Synchronet (DT)	Digital Dynamics		714-529-6328	714-529-9547
TBBS (D)	eSoft Inc.		303-699-6565	303-699-8222
TEAMate (U)	MMB Development	800-832-6022	310-318-1322	

Program Name	Vendor	Toll-Free	Local/Int'l	BBS
Telefinder (MS)	Spider Island Software		714-669-9260	714-730-5785
TurBoard (DT)	Software @ Work		615-756-8220	615-756-7810
WildCat! (DT)	Mustang Software	800-999-9619	805-395-0223	805-395-0650

Information Carrier Services

The following table lists some of the major online malls discussed in Chapter 8. The toll-free numbers listed are voice inquiry lines. Most of these services will provide a modem phone number for demonstrations, free trial packages, or demo disks. In many cases, you can subscribe online after test-driving a service.

Service Name	Voice Phone
CompuServe	800-848-8199
America Online	800-827-6364
GEnie	800-838-9636
BIX	800-227-2983
Delphi	800-544-4005
Prodigy	800-822-6922

Electronic Mail and Document Delivery Services

The firms in the following table provide electronic mail and modem-assisted document delivery services. See Chapter 9 for details.

Service Provider	Contact
AT&T EasyLink Services	201-331-4134
MCI Mail	800-444-6245
SprintMail	Any Sprint office
DASnet	408-559-7434

Internet Access Providers

The Internet, discussed in Chapter 10, has over 1.5 million host sites. However,it can be difficult to find one near you or one that offers the level of access you want. The vendors in the following table sell access to the Internet to individuals and corporations. Most will provide local access numbers in your area.

Vendor	Voice Phone
AterNet	703-204-8000
ANS	313-663-2482
HoloNet	510-704-0160
IDS World Network	401-885-6855
NETCOM	408-554-8649
PANIX	718-865-3768
PSInet	703-620-6651
PORTAL Communications	408-725-1580
Village Group	800-225-0750
WELL, The	415-332-4335
WORLD, The	617-739-0202

Books About Modems and Telecomputing

The following books are recommended reading for anyone interested in more information on subjects covered in *Modems Made Easy*.

Using Computer Bulletin Boards, 2nd Ed., John Hedtke, MIS Press, 1992.

Dvorak's Guide to PC Telecommunications, 2nd Ed., John Dvorak and Nick Anis, Berkeley, CA, Osborne/McGraw-Hill, 1992.

Introduction to PC Communications, Phil Becker, QUE, 1992.

The Modem Coach, Blankenhorn, Maxwell, et. al., New Riders Publishing, 1993.

Magazines and Newsletters

The online industry has grown so big and changes so fast that it has spawned its own circle of monthly and quarterly magazines and newsletters. Specialty publications can be hard to find, so we include a select list of publications for your consideration. Call the voice number to order sample copies or find out where to obtain a copy at a dealer near you.

Publication	Voice Phone
Boardwatch Magazine	303-973-6038
Making Money with Modems	913-478-3157
Online Access	312-573-1700
Shareware Magazine	800-245-6717
WIRED!	415-904-0660

Boardwatch Magazine's Readers' Choice Top 100 Bulletin Board Systems

Boardwatch Magazine has graciously given permission to reprint its 1992 list of the best bulletin board systems in North America, as determined by the people who call them. Between January 1 and July 1, 1992, over 11,000 BBS callers voted for their favorite BBS; over 1200 different BBSes were nominated.

The 1993 Readers' Choice contest was still in progress when this book went to print; it had already garnered over 15,000 votes from BBS connoisseurs as far away as the former Soviet Union. You can learn who the new winners are by calling *Boardwatch Magazine* (see Publications listings in this appendix).

#1	**Title:** Canada Remote Systems **Operator:** Neil Fleming **Location:** Mississauga, Ontario **Phone:** (416) 629-7000 **Lines:** 201 **Software:** PCBoard **Description:** Largest PCBoard in North America/30 Gb/3500 Confs/Usenet

#2	**Title:** Pleasure Dome **Operator:** Tom McKelvey **Location:** Norfolk, VA **Phone:** (804) 490-5878 **Lines:** 6 **Software:** Wildcat! **Description:** Social/adult files and discussions

#3	**Title:** Odyssey **Operator:** Michael Allen/Computer Prod. **Location:** Monrovia, CA **Phone:** (818) 358-6968 **Lines:** 128 **Software:** Major BBS **Description:** Largest multiline adult chat system in U.S.

#4

Title: PC-Ohio
Operator: Norm Henke
Location: Cleveland, OH
Phone: (216) 381-3320
Lines: 30
Software: PCBoard
Description: Shareware library with 5.2 Gb of files

#5

Title: Albuquerque ROS
Operator: Steve Fox
Location: Albuquerque, NM
Phone: (505) 299-5974
Lines: 12
Software: ROS
Description: 36,000 Files/online games/USA Today/Trade Wars

#6

Title: Micro Message Service
Operator: Mike Stroud/Paul O'Keefe
Location: Raleigh, NC
Phone: (919) 779-6674
Lines: 10
Software: TBBS
Description: Online since Oct. '92/Supports all computers/5 Gb files

#7

Title: San Diego Connection
Operator: Rich Famiglietti
Location: Spring Valley, CA
Phone: (619) 584-8456
Lines: 32
Software: DLX
Description: Adult multiline chat—social/political discussions

#8

Title: GLIB
Operator: Jon Larimore
Location: Arlington, VA
Phone: (703) 578-4542
Lines: -0-
Software: TBBS
Description: Gay/lesbian information bureau/AIDS info/news/weather

#9	**Title:** Stanford Palo Alto Comp Exch **Operator:** Owen Hawkins **Location:** Menlo Park, CA **Phone:** (415) 323-4193 **Lines:** 10 **Software:** PCBoard **Description:** SPACE—Computer industry database/50,000 shareware files

#10	**Title:** After Hours **Operator:** Conrad Ruchelman **Location:** Austin, TX **Phone:** (512) 448-3562 **Lines:** 16 **Software:** Major BBS **Description:** No information available

#11	**Title:** Zen Den Systems **Operator:** Jack Porter **Location:** Madera, CA **Phone:** (209) 675-8436 **Lines:** 1 **Software:** Wildcat! **Description:** Emphasis on film and Greenpeace/environmental issues

#12	**Title:** Lifestyle BBS **Operator:** Mark Laffer **Location:** Lake Grove, NY **Phone:** (516) 689-5390 **Lines:** 32 **Software:** Oracomm **Description:** Adult/member North American Swing Club Association

#13	**Title:** Random Access Information Net **Operator:** Janice Stevens/Greg Skinner **Location:** Cobett, OR **Phone:** (503) 695-3250 **Lines:** 16 **Software:** Wildcat! **Description:** Windows/OS/2/adult files and messages

#14	**Title:** The Garbage Dump **Operator:** Dean Kerl/Simon Clement **Location:** Albuquerque, NM **Phone:** (505) 294-5675 **Lines:** 37 **Software:** Major BBS **Description:** Largest system in Albuquerque—adult chat/multiline games

#15	**Title:** Chrysalis **Operator:** Garry Grosse **Location:** Plano, TX **Phone:** (214) 680-4337 **Lines:** 12 **Software:** TBBS **Description:** Connex Matchmaker, message and file areas

#16	**Title:** The Nashville Exchange **Operator:** Ben Cunningham **Location:** Nashville, TN **Phone:** (615) 383-0727 **Lines:** 20 **Software:** TBBS **Description:** 4 Gb files/many message areas/online games

#17	**Title:** Echo **Operator:** Stacy Horn **Location:** New York City, NY **Phone:** (212) 989-8411 **Lines:** 14 **Software:** Caucus **Description:** Unix conferencing system/call 212-255-3839 for access

#18	**Title:** Olde West **Operator:** Douglas Rhea **Location:** Bedford, TX **Phone:** (817) 572-4867 **Lines:** 3 **Software:** Phoenix **Description:** Old West theme/100 online games/bulletins

#19	**Title:** HH Infonet **Operator:** Lee Winsor **Location:** New Hartford, CT **Phone:** (203) 738-0342 **Lines:** 16 **Software:** PCBoard **Description:** Shareware library—excellent Windows file collection

#20	**Title:** Titan Software Solutions **Operator:** Clayton Manson **Location:** Pensacola, FL **Phone:** (904) 476-1270 **Lines:** 6 **Software:** Wildcat! **Description:** Adult files/games/3.2 Gb

#20	**Title:** Eagle's Nest **Operator:** Ron Olsen **Location:** Littleton, CO **Phone:** (303) 933-0701 **Lines:** 1 **Software:** QuickBBS **Description:** General user's board—files/messages/games

#22	**Title:** Aquila BBS **Operator:** Kevin Behrens/Steve Williams **Location:** Aurora, IL **Phone:** (708) 820-8344 **Lines:** 24 **Software:** PCBoard **Description:** Shareware library—excellent Windows collection/mail

#23	**Title:** Microfone Info Service **Operator:** John Kelley **Location:** Metuchen, NJ **Phone:** (908) 494-8666 **Lines:** 6 **Software:** TBBS **Description:** 7 CD-ROMS/active message areas/games/issues—5 Gb files

#24	**Title:** Modem Operated Remote Exchange **Operator:** Mel Silverman **Location:** Brooklyn, NY **Phone:** (718) 251-9346 **Lines:** 30 **Software:** TBBS **Description:** More BBS games/adult file areas/cooking
#25	**Title:** Studs BBS **Operator:** Hans Braun **Location:** San Francisco, CA **Phone:** (415) 495-2929 **Lines:** 14 **Software:** Wildcat! **Description:** Gay/homosexual issues
#26	**Title:** Metro Online **Operator:** Dave Harrison **Location:** Los Angeles, CA **Phone:** (213) 933-4050 **Lines:** 60 **Software:** Metropolis **Description:** Large file libraries/chat/mail
#26	**Title:** Multicom-4 **Operator:** Chuck Antonelli **Location:** Rochester, NY **Phone:** (716) 473-4070 **Lines:** 32 **Software:** Major BBS **Description:** Gay/lesbian/bisexual issues
#28	**Title:** ComputorEdge Online **Operator:** Ron Dippold **Location:** San Diego, CA **Phone:** (619) 573-1675 **Lines:** 8 **Software:** TBBS **Description:** Local San Diego Magazine BBS service

#29	**Title:** Channel 1 **Operator:** Brian Miller/Tess Heder **Location:** Cambridge, MA **Phone:** (617) 354-8873 **Lines:** 80 **Software:** PCBoard **Description:** Large shareware library/mail bbs

#30	**Title:** ECISD **Operator:** Jerry Cooper **Location:** Odessa, TX **Phone:** (915) 332-8128 **Lines:** 16 **Software:** TBBS **Description:** Ector County Independent School District teen chat lines

#30	**Title:** PKWare BBS **Operator:** Phil Katz **Location:** Brown Deer, WI **Phone:** (414) 354-8670 **Lines:** 4 **Software:** Random Access **Description:** Home of PKZIP archive/compression utility

#32	**Title:** Atlanta Mac Users Group **Operator:** Robert Story **Location:** Atlanta, GA **Phone:** (404) 447-0845 **Lines:** 5 **Software:** PCBoard **Description:** Macintosh files and support for local user group

#33	**Title:** Isles of Shae **Operator:** Scott Brinker **Location:** Ft. Lauderdale, FL **Phone:** (305) 321-2410 **Lines:** (unknown) **Software:** Major BBS **Description:** Multline chat/game system

#34	**Title:** Twilight Clone **Operator:** Paul Hellen **Location:** Silver Spring, MD **Phone:** (301) 946-8677 **Lines:** 19 **Software:** TBBS **Description:** Large Macintosh file area—OS/2 support
#34	**Title:** Blue Ridge Express **Operator:** Webb Blackman **Location:** Richmond, VA **Phone:** (804) 790-1675 **Lines:** 31 **Software:** RBBS **Description:** Support for Richmond area user groups
#34	**Title:** Intimate Visions **Operator:** Gary Dawson **Location:** Decatur, GA **Phone:** (404) 244-7059 **Lines:** 3 **Software:** Wildcat! **Description:** Exploring sensual awareness of our human potential
#37	**Title:** Windows Online **Operator:** Frank Mahaney **Location:** Danville, CA **Phone:** (510) 736-8343 **Lines:** 12 **Software:** PCBoard **Description:** Excellent Windows 3.*x* support and files/online newsletter
#38	**Title:** Doppler/Deep Cove **Operator:** Wayne Duval **Location:** White Rock, British Columbia **Phone:** (604) 536-5885 **Lines:** 16 **Software:** TBBS **Description:** Multiple PC Support/USA Today/Doppler Computer Centre

#39	**Title:** Index System **Operator:** Rodney Aloia **Location:** Woodstock, GA **Phone:** (404) 924-8472 **Lines:** 10 **Software:** TBBS **Description:** Multiline Chat/Atlanta BBS List/TBBS Support

A

#40	**Title:** Philadelphia Amiga Users Group **Operator:** Joe Mollica **Location:** Philadelphia, PA **Phone:** (215) 551-1485 **Lines:** 4 **Software:** Star-Net **Description:** Amiga support/files/FidoNet 273/50/runs on Amiga

#40	**Title:** S-TEK **Operator:** aka Eric Blair **Location:** Montreal, Quebec **Phone:** (514) 597-2409 **Lines:** 7 **Software:** TBBS **Description:** Gay/homosexual issues

#40	**Title:** Wolverine BBS **Operator:** Rick Rosinski **Location:** Midland, MI **Phone:** (517) 631-3481 **Lines:** 4 **Software:** Searchlight **Description:** Official BBS of the Midland Computer Club

#43	**Title:** Idiot Box **Operator:** Michael White **Location:** San Jancinto, CA **Phone:** (800) 354-2983 **Lines:** 4 **Software:** RBBS **Description:** Message board/minimal files/family oriented/serious user

#43	**Title:** Eye Contact **Operator:** Bill Montgomery **Location:** Mill Valley, CA **Phone:** (415) 703-8200 **Lines:** 32 **Software:** Oracomm **Description:** Online games and chat/1.3 Gb of files

#45	**Title:** Prime Time **Operator:** Bill Martin **Location:** Burbank, CA **Phone:** (818) 982-7271 **Lines:** 16 **Software:** Major BBS **Description:** Entertainment and online games/nationwide chat links

#45	**Title:** Digicom BBS **Operator:** Gary Barr **Location:** Evansville, IN **Phone:** (812) 479-1310 **Lines:** 3 **Software:** Remote Access **Description:** 1.7 Gb ASP approved

#45	**Title:** Radio Wave BBS **Operator:** Tyler Myers **Location:** Delran, NJ **Phone:** (609) 764-0812 **Lines:** 1 **Software:** PCBoard **Description:** Serving amateur radio operators around the world

#45	**Title:** Comm Post **Operator:** Brian Bartee **Location:** Denver, CO **Phone:** (303) 534-4501 **Lines:** 8 **Software:** TBBS **Description:** Emphasis on astronomy/star data/good files

#49	**Title:** The Source **Operator:** Chip North **Location:** Lawndale, CA **Phone:** (310) 371-3737 **Lines:** 4 **Software:** Wildcat! **Description:** File distribution system

#49	**Title:** Ghouls Lair **Operator:** Tim Pettigrew **Location:** Newtown, PA **Phone:** (215) 862-2088 **Lines:** 1 **Software:** Major BBS **Description:** General messages/games/small system

#51	**Title:** Chicago Syslink **Operator:** George Matyaszek **Location:** Berwyn, IL **Phone:** (708) 622-4442 **Lines:** 9 **Software:** TBBS **Description:** Home of Ferret Forum Echo/pet issues

#52	**Title:** Data Shack **Operator:** Judah Holstein **Location:** Eastchester, NY **Phone:** (914) 961-7032 **Lines:** 14 **Software:** TBBS/TDBS **Description:** TBBS/TDBS support—DOS/MAC/GIFS/Amiga/Adult Echos

#52	**Title:** Nix Pix Windy City **Operator:** Robert Copella **Location:** North Brook, IL **Phone:** (708) 564-1064 **Lines:** 19 **Software:** Wildcat! **Description:** Adult GIF Images

| #54 | **Title:** Higher Powered BBS
Operator: Bob Jacobson
Location: Sunnyvale, CA
Phone: (408) 737-9447
Lines: 3
Software: PCBoard
Description: General info/no games |

| #55 | **Title:** Argus Computerized Exchange
Operator: Pam Morrison
Location: Lexington, MA
Phone: (617) 674-2345
Lines: 65
Software: Major BBS
Description: Restaurant database/multiline adult chat service |

| #56 | **Title:** City Lites
Operator: John Lundell
Location: Grand Forks, ND
Phone: (701) 772-5399
Lines: 4
Software: PCBoard
Description: Support for Apogee, CHWare, and MSI software |

| #57 | **Title:** Interludes
Operator: Bill Sobel
Location: Cypress, CA
Phone: (714) 828-7092
Lines: 11
Software: DLX
Description: General-interest social chat system |

| #58 | **Title:** Hotlanta
Operator: Mike and Sheryll
Location: Roswell, GA
Phone: (404) 992-5345
Lines: 16
Software: DLX
Description: Adult multiline chat system |

| #58 | **Title:** KBBS
Operator: -0-
Location: Canoga Park, CA
Phone: (818) 886-0872
Lines: 32
Software: DLX
Description: Social networking for the 90s |

| #58 | **Title:** Data World BBS
Operator: Sean Dudley
Location: Knoxville, TN
Phone: (615) 675-6994
Lines: 9
Software: PCBoard
Description: 3.8 Gb/25,000 files/20 doors/doorway program |

| #61 | **Title:** Info Quest
Operator: Charles Stusz
Location: Carbondale, IL
Phone: (618) 453-8511
Lines: 3
Software: RBBS
Description: Computer hardware/software center catering to power users |

| #62 | **Title:** Tampa Matchmaker
Operator: Bobby Dominguez
Location: Tampa, FL
Phone: (813) 961-8665
Lines: 14
Software: Unix
Description: Matchmaker system on Unix/Usenet news groups |

| #62 | **Title:** Somerset Central BBS
Operator: Frank Petillo
Location: Somerset, NJ
Phone: (908) 940-2112
Lines: 8
Software: TBBS
Description: Computer sales/GIF images/CD-ROMS/online games |

#62	**Title:** Ask Fred's BBS **Operator:** Fred "Hardware" Martin **Location:** Boardman, OH **Phone:** (216) 783-9636 **Lines:** 24 **Software:** PCBoard **Description:** 11 Gb, featuring MIDI/games/adult image files

#62	**Title:** Binary Information Network **Operator:** George and Barbara Eppich **Location:** West New York, NJ **Phone:** (201) 617-8054 **Lines:** 4 **Software:** WIldcat! **Description:** No information available

#66	**Title:** The Drop Zone **Operator:** Mike Sanders (The Colonel) **Location:** Fairfax, VA **Phone:** (703) 425-3644 **Lines:** 16 **Software:** FALKEN **Description:** Multiline general chat service

#66	**Title:** Lambda Zone **Operator:** Toby Schneiter/Gloria La Hay **Location:** Park Ridge, IL **Phone:** (708) 827-3619 **Lines:** 6 **Software:** TBBS **Description:** Adult, alternative lifestyle BBS/gay/lesbian/bi//GaycomNet

#68	**Title:** Electronic Trib **Operator:** D.E. Carlson **Location:** Albuquerque, NM **Phone:** (505) 823-7700 **Lines:** 10 **Software:** Galacticomm **Description:** Online service of Albuquerque Tribune Newspaper

#68	**Title:** File Shop **Operator:** Walt Lane **Location:** Kansas City, MO **Phone:** (816) 587-3311 **Lines:** 12 **Software:** Wildcat! **Description:** 17.8 Gb/200,000 files/attractive screens

#68	**Title:** Starship II BBS **Operator:** Phil Buonomo **Location:** Lyndhurst, NJ **Phone:** (201) 935-1485 **Lines:** 16 **Software:** TBBS **Description:** Multiplayer games/shareware downloads

#71	**Title:** The Third Eye **Operator:** Mike Vetter **Location:** Nashville, TN **Phone:** (615) 227-6155 **Lines:** 4 **Software:** TBBS **Description:** The Electronic Erotic Magazine

#71	**Title:** Rusty & Edies BBS **Operator:** Rusty & Edie Hardenburgh **Location:** Boardman, OH **Phone:** (216) 726-2620 **Lines:** 124 **Software:** PCBoard **Description:** Large file library/adult GIF images/MIDI/games/15 Gb

#73	**Title:** The USA TBBS **Operator:** Eric Shore **Location:** Miami, FL **Phone:** (305) 599-3004 **Lines:** 16 **Software:** TBBS **Description:** News/games/messages/entertainment system

#73 | **Title:** Godfather
Operator: Jim Sharrer/Kathi Webster
Location: Tampa, FL
Phone: (813) 282-0023
Lines: 5
Software: PCBoard
Description: Modem news/GIFs/graphics utilities

#75 | **Title:** Casino PCBoard
Operator: Dave Shubert
Location: Pamona, NJ
Phone: (609) 561-3377
Lines: 2
Software: PCBoard
Description: Tourist info/RIME network/IBM files/since 1986

#76 | **Title:** Eagle's Nest Communications
Operator: Mike Labbe/Lea Walsh
Location: Warwick, RI
Phone: (401) 732-5292
Lines: 5
Software: PCBoard
Description: Friendly users/great message base/5.5 Gb/since 1983

#77 | **Title:** Data-Base BBS
Operator: Michael Walter
Location: Annandale, NJ
Phone: (908) 735-2180
Lines: 3
Software: PCBoard
Description: Database/programming/business/professional since 1985

#77 | **Title:** Bill N Bob's Place
Operator: David Houlihan
Location: Cleveland, OH
Phone: (216) 741-5888
Lines: 16
Software: DLX
Description: Adult chat service/swingers

#77
Title: EXEC-PC
Operator: Bob and Tracy Mahoney
Location: Elm Grove, WI
Phone: (414) 789-4210
Lines: 230
Software: Custom
Description: 350,000 files/largest BBS in America

#77
Title: Network East
Operator: Howard J. Hartman
Location: Rockville, MD
Phone: (301) 738-0000
Lines: 12
Software: PCBoard
Description: 50 online games/1 Gb files/RelayNet/U'NI-net/ILink

#81
Title: Cajun Clickers BBS
Operator: Mike Vierra
Location: Baton Rouge, LA
Phone: (504) 756-9658
Lines: 2
Software: PCBoard
Description: Computer club/DOS files/ILINK Echo Mail/games

#81
Title: MOGUR's EMS
Operator: Tom Tcimpidus
Location: Granada Hills, CA
Phone: (818) 366-1238
Lines: 5
Software: WIldcat!
Description: Eight mail networks/hub services/CD-ROMS 2.8 Gb

#81
Title: Susquehanna Speedway
Operator: Dave Mauretic
Location: Harrisburg, PA
Phone: (717) 652-9291
Lines: 1
Software: Wildcat!
Description: Adult message areas

#81	**Title:** Computer Confident **Operator:** Edward Zdrok (Doctor Z) **Location:** Franklin, MA **Phone:** (508) 528-2295 **Lines:** 16 **Software:** Maximus **Description:** FidoNet/Maxnet/OurNet/5 Gb files/online games

#85	**Title:** Walden's Puddle BBS **Operator:** Kevin Brokaw **Location:** Owego, NY **Phone:** (607) 687-6193 **Lines:** 2 **Software:** Wildcat! **Description:** Programming files/messages/echomail

#85	**Title:** Emerald Palace **Operator:** Gergory Shaheen **Location:** San Antonio, TX **Phone:** (512) 561-8150 **Lines:** 32 **Software:** Major BBS **Description:** Entertainment/chat/online games/nightly activities

#85	**Title:** 24th Street Exchange **Operator:** Don Kuhwarth **Location:** Sacramento, CA **Phone:** (916) 451-5829 **Lines:** 16 **Software:** TBBS **Description:** Computer and modem users community since 1983/ASP BBS

#85	**Title:** Locker Room **Operator:** Ed Golka **Location:** Santa Ana, CA **Phone:** (714) 542-5917 **Lines:** 1 **Software:** GAP **Description:** Sports theme

A

#85	**Title:** Winplus **Operator:** Bill Ryalls **Location:** Kent, WA **Phone:** (206) 630-8203 **Lines:** 10 **Software:** Major BBS **Description:** Christian/family-oriented BBS

#90	**Title:** Quebec Online **Operator:** Mark Smith/Danny Perreault **Location:** West Mount, Quebec **Phone:** (514) 935-4257 **Lines:** 10 **Software:** TBBS **Description:** Public domain/shareware/PC/MAC/CD-ROM file collections

#90	**Title:** AtlantaCOM BBS **Operator:** Kevin Whitney **Location:** Duluth, GA **Phone:** (404) 717-9867 **Lines:** 1 **Software:** Wildcat! **Description:** Home of programmers/analysts/business software

#90	**Title:** TechTalk BBS **Operator:** Jerry Russell **Location:** Titusville, FL **Phone:** (407) 269-5188 **Lines:** 4 **Software:** TBBS **Description:** Programs/utility files/ham radio/graphics/messages

#90	**Title:** BackDoor (Williamsburg) **Operator:** Fred Whittom/Peter Conway **Location:** Williamsburg, VA **Phone:** (804) 229-7269 **Lines:** 1 **Software:** Wildcat! **Description:** 53 adult conf/Studnet/Throbnet/adult GIFs/DOORnet

#90	**Title:** Ya WeBeCAD **Operator:** Dan Habegger **Location:** Evansville, IN **Phone:** (812) 422-9403 **Lines:** 2 **Software:** Wildcat! **Description:** AutoCAD/computer aided design interests 2.9Gb

#95	**Title:** Advanced Data Services **Operator:** Henry Prentiss **Location:** Frederick, MD **Phone:** (301) 565-9560 **Lines:** 23 **Software:** PCBoard **Description:** 5.6 Gb files/RIME network/computer sales

#96	**Title:** Geneva Convention Adult BBS **Operator:** Head Prevert **Location:** Clarksville, IN **Phone:** (812) 284-1321 **Lines:** 3 **Software:** Wildcat! **Description:** Adult image files and messages/erotic short stories/animation

#96	**Title:** Texas Talk **Operator:** Sonny Blair **Location:** Richardson, TX **Phone:** (214) 497-9100 **Lines:** 32 **Software:** TBBS **Description:** Friendly chat/matchmaker system/adult areas

#96	**Title:** Magic **Operator:** Mark Windrim **Location:** Markham, Ontario **Phone:** (416) 288-1767 **Lines:** 10 **Software:** FirstClass **Description:** Macintosh awareness group in Canada/MAC support

#99	**Title:** Wayne's World **Operator:** Wayne Greer **Location:** Tulsa, OK **Phone:** (918) 665-2711 **Lines:** 3 **Software:** Feathernet **Description:** Trade Wars/solar realms/online games

#100	**Title:** Radio Daze **Operator:** Michael Shannon **Location:** Mishawaka, IN **Phone:** (219) 256-2255 **Lines:** 4 **Software:** Wildcat! **Description:** Ham radio discussions/4.5 Gb/ChuckleNET headquarters

#100	**Title:** Round Table BBS **Operator:** Dan McCoy/Mike Brown **Location:** Wyomissing, PA **Phone:** (215) 678-0818 **Lines:** 5 **Software:** PCBoard **Description:** AutoCAD/engineering files/numerous networks/397 SIGS

A

NOTE: Since some winners tied, this list of best BBSs may appear to be out of numerical order.

APPENDIX

B

TROUBLESHOOTING

Chapter 13 explains ways to make your modem work better (see the section, "Getting Top Performance from Your Existing Modem" in that chapter); but sometimes, things just won't work the way they are supposed to, or won't work at all. Use this appendix to diagnose and correct major problems.

Rest assured that you will have such problems, but that they are almost always correctable in just a few moments. All modem users, including the author of this book, have days when they cannot dial local Directory

Assistance, let alone log on to the NASA Spacelink BBS. Do not get discouraged or panic; things are rarely as bad as they seem when a modem fails.

Actually, modems themselves rarely fail. Whatever the problem is, it is unlikely that you will have to buy a new modem to fix it. Let that thought comfort you when things look completely broken. Modems have no moving parts, and their circuitry can theoretically last forever. It is not uncommon to find ten-year-old 1200 bps modems in perfect working condition (usually at flea markets).

This troubleshooting guide is organized in a flow chart fashion. Each time you answer one of the questions at the beginning of the following sections, you will eliminate many possible sources of trouble from consideration. Start at the beginning. Answer each diagnostic question in order and follow the instructions to find the correct path to your specific problem and its solution(s).

Go slowly; do not make wholesale changes at random, hoping something will work. There are so many factors that can affect modem performance, and so many ways each factor can induce a malfunction, that it is difficult to diagnose a problem unless you take a controlled, disciplined approach. Using the procedures outlined in this appendix, *change only one thing at a time* as you try to correct a problem. For example, if you change your initialization string, change only one of the AT commands and test that change before changing another command. If you make multiple changes in one step, you could develop a *new* problem, and you will not know which change(s) are causing it or which change fixed the original problem.

Start Here: Can You Dial Out or Not?

If you can get a dial tone and the modem will dial a number, go to the following major section, "Do the Modems Connect?" Otherwise, continue reading and diagnosing from here.

Does the Modem Respond to Commands Normally?

When you load your terminal software, it will attempt to initialize the modem. You should see on your screen the commands the software sends and the modem's response, as in Figure B-1.

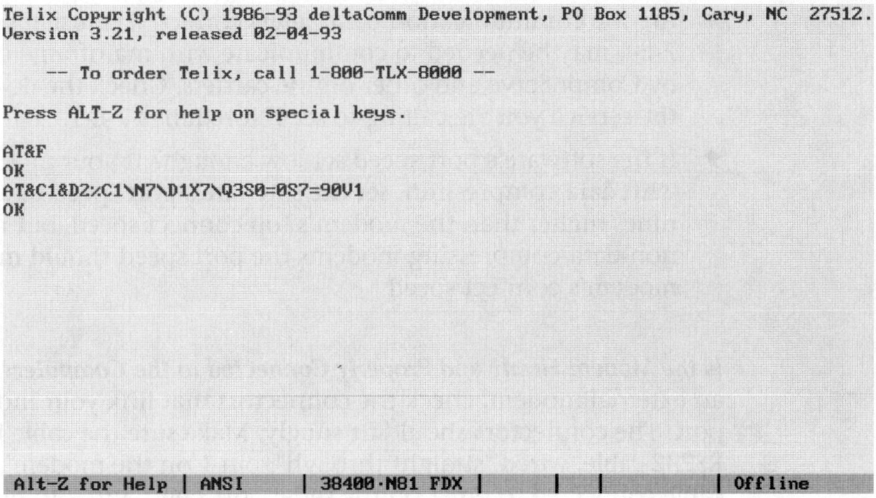

```
Telix Copyright (C) 1986-93 deltaComm Development, PO Box 1185, Cary, NC  27512.
Version 3.21, released 02-04-93

     -- To order Telix, call 1-800-TLX-8000 --

Press ALT-Z for help on special keys.

AT&F
OK
AT&C1&D2%C1\N7\D1X7\Q3S0=0S7=90V1
OK
```

B

Normal
initialization
and modem
response
Figure B-1.

```
Alt-Z for Help | ANSI     | 38400-N81 FDX |        |        |       | Offline
```

Is There NO Response from the Modem?

If nothing at all appears on your screen when you initialize the modem, make sure the modem's power is turned on. If that is not the problem, carefully type the following AT command and press ⟨Enter⟩:

```
AT E1
```

The E1 command turns on local echoing of characters typed from the keyboard. It is unlikely that your modem is configured not to echo commands back to you, but this test is so simple that you might as well get it out of the way first.

If an OK appears in response to the E1 command, you have corrected the local echo problem. Save your corrected configuration in the modem's memory so this problem will not happen again, type the following command, and press ⟨Enter⟩:

```
AT &W
```

Now type **AT Z** and press ⟨Enter⟩, to reinitialize the modem. This time you should get an OK response.

Is Your Terminal Software Correctly Configured? If turning on local echo does not cure the no-response problem, your terminal software may be incorrectly configured. Check the following settings:

✦ Is the correct COM port selected?

✦ Are the communication parameters correct? The usual settings are 8-N-1; 7-E-1 may be needed to communicate with mainframe computers used by CompuServe and other online carriers. Check the documentation of the service you are calling to see if it requires 7-E-1.

✦ Is the software's port speed set low enough? If your modem is equipped with data compression, set the software's port speed to a value four times higher than the modem's top connect speed, but no higher. For non-data-compressing modems the port speed should match the modem's connect speed.

Is the Modem Firmly and Properly Connected to the Computer? If you have an external modem, check the connectors that link your modem to the serial port. The connectors should fit snugly. Make sure the cable is a standard RS232 cable, wired "straight through": pin 1 on the modem's end of the cable connected to pin 1 on the serial port's end, pin 2 to pin 2, and so on.

If you have an internal modem, remove the cover of your computer and make sure the modem card is firmly seated in its slot.

Is the Modem Responding, but Abnormally?

Sometimes you will get a response, but not one you can read. It may consist of garbage characters—check marks, graphics characters, or a foreign alphabet. It's also possible that you may get a plain-English error message.

Is the Modem Responding with Garbage Characters? If garbage appears on screen when you initialize the modem, the simplest solution is to cycle the modem's power off and back on again. Just toggle the power switch on an external modem. If you have an internal modem, unload all software and cycle your computer's power off and back on.

NOTE: A warm reboot, pressing (Ctrl)-(Alt)-(Del), will not cycle the power to an internal modem. Turn the power off and on manually, or press the reset button if your computer has one.

Is the Modem Responding with an Error Message? If you get a plain-English error message, it may be as unhelpful as "ERROR" or more specific. A general ERROR message usually means you gave the modem a command it could not understand. Check the commands in your software's initialization string to be sure they are all valid and that the string ends with a carriage-return/linefeed character. See Chapter 6 for a tutorial on initialization strings.

If your initialization string contains a carriage-return/linefeed (^M) somewhere in its middle, that is, AT &F ^M AT V1 X4 ^M, your modem might need a moment to execute the first half of the initialization string before executing the second half. Insert three tildes (~~~) after the embedded carriage-return/linefeed to provide a 1.5 second pause.

More specific error messages are probably coming from your terminal software. A classic error message displayed by Telix is

```
CTS signal found off!
```

This message appears when Telix is trying to initialize hardware flow control, and the modem's hardware is not responding. Normally, it means your modem is not powered on. This problem usually happens with external modems. If it does, take a look at the modem's front panel; if no lights are on, turn on the power.

Can the Modem Get a Dial Tone?

If you tell your modem to dial but it does nothing, or responds with a "NO DIAL TONE" error message, the problem could be in the phone line and its connections or in the instructions your software gives the modem.

Is the Phone Line Properly Connected and Working?

To eliminate the phone line as the source of no-dial-tone problems, check the following factors:

✦ Is the phone line plugged into the jack on the modem labeled LINE, meaning the line running to your phone wall jack?

✦ Is the other end of the phone line plugged into the wall?

✦ Is someone else already using the line?

✦ Is there a dial tone when you listen to the line using a normal telephone?

If the problem is not in the phone line or its connections, then the modem is not getting the correct instructions.

Is Your Software Properly Configured?

Your terminal software must be configured to issue the following commands for every attempted dial. Check the dialing prefix stored in your terminal program's modem setup options.

✦ *AT* gets the modem's ATtention.

✦ *D* tells the modem to prepare to dial a number.

✦ *T* or *P* tells the modem to use touch-tone or pulse dialing.

✦ A valid phone number is necessary.

✦ A *carriage-return/linefeed* code (usually ^M) *must* end each attempted dial; otherwise the modem will not execute the command because it will not realize you have finished entering commands.

Is the Modem Dialing but Not Connecting?

If the modem dials a number but nothing happens, it means the problem begins after the phone number leaves your modem.

Make sure you have the correct phone number.

Verify that the phone line accepts touch-tone or pulse dialing, whichever method you are using to dial. Use a regular telephone to dial a number and see which dialing method works.

If you are calling from an office phone system that requires dialing a 9 to get an outside line, add a 9 and a tilde (~) to your default dialing prefix right after the T or P command.

Some phone systems will not dial a number until the caller enters an accounting code. If yours is one of these, add such codes to your software's dialing suffix.

When All Else Fails, Call the Phone Company

If you have followed the preceding steps and still cannot get a dial tone followed by a ringing pattern, you need help from your phone company's service department. If you are calling from an office phone system, check with the system administrator first to see if there is anything about the phone system that your modem or software needs to accommodate.

Do the Modems Connect?

If you can dial a number and get an answer, but you get disconnected after a few seconds, the two modems are not able to make an acceptable connection over which to exchange data. Causes can range from poor line quality to improper communication parameters or physical connections on your end, to rare problems with inflexible modems on the other end of your connection that will not adjust their connect speed to match their caller's connect speed.

Is the Line Quality Adequate?

Both modems must be able to detect the carrier wave signal over which data will be exchanged. Sometimes a line is too noisy, because static overwhelms the carrier wave signal.

The only indication of this problem with an internal modem usually is a relatively long period of squealing after the remote modem answers, followed by a disconnection.

An external modem's CD (Carrier Detected) light or LED should come on and stay on. If it never comes on or flickers, line noise (static) is overwhelming the carrier wave.

B

The quick solution to heavy line noise is to hang up and try again for a better connection. If you fail three times in a row to get a clean connection, it is best to assume there is a temporary problem in the local phone lines and try again later.

Is Your Long-Distance Carrier the Problem?

Sometimes long-distance carriers like AT&T, MCI, and Sprint have network-wide difficulties; any line you get will have static on it. You can use any of the alternative long-distance services for any specific call by prefacing your phone number with an *equal-access code* that specifies which long-distance service to use for that call only.

For example, AT&T's equal-access code is 10288. To dial 303-555-5555 using AT&T instead of your default long-distance carrier, you would enter **10288 1-303-555-5555**. Notice that you must add a 1 before the phone number, just as you would if dialing it using your default carrier.

There are dozens of long-distance carriers, and each has its own equal-access code. Your local telephone operator can provide the code for any carrier you can name. Some of the major carriers and their equal-access codes are

Carrier	Code
AT&T	10288
Sprint	10033
MCI	10022
Allnet	10044
LDS	10084

Are Your Local Phone Line Connections Good?

Check the phone jacks, cord, and modular connectors between your modem and your telephone wallplate. Reconnect or replace any loose or broken connections.

If the line noise is originating outside of your premises but not with your long-distance carrier, then it must be in your local telephone company's network (the *local loop,* as it is called). Call the phone company's service department and request a line-quality check. If a problem is found, the phone company must fix it at no charge to you.

The phone company's responsibility for wiring problems ends at the junction box that leads into your home or office. Everything from there to your modem is known as *inside wiring,* and any repairs will be your responsibility. If your phone company makes a house call to repair inside wiring, the cost can run $65 per hour and up. All phone companies offer an "insurance policy" for around a dollar per month that will cover inside wire maintenance, but most customers find it more cost-effective to hire a less expensive independent contractor for inside wiring repairs.

Other equipment that shares your modem's phone line may be causing noise problems, whether the other equipment is connected to a modem's second (PHONE) jack or to an extension jack in another room. Unplug any answering machines, extension phones, or fax machines and try again. If the noise problem goes away, test each device by plugging it in and using your modem; leave only one extra device plugged in at a time. When you find the culprit, have it repaired or replaced.

Are Your Communication Parameters Suitable?

Mismatched communication parameters are covered in some detail in a preceding section of this Appendix. Briefly, if a setting of eight data bits, no parity, and one stop bit (8-N-1) does not work, switch to 7-E-1.

Do You Need to Match the Other Modem's Settings?

Your modem should be configured to attempt first a connection at its highest speed and best available combination of error-correction and data compression features. All modems come preconfigured this way, prepared to negotiate the best connection they possibly can.

Unfortunately, the modem you are calling might not be as flexibly configured as your own. Most modems automatically adjust to the caller's speed, error-correction, and data-compression capabilities. This adjustment occurs during the *handshaking interval*, the time right after the remote modem answers during which the two modems squeal at each other. Sometimes, however, a remote modem is deliberately set up to accept only calls that meet certain requirements. For example, it might refuse a connection from modems that lack MNP error correction, or calls slower than 2400 bps.

Read your modem's documentation very carefully to learn what standard and enhanced AT commands will force your modem to call at specific speeds and using specific features. When you encounter such a finicky modem, you should try to talk to its operator and find out exactly which calls it will accept.

B

Is Data Scrambled or Missing?

Sometimes you will get logged on (perhaps with a struggle), but the data your modem starts displaying is a mess. It may be a total mess, or intermittently sprinkled with garbage characters.

Is Everything on Screen Unreadable?

If all of the characters that appear from the remote modem are graphics characters, check your communication parameters. Toggle from 8-N-1 to 7-E-1 or vice versa to see if you chose the wrong set.

Another possibility is that the remote modem is using error correction and yours is not. The garbage characters that solidly fill your screen are part of the error-correction handshaking attempts the other modem keeps making. If your modem has error-correcting protocols such as MNP, v.32, or v.32bis, make sure they are enabled.

Do Garbage Characters Come and Go?

If garbage characters appear intermittently and entire sentences or parts of menu screens seem to be missing, you might have a line noise problem. See the preceding sections "Is Your Long-Distance Carrier the Problem?" and "Are Your Local Phone Line Connections Good?"

If the errors occur only with every other letter of the alphabet, your terminal program's parity setting is incorrect. That is, if the characters that get scrambled always are A, C, E, and G or B, D, F, and H, change your parity setting. You might have to experiment with odd, even, and no parity to find the right setting.

If the errors occur only when data is rapidly scrolling down your screen or when you type quickly, then the problem might be flow control. Make sure you set your software to use RTS/CTS flow control. See Chapter 6 for detailed instructions.

Is There Garbage on a V.42 or MNP Connection

MNP, v.42, and v.42bis modems cannot have line noise; the modems remove line noise. If an error-free connection delivers garbage characters, your terminal software is receiving exactly what the remote computer sends, but it cannot properly display the information. Often the problem is traceable to improper terminal type selection in your software for the computer you are calling. If you do not have explicit instructions from the remote computer about which terminal types it supports, try switching from ANSI/BBS to VT100 terminal emulation. See Chapter 6 for a full discussion of terminal types.

File Transfer Failures

Few things are more irritating than having a file transfer abort during the 999th block of 1,000 blocks. Fortunately, the possible causes are fairly limited and easily fixed.

Do Failures Occur Only When Using Xmodem or Ymodem?

If the failures occur only on transfers using Xmodem or Ymodem protocols, your modem is stripping out XON/XOFF characters when it should just pass them on through. Even if you have XON/XOFF flow control disabled in your terminal software, the modem's internal settings have XON/XOFF enabled. Read your modem's manual and set the modem to pass XON/XOFF through in both directions.

Do Failures Occur at Every Speed?

If file transfers fail, no matter how fast or slow your connection is, your modem, terminal software, or both are not set to use RTS/CTS flow control. Set RTS/CTS on in both software and modem; turn off XON/XOFF flow control in both places too. See Chapter 5 for modem configuration instructions and Chapter 6 for terminal software instructions.

Do Failures Occur Only at High Speeds?

If failures happen only at high port speeds (19,200 bps and up), your modem needs a buffered serial port or UART. See Chapter 13 for details and where to buy them.

Trouble Can Be Fun Too

"Everything I did in my life that was worthwhile, I caught hell for."
—Former U. S. Supreme Court Chief Justice Earl Warren.

When trouble comes to roost in your modem, it can be difficult and frustrating to ferret it out. But before you drop-kick your modem into the next area code, remember why you bought it in the first place: to learn, to gain skills, and to have an adventure. Without challenges, none of these things is possible.

B

The nice thing about modem problems is their consistency. Once you solve a configuration problem, it will stay fixed. Line noise has the same look and the same solutions wherever it appears. After a few trying experiences, you will find it easy to defeat any problems the online universe throws at you.

A P P E N D I X

FAX/DATA MODEMS AND SOFTWARE

Chapter 3 offered a quick buyer's guide to fax/data modems (fax modems for brevity's sake). But the subject of fax modems is sufficiently popular and complicated to merit its own appendix.

According to PC Magazine (December 1992), fax modems will outsell stand-alone fax machines for the first time in 1993. The folks at Byte magazine also note that most fax modem users report problems with their modems and fax software, including hardware that claims to meet industry standards but does not, and software that does not work with standard hardware. It is possible to buy a fax modem/software combination that works for you, but you have to carefully pick your way through some difficult territory.

Fax modem buyers are in an uncomfortable place, on the "bleeding edge" of *three* rapidly changing technologies: facsimile, data communications, and related application software. Chapter 4 describes some of the problems of immature OCR (Optical Character Recognition) fax software; this appendix provides a better look at existing and evolving hardware standards, and the state of the art in other fax modem software.

Understanding Fax Modem "Standards"

It can be a chore just to understand what you are buying in a fax modem, because *two* sets of industry standards are necessary to describe a fax modem's capabilities. Anyone who has wrestled with the complexities of v.XX standards for data communications will rightly guess that fax modems can be a real puzzle. The following two sections attempt to simplify this complexity.

Fax Standards: Group 2, Group 3, and Group 4

The term "Group" applies to standards for facsimile transmission equipment, whether it be stand-alone dedicated fax machines or fax/data modems. Two existing standards — Group 2 and Group 3 — have been around long enough to have most of their bugs worked out, and have large enough installed bases to make it likely you will find a remote partner with the same fax capabilities you have. Group 4 fax is still very much in its infancy. Some very expensive products claim to be Group 4 compatible; but the Group 4 standard is still not formalized, so compatibility is a moving target.

Group 2 Fax: Old, Reliable

Group 2 is the oldest and most stable fax standard still in common use today. Group 2-compatible fax machines (or fax modems) can transmit fax images at up to 4800 bps, with an image resolution of up to 200 dots per inch (dpi). A Group 2 fax transmission can take well over two minutes to send a single page of fine graphics, and the 200-dpi resolution is well below the 300-dpi commonly considered "business quality" since laser printers became common. However, a Group 2-compatible fax device can communicate with any fax machine you are likely to encounter, and the slower speed is more reliable on noisy dial-up phone lines.

Group 3 Fax: Faster, Neater

Most new fax hardware is Group 3-compatible. Group 3 incorporates Group 2 capabilities in case the user must communicate with a Group 2 machine. The Group 3 standard specifies transmission speeds of up to 9600 bps and adds data compression functions, cutting transmission time by more than half when connected to another Group 3 device. Image resolution can range up to 400 dpi. Group 3 devices can switch to 200-dpi resolution for faster, draft-quality transmissions, or to *half-tone mode* for better transmission of gray-scale images. (Group 2 devices lack half-tone capabilities.) If you want your faxes to look their best, Group 3 compatibility is a must.

Group 4 Fax: an Evolving Standard

You will need over $10,000 to buy Group 4 capabilities, and you will not need them unless you spend most of your day faxing. Group 4 specifies transmission speeds of 19,200 bps over ordinary dial-up phone lines, and up to 64,000 bps over expensive dedicated lines used by corporate America. Group 4 includes better data compression than Group 3, so fax transmissions proceed even faster. Currently, there are no fax modems for individual use available with Group 4 capabilities. High-priced fax servers designed to handle the fax traffic of entire corporate networks are on the market, but their bugs are still being worked out.

Fax Modem Standards: Class 1, Class 2, CAS, SendFax, v.17

The "Group" standards apply to all fax-transmitting devices, including stand-alone fax machines. The following five sections describe standards that apply only to fax modems.

Class 1: Computer-Intensive Fax

Files generated by your computer must be converted to a format that can be faxed; that takes a lot of computer power. Class 1 fax modems put the burden of file conversion on the computer and fax software. The effect on the user is noticeable and often aggravating. Your computer may be unavailable for other work while converting a file to faxable form, or at best foreground tasks will slow to a crawl. Class 1 fax software also takes up large chunks of RAM (often over 100K), creating conflicts with other complex application software when you want to keep your fax software resident in memory.

Class 2: Modem-Intensive Fax

The obvious solution to the problems with Class 1 is to move the processing out of the main computer; Class 2 fax modems move it to the modem hardware itself. Class 2 fax modems include built-in microprocessors, RAM, and software that does the conversion work while the CPU is freed for other tasks. The result is that CPU-resident software can be smaller, and you will reclaim your computer's full processing power much faster.

Another benefit of this move towards putting fax processing chores into the modem is software independence. Modern fax software loads a driver into your computer, which compatible word processors, spreadsheets, and database managers recognize as just another printer attached to the computer. Users do not have to learn new procedures, configure their existing software for faxing, or worry about compatibility between the data formats they normally use and their fax software.

CAS: An Unofficial Fax Standard

Intel Corp. and DCA (Digital Communications Associates) are two heavyweights in the modem industry. The two companies came up with their own fax modem standard, called the *Communications Application Specification (CAS)* and are doggedly marketing it. CAS, in theory, provides a vendor-independent fax interface between software products. In other words, you can use your favorite spreadsheet, database manager, or word processor just like you always do, but send a fax just as if you were printing a file or report to a printer. A great idea, but CAS' unofficial status limits the number of software vendors supporting it. Some recently discovered bugs in Intel's CAS-compliant modems have prompted massive defections to other products.

SendFax: Send-Only Capability, Small Software

Laptop computer owners used to have limited disk and RAM space. Mobile computer users generally send faxes, but do not receive them often. So Sierra Semiconductor developed the SendFax specification to solve the space problem while meeting the biggest user need (sending capability). Today, mobile computers often have as much RAM and disk space as their deskbound counterparts, so SendFax is something of a dinosaur.

CCITT v.17: 14,400 bps Modem-to-Modem Fax

A very new international standard, v.17 specifies modem-to-modem fax operations at connect speeds up to 14,400 bps. The speed will drop to 9600 bps if a stand-alone fax machine is on the other end of the connection, because v.17 is implemented only in modems, not dedicated fax machines. Buying a v.32bis modem with v.17 fax capability is a state-of-the-art investment; you will have 14,400 bps capability in both fax and data transmissions. But it may be some years before your correspondents do, so you may not get to use v.17 very often.

Software for Fax Modems

The following sections describe essential features and some of the "real cool" capabilities found in modern fax software. Generally speaking, the more bells and whistles a fax program offers, the more you need an 80386 or 80486 computer, and lots of RAM (4MB or more).

Plan on switching to the Microsoft Windows operating environment if you want to keep your fax software resident in memory most of the time (either in receive mode or to use in conjunction with other application programs). MS-DOS fax software is a poor compromise; the DOS operating system just does not support the multitasking functions needed for trouble-free fax modem use.

Basic Fax Software Features

Fax software must have certain features in order to be genuinely useful. Avoid buying any software that does not include the following basic capabilities:

✦ *Essential data conversion* Every file you fax must be converted into a fax format. Good fax software has conversion routines built into it for ASCII, PCX, TIFF, and DCX data formats. Be sure the fax software you select can convert the types of data you most often fax "on the fly," without requiring you to run an external conversion program before faxing.

✦ *Background send/receive operation* Fax data conversion and transmission take a significant amount of time; you do not want to sit around waiting for a fax program to send or receive a fax. Virtually all modern fax software can operate in background mode, allowing you to leave the receive-fax portion of a program in memory at all times.

✦ *View-fax utility* Paperless operation is one of the main attractions of computer faxing. Printing a fax is a time-consuming operation, one best avoided if possible. Fax software should let you examine a fax file on screen before deciding whether to print or delete it.

✦ *Scheduled sending* While most faxing is urgent, quite a few faxes can wait until the middle of the night when long-distance telephone rates are low. Fax software should include a scheduling function that will send faxes at any time, without your assistance.

The basic features described above are enough for most occasional, informal fax needs. If you want to compose and fax unsigned letters without printing and scanning them into a stand-alone fax machine, and receive faxes you can later print out, the basics will do just fine.

Fax Software Image Editing Features

While not essential to basic fax operations, the ability to edit faxable bitmapped image files can add a great deal of professionalism and convenience to your fax correspondence. Editing functions fall into two categories: sending-preparation and received-fax editing.

Sending-Preparation Functions

These features make it possible, easier, or faster to prepare a document for faxing:

✦ *Merge-files* Select and combine multiple image files into one document for faxing. Such files might include scanned signatures, the outline of your letterhead, a logo, or any other image file you wish to include to dress up your fax. The ability to merge data of different formats into one file is often handy; for example, merging a spreadsheet into a word processor document.

✦ *Direct Scanner Support* Often a document starts out on paper, and must be scanned into an electronic file before it can be sent via fax modem. Choose fax software that accepts scanned images directly from your choice of scanner; avoid programs that make you go through an extra step of using an external scanner utility program.

✦ *Broadcast Fax Support* Sometimes you will want to send the same document to everyone in a particular group of correspondents; a sales manager's memo to subordinate sales reps is one good example. Fax software should include a dialing directory that lets you create a named group, such as "Eastern Region Sales Reps," and schedule multiple transmissions to everyone on the group list with just one selection.

✦ *Cover Page Library* Fax etiquette calls for a cover page with each transmittal. Fax software may include a library of customizable cover page files. Some cover pages are businesslike and dignified, while others can be blatantly self-promoting or just fun.

✦ *Voice Annotation* This feature really gets attention if you can use it within your circle of correspondents. Some fax software will let you record a digitized audio message and attach the sound file to a fax document. Such files must be faxed directly to another computer, not to a stand-alone fax machine. The recipient must also have appropriate software to play back your recording while reading your fax.

Received-Fax Editing Functions

When you receive a fax, you may be expected to do something with it (besides just read it). Often price lists, proposed contracts, and other documents must be reworked before being passed on to other people in your company, or keyed into a database or spreadsheet for further processing. Fax modem software can make these editing and data-entry tasks easier.

+ *Optical Character Recognition (OCR)* This is the ability to identify bitmapped images and correctly convert them into ASCII text suitable for importation into other application software. The key word here is "correctly"; you do not want your company's financial data misinterpreted on its way to the general ledger. Most OCR software falls far short of perfection; the best you can expect under real-world conditions is 95 to 99 percent accuracy in converting graphics to ASCII. That means you can expect 20 to 100 errors per 2000-byte page, making OCR totally unacceptable for translating critical numeric data. OCR is best used for text document conversion, with consistent proofreading.

+ *Image Editing* A bitmapped fax image can be cut, rotated, reversed, and otherwise transformed before being printed. Adding elements to a received-fax file is another handy function. The ability to change typefaces, highlight or underline text, or adjust the gray-scale intensity of a picture, are some of the other editing capabilities you might need. *Anti-aliasing* smooths out the ragged edges of letters and images caused by the mismatch between the dot-pitch resolution of a fax and the resolution of the original document, making a received fax easier to read.

+ *Annotations* Distinct from editing functions in that they are stored as separate files to preserve the original image intact, annotations are little notes you can write *about* the original received-fax file.

+ *Retransmission/Forwarding* The ability to send a fax file you have received to another fax modem seems like an obvious, almost essential feature. But some fax software cannot convert received fax files into faxable files! If you plan to run a truly paperless operation, retransmission of received faxes is an important feature.

The Future of Fax

Virtually all modems will soon have built-in fax capabilities, for little or no additional cost. OCR software will continue to improve, but will probably never achieve 100% accuracy. Editing and annotation features will bring us ever closer to the paperless office ideal.

One Holy Grail of the hardware business is the all-in-one fax, modem, laser printer, scanner, and copier machine. Vendors love the idea, because such machines offer bigger profit margins. But while such marvels have strong appeal to anyone whose office is short of desktop space (and whose isn't?), considerable thought should be given to what you will do if just one of the components breaks down. Independent machines provide comforting redundancy in case of malfunctions. You can always send a document via modem if your fax machine is in the repair shop.

About the Author ...

David Hakala is the director of the BBS Incubator and is a freelance writer specializing in telecommunications in Denver, Colorado. As a reporter for *Boardwatch Magazine*, he has reviewed and chronicled thousands of online services, modem-based business tools, hardware and software packages, and the online world. He is coauthor of **Hot Links: The Guide to Linking Computers**. David may be found on CompuServe (74720,3377), the Internet (david.hakala@ boardwatch.com) and better Bulletin Board Systems everywhere.

INDEX

THOUSANDS OF FRESH BBS PHONE NUMBERS!

The Bonus Disk set also includes the latest editions of BBS lists containing thousands of phone numbers you can call with your modem. Each list includes the name and phone number of the BBS where you can find later editions as needed.

A BONUS ON TOP OF YOUR BONUS!

But that's not all! Buyers of the Bonus Disk set will also receive with their orders a full year's subscription to **The Modems Made Easy Bulletin Board System** (normally $30.00/year). Osborne/McGraw-Hill assumes NO responsibility for the fulfillment of this offer. The MME BBS is maintained by your author to provide a place where readers can suggest improvements to the next edition of Modems Made Easy, exchange information with other novice and expert modem users, and download the many megabytes of outstanding resources that would otherwise fill dozens of disks.

- -

Yes! Send me the Bonus Disk set and my password for a full year's access to The Modems Made Easy Bulletin Board System. I enclose a check or money order for $12.95, payable to

David Hakala

Suite C-114

860 South Oneida Street

Denver, CO 80224

SHIP MY BONUS DISK SET TO:

NAME: _____

ADDRESS: _____

_____

CITY: _____ STATE: _____ ZIP: _____

Please specify disk size: _____5.25" disk or _____3.5" disk.
Allow 4 to 6 weeks for delivery.

Osborne **McGraw-Hill** assumes NO responsibility for the fulfillment of this offer.

SPECIAL TWO-DISK BONUS OFFER!

Many computer-related books now include disks full of shareware and "special editions" of commercial software. Your author wants to give you something more and better.

You see, any software packaged with a book may be obsolete by the time you buy the book. It is not unusual for a shareware program to be updated and improved three or four times a year. Also, the online world changes so fast that many lists of bulletin board systems and other electronic publications change every month.

The Modems Made Easy Bonus Disk set is offered by mail so that your author can personally fill your order with only the most up-to-date, useful shareware utilities and electronic publications. These resources are handpicked from dozens of files your author downloads or receives from vendors every month, sparing you enormous trouble and expense.

For just $12.95, you receive the latest shareware versions of these and dozens of other useful modem-related utilities:

- ✦ **MODEM DOCTOR:** the best all-around modem diagnostic utility. (See Chapter 14.)

- ✦ **LITES11:** displays onscreen "status lights" for internal modems. (See Chapter 14.)

- ✦ **PERSONAL-E MAIL:** set up your own 24-hour e-mail network. (See Chapter 11.)

- ✦ **GIFLINK & GIFLITE:** view GIF image files while downloading, compress the "keepers" to save disk space. (See Chapter 14.)

- ✦ **WIZLINK:** take remote control of another computer by modem; send/receive e-mail or compressed files, chat, and more. (See Chapter 11.)

- ✦ **CISREF:** save money by downloading Forum file directories, searching and tagging files offline.

- ✦ **CISBILL:** keeps track of your CompuServe charges.

- ✦ **BBSMETER:** tells you how much money you are spending while connected to a BBS, CompuServe, or other online service.

- ✦ **TXTFON:** converts BBS lists to dialing directories for Procomm, Telix, Boyan, Qmodem, GT Powercomm terminal programs. Saves typing!